The Hunger Book

21st Century Essays

David Lazar and Patrick Madden, Series Editors

The Hunger Book

A Memoir from Communist Poland

Agata Izabela Brewer

Mad Creek Books, an imprint of
The Ohio State University Press
Columbus

Published by Mad Creek Books, an imprint of The Ohio State University Press.

Library of Congress Cataloging-in-Publication Data

Names: Szczeszak-Brewer, Agata, author.

Title: The hunger book : a memoir from Communist Poland / Agata Izabela Brewer.

Other titles: 21st century essays.

Description: Columbus : Mad Creek Books, an imprint of The Ohio State University Press, [2023] | Series: 21st century essays | Summary: "Personal essays exploring the author's experiences growing up in Communist Poland against a backdrop of food insecurity, parental mental illness and addiction, and the hardships of living under a totalitarian regime"—Provided by publisher.

Identifiers: LCCN 2023011456 | ISBN 9780814258781 (paperback) | ISBN 0814258786 (paperback) | ISBN 9780814282984 (ebook) | ISBN 0814282989 (ebook)

Subjects: LCSH: Szczeszak-Brewer, Agata—Childhood and youth. | Szczeszak-Brewer, Agata—Family. | Mothers and daughters—Poland. | Adult children of alcoholics—Poland. | Food security—Poland. | Communism—Poland—History—20th century. | Poland—Social conditions—20th century.

Classification: LCC CT275.S998 A3 2023 | DDC 943.805092 [B]—dc23/eng/20230522

LC record available at https://lccn.loc.gov/2023011456

Cover design by Melissa Dias-Mandoly

Text design by Juliet Williams

Type set in Constantia

∞ The paper used in this publication meets the minimum requirements of the American National Standard for Information Sciences—Permanence of Paper for Printed Library Materials. ANSI Z39.48-1992.

for Tomek
whenever you're ready

Contents

Acknowledgments

I want to thank Grandma Iza and Grandpa Wincenty for loving me and keeping me alive; Jakub, Izabela, Josh, and Pixie, for unconditional love; Tomek, for everything; Ryszard Szczeszak, for his memories of Communist Poland and for checking copyright info; Sławomir Stelmaczonek, for warm encouragement and for his accounts of Mother's childhood and adolescent years; Jerzy Kosewski and Włodzimierz Kosewski, Grandma Iza's younger brothers, who shared their homes and memories with me; Anna Organiściak-Krzykowska and Róża Ziajka, for details about Mother's high school years; Paula Dobrzeniecka-Perl, for reading early chapters and advising on copyright restrictions in Poland; Michał Perl, for teaching me how to cook blood soup; Mandy and Michael Meloy, for friendship and kaszanka; Christie Buyn, for crafting breaks and reality checks; Ania Spyra, Kristen Elias Rowley, Erin Wood, Natasha Williams, Charlotte Maya, Liz Kleinfeld, Jodie Sadowsky, Dinty Moore, Jina Moore, and Violet Benge, for generously reading full drafts or parts of the manuscript; Dinty Moore, Allison K. Williams, Leslie Jamison, Jill Talbott, and T Kira Madden, for inspiring me and kicking my butt in their workshops; Joy Castro and Eric Freeze, for advice and encouragement; Julie Lambert and Jay Deitcher, for keeping me writing on Sunday evenings; Karin Wimbley, for Monday writing dates on Zoom; Kaye Holcomb, for helping me heal;

Sarah Parker and Paula Dodd, for vestibulars; Andrew Taylor, for Darkroom magic; Bożena Pysiewicz, chief curator of the Poster Museum at Wilanów, for poster copyright assistance; Jim Brown, for expertise in physics and nuclear reactions; and Wabash College, especially the Collett Chair, the John J. Coss Faculty Development Fund, and the Dean's Professional Travel Fund, for covering my travel to archives and interviews.

Parts of this memoir appeared in print before this publication: "Leaving Lviv" in *Guernica* (March 9, 2022); "Birds" (winner of the 2019 Black Warrior Review Nonfiction Prize) in *Black Warrior Review* (46.2, Winter/Spring 2020); "Mushrooms" in *Hektoen International: A Journal of Medical Humanities* (Summer 2018). My account of Polish martial law and the 2021 US Capitol coup are forthcoming in "The (Face)Book of Academic Motherhood: Online Communities Respond to the Traumatic and the Mundane," with Laura Quaynor, in *Academic Mothers Building Online Communities: It Takes a Village* (edited by Sarah Trocchio, Lisa K. Hanasono, Jessica Jorgenson Borchert, Rachael Dwyer, and Jeanette Yih Ha; Palgrave Macmillan).

I used numerous sources to research the history of Communist Poland and the biology and sociology of addictions, as well as mycology, nuclear fusion, and more. Most extensively, I was inspired by Merlin Sheldrake's *Entangled Life: How Fungi Make Our Worlds, Change Our Minds & Shape Our Futures* as well as Bessel van der Kolk's *The Body Keeps the Score: Brain, Mind, and Body in the Healing of Trauma.* The Polish poems and stories were translated by Czesław Miłosz, Rober Hass, Leonard Nathan, Renata Gorczyńska, and Celina Wieniewska.

This is a work of creative nonfiction. While all the stories in this book are true, some names and identifying details have been changed to protect the privacy of the people involved.

Mushrooms

She follows me all the way across the Atlantic Ocean. Farther and farther west I flee, by plane, in a rusty Honda, in a bright-yellow Penske moving truck, until I am sheltered by cornstalks and windswept ravines in Browns Valley, Indiana. But her tentacles reach me even here. I know it before I pick up the phone.

That day, I throw acorns into lake water with my two-year-old son. We sing a Polish tune about a cucumber in a green suit and squint at the morning light spreading like silver glitter across the canvas of muddy water. As we walk down our gravel driveway and inside the house, a ringtone pierces the soft air.

"*Proszę matkę stad zabrać. Proszę ja uspokoić.*" The voice is high-pitched, frantic. The Polish *ess*es and fricatives tell me to come get Mother and calm her down.

The alarm system my body has been suppressing for years goes haywire. I can no longer feel my son's squishy diaper against my skin. I can no longer feel his weight on my right hip. The phone disappears from my grip. I am now a six-year-old girl with a disheveled braid, tears streaming down on Mother's dirty jacket as I try to prop her up and make her walk again, while she remains prone on hard pavement. I want us to be home, where nobody can see her, where nobody can see us.

"Who is it?" I say, but I know even before I ask. The voice

belongs to a Bronx doctor, a Polish immigrant who hired Mother as a live-in nanny for her infant daughter.

"She's throwing rocks at my windows. There is glass everywhere. My baby is with me, inside."

"Let me talk to her." I hand over my toddler to Josh.

"Are you insane? I'd have to open the door first." She's breathing fast. "Your mother is dangerous, don't you understand? I called the police."

The air conditioner kicks in with an angry roar. It's late spring in Indiana, but the humidity is already unbearable. The voice travels 700 miles on an electric current and exits my cordless receiver without effort, but all I hear is echo. Rocks. Glass. Dangerous.

When our connection cuts off unexpectedly, I imagine blood splattered on a broken window.

Then the phone rings again.

"This is NYPD."

By the time I convince the officer to drive Mother to JFK instead of jail, I make a decision—not for the first time—to sever our ties. I gather later from the shreds of stories and accusations that Mother had been fired from her nanny job, drank all night in her room and, instead of packing for her scheduled flight back to Poland, plotted revenge against her employer, who refused to pay her the full promised wage. Disheveled, in a white nightgown with a pink floral pattern, she confronted the woman in the morning and was pushed out of the house when she became unhinged. That's when the rocks started flying, striking the glass with a ferocity nobody would expect from a fragile sixty-year-old. The NYPD retrieved Mother's belongings from the house, and since her employer had hired her without proper documentation, she didn't press charges against Mother. Still in her nightgown, Mother arrived at JFK in the back of a police car and called me from the departure hall.

* * *

That night, a dream returns. I walk down a wide forest path, holding hands with my younger brother, Tomek. Behind us are Mother, Uncle, Grandma Iza, and Grandpa Wincenty, each holding a basket. We are mushroom hunting. I see us all as if from behind a moving camera taking a long wide-angle shot. Tomek and I skip ahead and hold on to each other, smiling. What we don't see, can't see, is that behind us, our family steps off the path, into the thick shrubs. In an instant, they disappear. By the time Tomek and I realize that we are alone, they are long gone. The dream ends with a feeling of dreadful abandonment. Where do we go now? How do we find home? What's the point of going home if nobody is there?

* * *

"Can you believe what this bitch did to me? Fucking whore." Mother's voice is shaking, high-pitched. I hear the hum of the JFK departure hall in between her words. "Where am I supposed to change into my clothes now?"

"Bathroom. Then go through the check-in so you don't miss your flight." I want her gone. I want her back across the Atlantic, at a safe distance from me, at a safe distance from my child.

"Can you believe it? *Kurwa.*" She rolls the *r* long and hard, at a low pitch, the cuss word now more threatening than frantic, rumbling toward the doctor, toward the NYPD, toward me, toward my son.

"It's quite horrible. Just breathe." If I say anything to offend her, she may still turn around and find her way back to us. I really need her to be on that plane.

"Mama? *Lody*?" My toddler is back at my feet, asking for

ice cream. I promised him a treat if he came back home from our acorn throwing without a fuss. I reach out to touch his hair but jerk my hand back on my hip. It's shaking. I don't want to frighten him.

"Fuck this. I'm gonna fly in my fucking pajamas."

"OK. Now go to the check-in counter."

Please.

"I'll call you when I land in Warsaw."

I suddenly feel the kind of calm that comes from having just arrived at a firm decision, one that will help me regain equilibrium and keep my family safe. I will not pick up the phone when she calls me from Warsaw. Or from Olsztyn, the city where I grew up and where she lives in a tiny one-bedroom apartment, next to a dry cleaner's, inside nicotine-stained walls. But deep down I worry, too, that she is not going to leave me alone. Like a toothache that cannot be ignored, this anxiety makes itself known as I lie down in my bed that night, gasping for air, too numb to move. I watch my body from above, a limp, breathless carcass opening and closing its fish mouth.

* * *

In my parents' sepia-colored wedding photo, Mother's bulging belly hides behind a white rose bouquet. She is wearing a white satin dress and a blazer, fancy for Communist Poland. The hair band tied under her bob cut makes her look like a flapper. Knocked up by a married man, she must have stood out in a Catholic country where priests were infallible gods and the church's doctrine was the only oracle, despite the Communist government's attempts to teach Marx, Engels, and Lenin in schools and factories. She is smiling but, unlike Father, who is staring confidently at the camera, she's looking sideways, into the distance, as if the smile she's wearing were just a pretense of bliss, as if she were trying to cover up some hesitation, some fear.

That photo was taken in October 1978. Father's first marriage had officially ended that September. I was born two months after their wedding.

* * *

After Mother's flight back to Poland from JFK, I ignore her phone calls and decide to move my childhood photos to a plastic bin in the basement. Instead of getting rid of the pictures quickly, I pore over the birthday celebrations, seaside trips, and school assemblies. In one photo, a bored teenage Santa holds two small girls on his lap. One is a queen—she's wearing a yellow handmade crown and a crepe-paper cape draped over her shoulder. The other girl is dressed as a poisonous mushroom. That other girl is me.

I'm wearing a construction-paper toadstool cap—rounded, the top red, with white spots—and a white gown, which is the stem. The gown has a starched lace hem, itchy and uncomfortable. I smile innocuously, but you know what hides behind the cheerful-looking toadstool. Even one bite releases a potentially deadly toxin.

* * *

So why a toadstool? My family, like most families in Poland, loved mushroom hunting and developed expertise in recognizing the poisonous ones and spotting sites rich in porcini and chanterelles, bay bolete and scaber stalks. Mushroom hunting is a national sport in Poland. Step into a forest anytime in September and you will see hordes of people carrying wicker baskets, metal pails, and discount-store plastic bags to their secret mushroom spots. Or read last year's report about mushroom pickers in Poland who interrupted US military exercises in a forest near Żagań despite numerous warnings in both Polish and English about heavy artillery shooting. But hey, it had rained a couple of days before, and it was early fall—perfect timing for mushroom hunting, tanks or no tanks. The US command had to cancel the maneuvers.

Mushroom hunting is a free-for-all in Poland, probably not an environmentally friendly idea but one that results in delicious fungus-based dishes on our tables. And so each year Poles pick around 6 million kilograms of mushrooms—and that's only the amount they sell to stores and farmers' markets, since nobody bothers measuring how much an individual family collects and eats.

During Communism, mushroom and berry picking was a major source of food, and it still sustains a lot of families in rural areas. They leave their homes right after dawn for their special spots rich in chanterelles, wild blueberries, wild strawberries, and raspberries, and by noon, they line up alongside country roads, selling their goods to city folk, who often stop with screeching tires the moment they see someone with buckets and wicker baskets in a roadside ditch.

Recognizing poisonous mushrooms used to be an art passed down from generation to generation. My maternal grandfather Wincenty learned about mushrooms from his father in what is now Belarus. Mother, who loved mushroom hunting, learned it from Wincenty and passed this knowledge to my brother. We were told never to pull or kick a mushroom and to preserve the ecosystem by cutting the stem with a knife. While Mother hunted for mushrooms on her own, a cigarette in one hand, a red plastic bucket in the other, heavy rainboots stomping on moss with a soft squelch, my grandparents would make a team—Grandma Izabela cutting the stems with a short blade and Grandpa Wincenty carrying the increasingly heavy buckets. He always watched carefully what she picked. She was a city girl, brought up in Warsaw, so he didn't trust her foraging skills.

To find Mother, who would often hide behind trees and bushes, you'd simply follow the smell of tobacco.

She rarely wanted to be found.

My younger brother and I, on the other hand, could be easily located from far away because we smelled like raw onions. That's because Grandma would cut an onion in half and rub it all over our skin to deter mosquitoes. On our way back, our tiny red Fiat smelled of fresh forest and onions, and we'd each have at least one heavy bucket of mushrooms on our lap. Our pungent skin made my eyes water.

* * *

After my parents first met, Father's dark hair, hippie beard, and large eyes charmed Mother into a tiny hotel room where they danced to Leonard Cohen before falling on the bed. He couldn't have children, he said, and when she later told him she was pregnant, he divorced his first wife. He vowed to take care of the baby girl. This he did for a couple of years. Then a sickly, gray-faced boy appeared, and their lives, already filled with poop, colic, and day-care lice, became a cacophony of screeches, yelps, ashtrays exploding against walls, and the staccato of train wheels because Father had to go to the capital for canned milk and gluten-free flour for his celiac son, courtesy of international aid boxes for the Eastern Bloc. When he came back one night, arms filled with cans and hair smelling of another woman's perfume, she greeted him with a slurred "Bastard," one child on her hip, the other wailing in her bed. She took another swig of vodka and thought she should stop before she dropped the boy and before her balance was too unsteady to change the girl's wet pajama pants. But then, she didn't really want these children, did she?

Father visited us every other week after their divorce. He took me on hikes while Mother sat at a Formica table stained with yellowish-brown circles where she put down her cigarettes. When she hung the rope in the bathroom for the third time, I imagine she felt nothing, not even the need to hold the smooth bottle neck in her hand. But then, she didn't really want these children. Did she? She left the rope suspended on the pipe and decided to light another cigarette.

***

I grew up inhaling the earthy smells of drying mushrooms in Grandma Iza's kitchen, touching the rough, wrinkled skin of fungus, strung in garlands over radiators, and then tasting the first mushroom and sauerkraut pierogi of the season. Sometimes I'd put the mushroom necklace on and strut around our two-bedroom apartment like a model, blowing kisses to admirers and photographers, even though my only witnesses were indistinct figures in Grandma's cheap reproduction of Van Gogh's *Café Terrace at Night,* hanging right above her fold-out sofa, and grim cockle pickers with curved backs in another painting on the opposite wall. This whole putting-things-around-our-neck habit is one of my most vivid memories from Communist Poland. We all displayed proudly our most prized purchases, like toilet paper, which we had to line up for in front of the store for several hours, blowing on our freezing hands and then strutting home with toilet rolls strung on a rope and swinging from our necks, our precious Eastern Bloc lei.

Those fungal garlands sitting on radiators helped us during harsh winters. When I think of September and October back home, I recall the sylvan scent of drying mushrooms. Yet I hear that there are fungi out there that smell like raspberries or like herring and pickled cucumbers. Some mushrooms smell like coconut, others like radishes, or lavender, or anise. The ones drying on our radiators were not fancy at all. They smelled of soil, moss, and wet leaves.

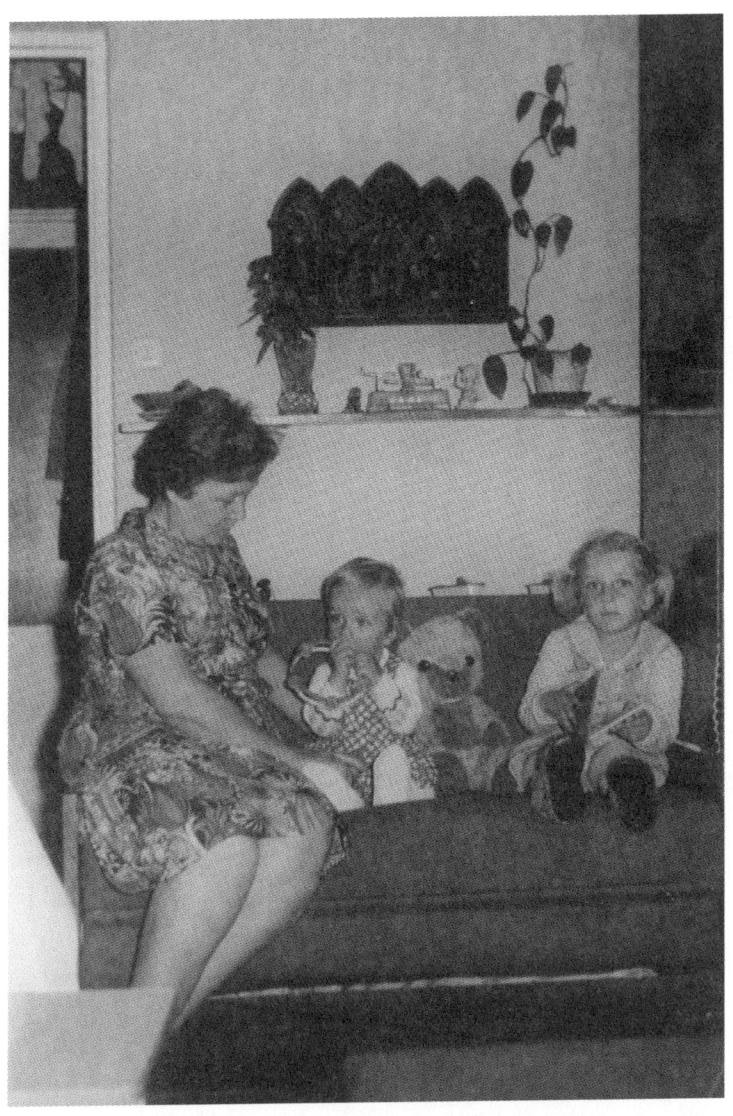

Grandma Iza, Tomek, and me; Ostróda, Poland, 1982. Photo by Ryszard Szczeszak.

* * *

1983. The green crayon in my hand moves slowly, steadily across thin paper and makes the wobbly table underneath whimper like an injured dog. Grandma sits in a brown armchair, her elbows on fake leather armrests, her face in the shadow.

"Your mother was poisoned. Mushrooms." She lifts her arms in the air to welcome my brother and me to a family hug, but her hands are shaking, and I hesitate. Tomek is already on her lap. I join in and feel her plump cheek against my forehead.

"The priest is at the hospital. He'll put holy oil on her forehead so her sins are forgiven. He'll stop by here afterwards. Priest Zdzisław. Do you know what this means? The doctors are trying to help, but they say she may go to heaven soon."

We all kneel on rough carpet, facing the black night outside the living room windows. *Hail Mary, full of Grace, the Lord is with thee. Blessed art thou amongst women, and blessed is the Fruit of thy womb, Jesus. Holy Mary, mother of God, pray for us sinners, now and in the hour of our death. Amen.* In the quiet of the night, we say the prayer over and over again until my eyelids grow heavy with sleep.

I don't remember the priest's visit. He must have come—he was a family friend, my First Communion guide, my mentor. Lanky and jovial, Priest Zdzisław was always surrounded by kids, singing and dancing in church and playing soccer with us after catechism classes. He must have come and comforted us that night, but my memory fails here. What I can recall vividly from that night when I was five is finding Mother unresponsive in her bed, dressing my younger brother in wool pants and winter boots, and trekking with him through muddy snow to reach Grandma's apartment, then listening to Grandma as she sat in that ugly chair to tell us about the mushrooms.

* * *

Grandpa taught us to look under the mushroom cap to make sure it is not poisonous. If under the cap there are gills, something that looks like bicycle spokes, he'd say, it's best not to pick it.

You can't tell by the taste whether a mushroom is poisonous or not, and they are often deceptive. The death cap, one of the world's most poisonous mushrooms, apparently has a mild taste—no warning in that first or second or third bite. Because it looks like a straw mushroom, it's tricky to distinguish from other edible fungi. You can't kill its amatoxins with heat, unless you crank it up to over 300 degrees Celsius, so cooking it on a stove won't help at all. It causes intense vomiting, diarrhea, dehydration, organ damage, and eventually death. This mushroom is responsible for over 90 percent of fatal mushroom poisoning globally. Pope Clement VII is said to have died of accidental death cap poisoning, and there's a rumor that the Roman emperor Claudius did, too.

There's dark humor in some translations of poisonous mushroom names. What we call in Polish *muchomor jadowity* means in direct translation a "poisonous fly-killer," but it has a different English designation—destroying angel. With a white stalk, gills, and cap, it does look innocent and is often confused with a button mushroom. But its name in English doesn't imply a danger to insects; rather, it implies the wrath of Yahweh and the slaying of the Israelites. *And God sent an angel to Jerusalem to destroy it: and as he was destroying, the LORD beheld, and he repented him of the evil . . .*

I often sat in Grandma's living room, which doubled as her bedroom after my grandparents took me and my brother in (an on-and-off arrangement that fluctuated depending on Mother's ability to care for us), and pored over a large mushroom atlas, looking at poor-quality photos of edible and poisonous fungi, trying to guess which ones almost killed my mother. Whenever I asked, my grandparents and uncle would quickly look away and change the topic, which I should have interpreted as a sign that Mother must have been poisoned by something else, with the determination of a freshly divorced alcoholic. But the word *suicide* was not yet in my vocabulary, and I transferred all my anger and helplessness from that night onto the pages of the atlas. When I found it years later, its hardback covers were chewed off on the edges, and the paper inside was stained and creased.

* * *

My costume in that Santa photo was a fly agaric. I believe the photo dates from before Mother's attempted suicide. Fly agaric is potentially deadly, but it mostly causes digestive issues. People in Eastern Europe use it as insecticide because it attracts houseflies when you crumble up the cap into a saucer of milk. It contains toxins that paralyze the central nervous system in humans and cause symptoms such as vomiting and vertigo, as well as euphoria and visions—that's because muscimol and ibotenic acid in fly agaric are psychoactive. There's a story that Lewis Carroll hallucinated after eating dried fly agaric, and that this experience influenced a scene from *Alice in Wonderland,* the one where Alice shrinks and then grows tall after biting opposite sides of a mushroom.

* * *

On a rainy evening in west-central Indiana, I prop my infant son's head in the crook of my arm and hold a cheap edition of *Alice* in front of us. He doesn't yet understand the words, but I've been reading to him since I spotted two red stripes on the screen of a Walgreens pregnancy test in my bathroom.

"Who are you?" said the Caterpillar. This was not an encouraging opening for a conversation. Alice replied, rather shyly, "I—I hardly know, sir, just at present—at least I know who I WAS

when I got up this morning, but I think I must have been changed several times since then."

"What do you mean by that?" said the Caterpillar sternly. "Explain yourself!"

"I can't explain myself, I'm afraid, sir" said Alice, "because I'm not myself, you see."

"I don't see," said the Caterpillar.

"I'm afraid I can't put it more clearly," Alice replied very politely, "for I can't understand it myself to begin with; and being so many different sizes in a day is very confusing."

Father used to read *Alice in Wonderland* to me, even after my parents' divorce when he visited us once every two weekends. I envied Alice her ability to change sizes and did not realize back then that Alice found it disconcerting and scary because changing sizes wasn't her choice, at least not at the beginning. I also didn't see how close to that state of bewilderment I myself was as a child, how much a lack of agency shaped my personality, how the unexpected and forced assumption of responsibility over the family's well-being warped my sense of security. At that time, I firmly believed the family folklore about mushroom poisoning, and I begged Mother to retell her story about seeing a bright light as she lay dying in the hospital that night.

* * *

I turn to Alice in moments of terror. Some nights my ample body shrinks and almost disappears.

* * *

I search for information on fly agaric's hallucinogenic properties and find a Polish website with recipes and doses. You can mix it with honey, but it's best when dried in the sun first to release the mushroom's psychoactive properties. You can also boil it for an hour and drink the stew, hoping to get a trip instead of serious stomach poisoning. It is said that fly agaric was often added to the haoma drink used in Zoroastrian practices, stimulating alertness and increasing sexual drive. On the other hand, the mushroom is credited for Berserkers' trancelike fury when these Norse warriors attacked their enemies. When you read Icelandic sagas, you learn about Berserkers foaming at the mouth, howling like wild animals, and charging at the enemies, immune to fire and weaponry, only to become weak and timid after the battle. Some historians theorize that fly agaric was the secret to their frenzies.

Mother's poison of choice was alcohol, though, not dangerous mushrooms, and that night when I couldn't wake her up she had mixed it with a bunch of potent sleeping pills. Like Berserkers, she was capable of unstoppable fury, though her trigger was alcohol withdrawal. Once she charged at me with a large, curved shard of glass. This indelible memory—Mother running toward me through the hallway, the sliver moon of glass in her raised hand, eyes wide open, nostrils flaring—makes it hard for me to acknowledge that she was, in fact, a small, fragile woman, with delicate facial features and thin arms ending in tobacco-stained fingertips. No doubt I provoked her fury. I was an insubordinate teenager despite my grandparents' attempts to civilize me, and, if I recall correctly, the glass was there because I shut the door to my room with a large bang, shattering glass all over the hallway. But that wasn't the only instance of aggression on her part. She'd bite Grandma after discovering her secret alcohol stash gone. She'd yell obscenities and kick when we tried to drag her home from a libation at three in the morning, hoping that somehow nobody heard her; she was a high school teacher and, apart from our grandparents' retirement money, the only source of income in the house. The fear that she'd lose her job one day was always there, especially after we overheard on a crowded bus that someone's English teacher was drunk in class again. It wasn't just the money that we'd lose then. We intuited even as children that for her, work was the only thing between semifunctional alcoholism and a full-on escape into the bottle.

* * *

Mother grew up in the provincial town of Biskupiec in northeastern Poland. Stalin was dead by the time she was born, but the totalitarian regime still held the Eastern Bloc in its tight grip, outlawing political opposition, jailing dissidents, manufacturing historical narratives that fit its Communist agenda and maintained the mirage of Soviet-Polish friendship, and keeping all except the party apparatchiks in poverty.

Mother's high school friend tells me that she has always been different.

"She was ethereal, unconventional, reserved," she says when I call her from Indiana. I found her on Facebook, over thirty years since I last saw her back in Poland. She agreed to talk to me after we exchanged a few private messages about my academic career, my new family, my emigration. "Some may say arrogant or aloof, but I called her unorthodox."

"Did she drink in high school?" I ask, groping in the dark for an answer to a question I haven't quite formulated yet. Or was it me that made her reach for a bottle of vodka each day?

"She did drink," Mother's friend says, "but so did everyone else."

I try to understand why I feel relief in my chest when I hear about Mother's high school parties and alcohol-soaked mushroom-hunting excursions.

* * *

Whose idea was it to dress me as a poisonous mushroom for the Christmas party? Did I say no to being a princess or a doctor or a butterfly? As I ponder this question, I discover a curious connection between fly agaric and Santa, and a vague image comes back to me of a glittering fly agaric tree ornament in our home. My brother Tomek and I, still in pajamas, pretend that the Christmas tree is an enchanted forest, and we make our cardboard angel ornaments jump from one glittering mushroom to another, searching for a fairy. The morning sun lights up the tinsel in a million silver flashes. Much later, when I listen to an NPR segment with the catchy title "Did 'Shrooms Send Santa and His Reindeer Flying?" I learn that fly agaric mushrooms were a common aid in shamanistic rituals in the Far East. In Siberia not only shamans but also reindeer ate fly agaric and enjoyed vivid hallucinations. So the biologist interviewed on the radio asked whether reindeer were flying, or perhaps "flying"—that is, did people simply have visions in which reindeer flew? Intoxication—through mushrooms, alcohol, potent white and gray and brown powders, liquified opioid sucked into a needle from a heated spoon, or pills found in medicine cabinets—has been a catalyst for unique art, a power behind myths and religious systems, but also the destroying angel lulling humans into submission, turning them into hollow shells, blinding them to love.

As children, we loved fly agaric's attractive coloring and the cheerful little dots, but we never touched it in the forest. We knew even then that we could die from eating it and also that destroying one would not protect other people from picking the mushroom because that bright little cap was just the fruiting body of a huge network of the fungus deep underground.

As an adult, I am in awe of the vast ecosystem of mushrooms, their hyphae reaching down, down, their mycelia often surviving for thousands of years. Those who kick or cut away mushrooms from their lawns or mossy forest beds only remove a tiny part of a resilient, beautiful organism hiding patiently away underfoot, ready to produce more bodies when temperatures drop and the rains come.

And that vast underground network is apparently one of the ways trees communicate with each other. In an incredible symbiosis, trees provide fungal cells with carbohydrates while fungi help trees collect water. Fungi are information superhighways linking roots through their thin underground threads, sending information and nutrients from plant to plant, and helping established plants sabotage invasive species. Mycologist Paul Stamets calls fungi "earth's natural internet," and it's an apt analogy.

How do we reconcile the mushrooms' nutritious potential with their destructive abilities? Their fragile fruits, susceptible to hooves and galoshes and drought, with an almost indestructible network of mycelia dwelling underground, ready to regenerate whatever dies aboveground? Fungi are like foster care. Nurturing and protective, their underground threads attach themselves to tree roots, providing nutrients, protecting them from invasive species, and even boosting the "immune system" of the plants and training them to resist disease. Large, older trees help younger and weaker ones through carbon transfer along the fungal mycelia. When trees and other plants like tomatoes or broad beans are attacked by toxic fungi, they release a warning to neighboring plants through the mycelia. Because of the help from the fungi, trees are actually social beings, helping each other survive. But those mycelia often facilitate theft of nutrients. For example, phantom orchids steal carbon from neighboring trees because the orchids don't have their own chlorophyll. Lots of other unfriendly plants, like the black walnut tree, release toxins toward their neighbors in fierce competition for water and food.

Living with an addict means living with the same baffling contradictions. Was Mother's "mushroom poisoning" an escape from a life she never wanted to live, the boredom of unplanned mothering, the harsh realities of single parenthood, and the mayhem of two kids under five? Was she fit at all to have children? What does it mean to be fit to have children? Were we stealing her air? Did we finally suck her dry of life-giving nutrients? After all, she divorced my chronically unfaithful father when we were tiny, and she had a full-time teaching job, not to mention the often-impossible task of finding food and basic toiletries in Communist Poland.

Would she be a tad warmer, more loving toward us if she had loved herself in the first place?

Luckily, our grandparents intuited early that things were not going well. They moved from their sleepy town to a bigger city to be near us and rescued us time and again from a woman who was probably never mother material. Though I was the one dressed as a toadstool, and though I thought of myself in unflattering terms throughout my childhood, transferring the blame for Mother's aggressive and sometimes withdrawn behavior onto myself, it occurs to me now that perhaps I was not the one poisoning our fragile ecosystem.

* * *

After talking to Mother's high school friend on the phone, I sink into midwestern darkness.

I slam the door and glass explodes into air a shard falls moonshaped next to Mother who is a bundle of sinews and synapses out of sync clenched fists flared nostrils black wool rising and falling rising and falling where the heart should be and fuck she picks up the moon caresses its sharp edges with her gaze and fuck it glints above her shoulder then ear then hair and she runs eyes unseeing heaving spitting the moon closer and closer and fuck no fuck no fuck no. A flower opens where my heart should be.

* * *

When Grandma and Grandpa took us in after Mother's first attempted suicide, they took her in, too, hoping they could keep her away from self-destructive binge drinking, but she would always find a way to sneak alcohol into their apartment and hide it in most unlikely places—behind the radiator in Grandpa's dark room, behind the washing machine, among flower pots on the balcony where she smoked, between books in her large purse, in a utility closet, and even in a toilet tank. Initially, whoever found her little bottles of vodka would throw a fit, spilling the contents in the kitchen sink, and beg her to "think of the children." At some point, those dramatic displays faded and life became somewhat quieter, but I could always detect tension in the secret looks between my grandparents. Mother drank as much as before. Eventually my grandparents decided to focus on us and provide as much stability and peace as was possible for five people, a disruptive alcoholic among them, living in a tiny two-bedroom apartment. They were both retired by then—Grandma from her work in accounting, Grandpa from his political positions and from teaching economics—and though they were busy doing volunteer work and growing, preserving, and preparing food, they always made sure that our homework was done, that we got enough food and sleep, and that we knew we were loved. While Mother must have given us hugs and must have told us she loved us, I don't remember these moments. Her body was tense, lean, hard. Her teeth clenched tight. Her eyes angry or unhappy, depending on the alcohol level in her blood. I would sometimes look at old photos of her, from when she was a university student, and wonder where all the charm and glee I saw on her face had gone. Would she ever smile at me the way she smiled at her friends in these photos? Mother's whole mysterious world of experience and emotion, intellectual discovery and adventure, was inaccessible to us, buried under a mask, or rather masks—either the angry or the comatose one.

She neglected her collection of books packed tightly onto her living room shelves. She gradually stopped playing our antique piano—an 1876 gift to a Prussian princess, if the inscription inside the instrument was genuine; dark brown and majestic, with lions carved into its legs, it had been purchased from an acquaintance for a bottle of vodka and, eventually, sold for three bottles of vodka after Mother ran out of family gold. A capitalist would call it an excellent return on investment. When Mother reported over the phone that she had sold the piano, I could tell she was already drunk.

She never gave up mushroom hunting, though, and she'd occasionally help Grandma in the kitchen after a trip to the forest, threading mushrooms for hours into brown and orange garlands.

***

Mother's third-floor apartment was sterile and drafty, with wind howling through the pipes and the sound of city buses waking us up before dawn. When I think of her kitchen, I think of my brother Tomek sitting with me on top of the table, peeling large swaths of skin off his thumb and showing them to me with pride. I now recognize we must have suffered from serious vitamin deficiency, but back then, we couldn't wait for pieces of our skin to come off so we could compare their sizes and declare a winner.

But our grandparents' home always smelled of cooking and baking: sautéed onions, potato pancakes, cabbage soup, simple pastries. And mushrooms—lots of them, especially in winter, when our garden lay barren, and meat, as usual, was mostly unavailable. We dried mushrooms, but we also pickled them and prepared them fresh—steamed, sautéed, deep-fried, mixed with sauerkraut and stuffed into pierogi dough, added to soups and sauces, mixed with pasta or potatoes or buckwheat. And though most people in the US would consider the smell unsavory, one of the most distinct odors of the Polish kitchen, including my grandparents', is that of *bigos*—mushrooms stewed for three days with sauerkraut, red wine, honey, prunes, kiełbasa, and meat scraps, served with rye or sourdough bread. After days on the stove, the stew thickens and becomes dark brown. As you eat, its sweet and sour taste gives way to an umami sensation that comes from the mushrooms and cabbage, lingering on the roof of the mouth and in the back of the throat.

* * *

BIGOS

2 pounds sauerkraut
1 pound kiełbasa and other meats (pork roast, duck roast, bacon, etc.), cubed
a handful of boletus mushrooms (or other kind)
1 large onion, chopped
2 Tbs lard
10 prunes
1/4 cup dry red wine
1/8 cup honey
Salt, pepper, marjoram to taste
1 Tbs tomato paste (optional)

Rinse sauerkraut briefly. Chop sauerkraut and mushrooms and simmer in beef or vegetable stock just covering the cabbage for about 20 minutes. (If you're using dried mushrooms, soak them in water overnight.) In a skillet, sauté a finely chopped onion and meat in lard. Add to the simmering cabbage, together with chopped prunes. Add wine, honey, tomato paste (if using), and seasoning. Bring back to simmer for another 60 minutes. Store in the fridge for 24 hours. Reheat and serve the next day. Bigos is best with whole-wheat or dark rye bread.

Bigos tastes like a snuggle under a warm blanket with Grandma Izabela while the window panes are covered with frost and you wait for the TV screen to stop jumping so you can watch your favorite show about a brave Soviet tank crew and their dog, or the cartoon about Bumblebee Maia who is caught in the storm and finds refuge under a giant mushroom while the waters about her rage and swell and swallow tiny forest creatures too far from dry land to be rescued.

* * *

I slam the brakes in my Subaru and wait for the dust to settle before I open the door.

"Mama? What happened?" My tween asks from the back seat. The sudden stop makes him lift his head from the phone screen, but his thumb is still hovering over the blue glow.

"Put down your phone. I need your help."

"What . . ."

But I'm already out in the wet grass, heading for a patch of large white globes by the edge of the woods. He hurries after me.

"See this?" I point at the puffball mushrooms.

"Wow. What is it?"

"Dinner!"

I grab the mushrooms and twist them gently to dislodge them from the mycelia.

"Eeew . . . I'm not eating that. Not touching it, either."

"*Proszę.*" Please. "I parked illegally. We gotta get back to the car."

We carry the large, spongy globes to the trunk. One is bigger than my head. I'm already planning to slice it up and bake it as a pizza crust, with pesto and shredded mozzarella and Asiago on top.

"Mom, you know we don't have to scavenge for food. What if someone sees us?"

* * *

My American family won't touch the cooked puffball. I try to convince them that this mushroom tastes mild, that it tastes like tofu.

"And why would I find that appetizing?" My son has already poured frozen chicken nuggets on a plate and is reaching for the microwave. Soon my husband will fix himself a quesadilla.

I munch on my "pizza" in silence, wallowing in self-pity. At this moment, I resent my adopted country. I resent its opulence. I resent the ease with which middle-class people like us can find and fix a meal. I resent the blandness of the chicken nuggets and the nauseating sweetness of American ice cream and the spongy store-bought bread and the rubbery chicken wraps in school cafeterias and the syrupy canned peaches and the breaded fish sticks that taste like sewer. In moments like this, I forget how desperate I was to leave Poland.

"But I can make us brownies!" My son pulls out a cake pan and powdered cocoa.

* * *

Soon I will load the dishwasher and put my kids to bed, and I will sink my head into a fluffy pillow. When I finally drift away, I will slam the door and glass will explode into air, and Mother will be running running running toward me with a moonshaped shard.

Birds

A few months before Mother swallowed the whole container of pills, chased it with a bottle of vodka, and lay down in her bed to die as my brother and I played with our clay zoo in the next room, she got hold of a whole chicken on the black market. City folk like us had little access to meat of any kind in Communist Poland, and I still don't know who sold the chicken to her. She wasn't much of a cook, my mother, but she was determined to make a feast for us all, and she stuck that bird into our rotisserie oven—possibly the first and the last bird that was cooked there. She sat at the laminate table by the window and waited, smoking one filterless cigarette after another. Suddenly, she screamed "*Jezus!*" and ran out of the kitchen and out of the apartment, leaving a trail of tobacco smoke behind. Father was still living with us then, or maybe he was just visiting. When he checked the oven, he realized that Mother had not removed the chicken's trachea, and now, as the air was circulating through it, the chicken made an eerie *eeeeeeech eeeeeeeeech eeeeeeeech* sound, the notes rising with each rotation. I don't remember the taste of that chicken. I do remember that we ate it without her.

Poles eat most parts of the chicken, including the giblets and sometimes the feet. Dry-fried chicken liver smothered in garlicky butter is still one of my favorite dishes, its silky, rosy flesh melting on my tongue. The traditional Polish way to serve roasted chicken is with young potatoes sprinkled with dill and a side of *mizeria*—fresh, thinly sliced cucumber, sour cream, and sugar. We couldn't always get sour cream or sugar or chicken, but we could always get cucumbers.

Sometimes, though, Father came in through our front door with a large box filled with exotic treats, and we'd take a break from cucumbers. He often traveled with the orchestra he worked for as a manager and occasionally as a substitute oboe player filling an unsightly gap in the ensemble when someone got sick or absconded behind the Iron Curtain. He would go on tour to Berlin, Moscow, Sofia, or Bucharest, and when he was away, I looked for these places on the map and drew tiny little clefs with a red pencil next to the cities he visited. Then, before going to sleep, I studied the map, measured distances, and retraced the flow of rivers with my fingertips. I knew that Sofia was not far from the sea that resembled a giant slug, and that the roads leading to Moscow looked like spider legs. Before Father went to West Germany and France, though, he had to get permission from the government, and I was not surprised that it was hard to go there because one of my teachers had told me that there were thieves in the West—it was full of people who stole from the poor and gave to the rich. So when Father came back from the West loaded with real chocolate and beautiful red-haired dolls and Lego blocks and oranges and Haribo gummy bears, I was afraid that he also stole from the poor.

Right after he came back from one of these trips, my parents began whispering behind the closed kitchen door, and then my father moved to another city. "It's not a divorce, sweetheart. It's separation," Mother said as she took another swig of stinky beer. I didn't know either word at the time, but I would repeat that sentence, with an air of being initiated into the secret world of adult relationships, to anyone who later asked me about Father's disappearance.

My parents were friends before they became lovers. Mother was quiet but unpredictable, her blond hair framing her delicate features. Father towered over her, tall, dark, and reckless, his stories echoing at parties, his energy palpable the moment you entered the room. I'm pretty sure Mother knew that Father was married when they both checked into a dingy hotel room in Poznań, where Mother studied in a low-residency English program after graduating from the Nicolaus Copernicus University with a master's degree in Polish literature. Father told me I was conceived to the accompaniment of Leonard Cohen songs streaming from a black plastic-cube radio perched on a shelf above their narrow bed. *And you know that she's half-crazy, but that's why you want to be there.* He still has the hotel check-in slip from that night, he says, though he never shows it to me, so I imagine a grumpy, wrinkled concierge handing them a key to their room, a cardboard-thick tag attached, and a registration under a fake name for both of them because it's late 1970s Catholic Poland and people are always in your business when they tire of watching Communist propaganda on TV.

Like a bird on a wire
Like a drunk in a midnight choir
I have tried in my way to be free.

In my mind, the four walls of that dark hotel room are a shelter, a portal to an imagined freedom and recklessness and love—love that would soon prove just as confining as the lives they escaped for that one night in a bed jingling to Cohen's voice.

* * *

After their shotgun wedding, my parents moved to Olsztyn, a formerly Prussian city in the lake district not far from Mother's hometown. They rented a tiny studio with a kitchen annex and

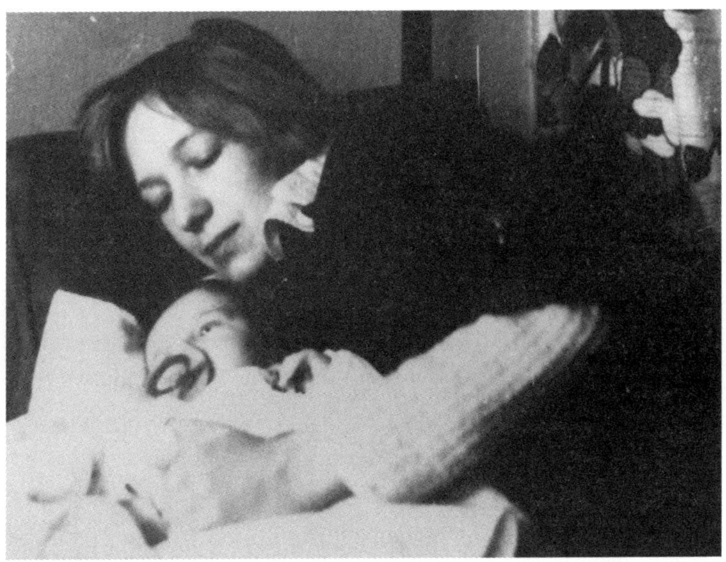

Mother and baby me, late 1978 or early 1979. Photo by Ryszard Szczeszak.

a shared bathroom down the hallway. It was in that apartment they celebrated Mother's birthday on the night of December 8, and according to my uncle who joined them and several other guests, Mother "had a drink or two," which I suppose was not unusual for expecting mothers back then. She was eight months pregnant. The next day, she and her brother braved slippery sidewalks and boarded a train to visit their parents. Halfway through their trip, Mother's water broke, filling her winter boots with amniotic fluid and sending my uncle into a frenzy. As he ran up and down the narrow corridor, looking for a doctor on the moving train, flailing his arms and saying "*Mój Boże*," my God, under his breath, Mother leaned against her plastic seat and focused on its bright-red color, groaning from time to time. Whenever I was told this story as a teenager, I admonished Mother for making it to the hospital just in time. Had she delivered me on that train, I'd have had honorary free train tickets for life. "I'll buy you a train ticket. Where do you want to go?" she'd mumble without taking her cigarette from between her lips.

* * *

In 1979 Father got a job at a theater in Olsztyn as a marketing specialist, but three years later he returned to his previous position at the Baltic Opera and Philharmonic in Gdańsk, which allowed him international travel, an unheard-of luxury for most Poles at that time. After his first trip to the West, we ate oblong yellow fruit that tasted like soap, black licorice candy we pretended to like, juicy oranges, kiwi, and canned meat. No cucumbers for an entire week! We let them grow and ripen, untouched, in our garden. Afterward, we went back to our usual diet of cucumbers on bread for breakfast, cucumbers in sour cream for lunch, and cucumbers with white cheese for supper. Sometimes, in preschool, we got cucumbers in our omelet. We would eat the eggs, but the pale-green, soggy cubes always ended up in a huge smelly metal bucket that the cleaning ladies carried around the tables, grunting, "You should eat cucumbers. They are very healthy, and besides, we have nothing else to eat."

So I was surprised when Mother did not sit down at the table with us to eat that singing roasted chicken. It did not occur to us to save any meat for her. We ate it all, leaving the carcass for the next-day broth. Now that I think of it, she was never an avid carnivore, perhaps because she loved animals. She stopped us from killing spiders and bees. She stepped into pet stores and played with hamsters and mice, clicking her tongue at them and sticking her yellow fingers between the bars. She even let me adopt a pustule-covered black female rat I brought home one day as a teen, when a friend from my punk posse asked me to take care of it before he headed to jail for robbing a kiosk. Mother was the one who applied special ointment on the rat's blood- and pus-covered skin, who tenderly stroked its mangy black fur as she watched *The Thorn Birds* on TV. She was gentle and cuddly with our dogs, although she often forgot to feed them.

Mother bought our first dog, Aza, with a bottle of vodka. In a country where official currency was pretty useless, half a liter of vodka became real tender. Aza was a black mutt, a traveling dog. She would sneak out of our apartment whenever the door was left ajar, run to the nearest bus stop, hop on a bus, and hop off at another stop before running back home, panting with excitement and telling us all about her adventures with her wagging tail. Neighbors would often report which bus line they spotted her on: "I saw Aza on Number Two this morning. Is she back yet?" "She sat on someone's lap on Number Twenty-Five and jumped off before the primary school." "The driver kicked her off Number Fifteen." When Aza came back, Mother would pet her shiny black fur and say: "I gave half a liter of vodka for you, so you better not run away for good."

* * *

My hunger for Mother's affection wedged itself into my stomach, gnawing and churning, making sure I was ready at all times to defend myself, to scavenge, to plead. But this hunger was occasionally lifted by life-giving substitutions. I lived in a gray world of totalitarian lack—of freedom, of hope, of basic necessities—but also in the wonderland of Grandma's kitchen, with its tea-stained glasses and the earthy smell of gingerbread. As with our beloved mushrooms, my world was both toxic and life-giving, and I learned to navigate Mother's land mines, to receive her blows, and to recover on Grandma's lap, regaining strength to weather the next family crisis.

* * *

Several years ago, I visited a distant family member in a Polish village close to the eastern border. As we sat in her living room and watched sparrows tapping at the windowsill, Teresa said, "Most village people ate them right after the war. Boiled in hot water, feathers off. Good source of protein."

I licked the spoon clean of her rose petal jam, ready to open the jar of dandelion "honey," which she makes by boiling flowers with sugar. She spoke slowly, giving the memories time to take shape. There was softness in her wrinkled face, and her voice sounded girlish, almost melodious, with surprising cadences in her consonant-heavy, rustling Polish. Teresa's affricates and swishing phonemes made me think of autumn leaves parted by unhurried feet. I felt no discomfort in her long silences, but I was intrigued about the sparrows. I asked about them again.

During the war, she said, her family couldn't eat sparrows because the Nazis took their horse barn. But after the war, you'd go to the barn or pigsty, which was covered with hay. The sparrows had their nests under the thatched roof to hide from the cold. Late in the evening, Teresa's mom would take a paraffin torch, her dad a hazel tree branch, and out they went into the snow. The intense light from the torch disoriented the birds, and the steady beat of the hazel stick scared them out of their nests. When they flew away toward the light, tiny fuzzballs chirping their confusion, Teresa's dad would catch them in a linen sack. Sometimes little Teresa helped by grabbing the sparrows mid-flight and putting them, still alive, under her shirt.

"You didn't mind?" I asked. The dandelion honey had a sharp aftertaste, not altogether unpleasant. I reached for more.

Teresa leaned back against the creaky chair, stretching her swollen legs. No. Sparrows are clean because they eat grain, sometimes worms. Her neighbor ate crows. He'd climb trees using homemade wire pole climbers attached to his shoes, strap himself to a linden or oak, and scoop up young crows that were already in feathers, almost ready to fly. Omnivorous scavengers, those crows.

"Was it the hooded crow or the carrion crow?"

Teresa didn't know. To her, it did not matter whether the plumage was ash gray or glossy black, as long as there was meat on the bird's bones. I think of winter mornings forty years after the end of the war, in my hometown not far from Teresa's house, when the crows' *kraa kraa kraa* pierced the chilly gray air, a sign I had to put on my boots and brave the cold to be in preschool on time. To this day the sound wrenches me away from my warm bed in small-town Indiana and carries me thousands of miles across the Atlantic toward the freezing half-light treks to preschool.

On the Faroe Islands, they used to believe that if a girl threw a stone, a bone, and a clump of turf at a crow, and the crow flew toward the sea, she would marry a foreigner. Did I ever throw anything at crows as a girl? And what would the Faroese think of Teresa, a hungry girl sucking greedily the fat from a crow's skull?

Teresa shifted in her chair. Crows were a rarity back then, she explained. At home, it was mostly sparrows. Before boiling the birds, you cut off their heads and de-feathered them that same evening or late at night. Sometimes they'd fry them in whatever grease they had—usually linseed oil pressed on site. There's not a lot of meat on a sparrow, so Teresa ate hers carefully, paying attention to the last bites from around the tiny ribs.

"Isn't that what your village was called," I asked, "Ribs?" *Żebry* means "begging" in Polish, Teresa explained, not ribs. They never begged.

But they were often hungry. After the war, the kids would go to the river, dig canals in turf, and catch golden-bronze crucian carp there with triangle-shaped nets. They ground the fish—head, bones, and all—and made fish balls. Sometimes, after taking the cows to graze, the kids baked the freshly caught crucians in gray river clay, which they kneaded on the spot. It was great clay, says Teresa, that didn't even stain their hands when they squeezed and molded it. The girls wrapped the fish in that clay and threw it in a fire. When they took it out and broke the clay, one part of the fish would be on one side and the other on the other side, the scales stuck to the clay, so it was easy to clean the fish. The entrails and bones would separate from the tender meat. Their stomachs full, they'd make dolls out of the river clay while minding the cows and chewing on rye grains.

"How old were you then?"

"Five or six." Teresa dropped a spoonful of dandelion honey into her tea.

My mind moved quickly to the back seat of my SUV gliding along I-74, a five-year-old boy, my son, secure in a booster seat, a handful of chicken nuggets in his cup holder. Out of nowhere came a question: "Mama, do you know that some people eat peacocks? How can they?" He sniffled for a while but forgot all about beautiful peafowl a minute later. I heard him sing with his mouth full.

For here am I sitting in a tin can
Far above the world.

* * *

Werner Herzog's film *Stroszek* ends with a scene in which hypnotized chickens dance in a tourist-trap arcade after the main character drops coins into the slot. Herzog famously confirmed his fear of chickens when he said, "Look into the eyes of a chicken and you will see real stupidity. It is a kind of bottomless stupidity, a fiendish stupidity. They are the most horrifying, cannibalistic and nightmarish creatures in the world." Although this contradicts current knowledge about chickens' intelligence—as researchers rename parts of the avian brain and stipulate that the chicken brain processes information in a way similar to our own cerebral cortex—it does help us understand Herzog's other claim that chickens are a metaphor for something. The final *Stroszek* scene seems to tell us that life is a series of dumb entertainment vignettes fueled by money as we try to forget about our mortality. We watch what disgusts us. We cannot turn away. We move from one shallow entertainment to another, from a dancing chicken to a piano-playing chicken, to a drumming duck. As the birds entertain the film's audience, Stroszek himself rides up and down a mountain in a cable car, an "Is this really me!" sign on the back of his seat and a frozen turkey and a shotgun on his lap. When he disappears from view, a single shot rings out.

* * *

We may bristle at sinking our teeth into sparrow flesh, but eating birds other than chickens and turkeys really isn't a novel idea. The medieval Western world, especially the upper class, loved swans and peacocks on their feast tables. An Italian book on feasts, published at the beginning of the sixteenth century, has a chapter on how to "*make Pies that the Birds may be aliue in them, and flie out when it is cut vp.*" I had thought the Mother Goose rhyme about four and twenty blackbirds baked in a pie was just a flight of imagination, until I stumbled upon that Italian cookbook.

When the pie was opened
The birds began to sing—
Wasn't that a dainty dish
To set before the king?

Mother, who taught high school English until her self-destructive behavior made it impossible to show up in class sober, sang Mother Goose nursery rhymes to me as she sat at the kitchen table sipping on her vodka. After an hour or two of drinking, she'd switch to singing Polish revolutionary songs about starving peasants. “Sing a Song of Sixpence” was in her repertoire. Although some say that this rhyme is really about King Henry VIII’s break from the Catholic Church, with the birds representing the church, and the maid who appears later in the song representing Ann Boleyn, the dish with live birds really existed. On occasion, cooks would replace birds with frogs, rabbits, or even poetry-reciting dwarfs. Nowadays some bakers use so-called pie birds—hollow ceramic figures of birds placed in the middle of their pie—to provide ventilation and prevent the contents of the pie spilling over as the heat rises.

What was once an elaborate, fancy meal on the tables of nobles in Genoa and Paris and a source of entertainment between dishes became a base form of sustenance in lean postwar Poland, especially in the countryside. Teresa’s family bent over the sparrows’ boiled flesh sprinkled with salt and with deft fingers picked around the keel-like sternum, the furcula, the humerus, radius, and ulna, stripping the birds of the now-beige meat.

These must have been Eurasian tree sparrows, which, despite their name, often build nests on buildings, like their slightly larger urban cousins, house sparrows. Their chestnut-colored crowns and white cheeks with a contrasting black pattern bob up and down as they search for seeds and worms. With a clutch of about six eggs, they breed fast and used to be plentiful in the Polish countryside, especially before the widespread use of herbicides that now contribute to their declining population. Their high-pitched chirps and cheeps carry a long way from the roof cavities of empty buildings or from pollarded willows. They sometimes breed in nests abandoned by magpies and storks. Their own untidy nests are made of sticks, grass, hay, and wool and are insulated with feathers.

Both parents incubate their small, blotchy eggs. Sparrows are an altricial species, which means that their young are incapable of taking care of themselves. As they emerge from the eggs, young sparrows need to be nurtured and protected as they fledge and before they take flight. The parents guard the little ones against owls and hawks. Some nests are attacked by weasels and rats. In postwar Poland, they were also raided by hungry humans.

Hungry Poles were their predators, but so was Mao Zedong, who ordered 3 million Chinese peasants to eradicate sparrows in the Four Pests Campaign of 1958 to reduce grain crop damage. Sparrows were declared the enemy of Communism. Like bloodsucking capitalists, sparrows stole the products of people's labor, filling their plump bellies without hard work. During the campaign, they mostly died of exhaustion, as the favored weapons against them were pots, pans, and spoons. Sparrows cannot stay in the air for long. They need to perch and rest often. When they cannot do that, their little hearts fail. Humans made so much noise with their cooking utensils in the countryside that sparrows couldn't land in their nests or on trees and eventually dropped dead to the ground. They were also attacked in cities, including Beijing, where the military as well as volunteering schoolchildren killed them en masse. Ironically, some sparrows escaped to the grounds of the Polish embassy in Beijing, which proved a sanctuary for them because the diplomats there refused to let the Chinese enter and kill the birds. In the end, the embassy was surrounded by people with pots and pans, and a few days later, the embassy staff had to shovel out thousands of dead sparrows. As with other campaigns designed to meddle with the environment on a massive scale, this one backfired. The sparrow population diminished in China, and the number of locusts and other insects increased, which contributed to the 1959–61 famine during which 30 million people died. By then, there were almost no sparrows left to eat.

* * *

When I visit a local butcher in my small midwestern town, I ask about chicken livers.

"I only have lamb livers today. Dogs like those, too."

"It's for me." I blush as the lanky young man wipes his gloved hands on his bloodstained apron and sizes me up. The crazy foreigner, he probably thinks. My accent always betrays me, even though I think I do a good job passing among Indiana farmers, shop assistants, teachers, and lawyers. I feel invisible until I open my mouth, and then the inevitable "Where are you from?" sounds out. "Poland? Wow. I know someone from Australia!"

"Oh, sure," the butcher says. "I love livers, too. Just not something a lot of people around here eat, you know?" He promises a bag of chicken livers next week and writes down my name. He's older than I thought. Now I see small wrinkles in his eye corners and loose skin around the sinews on his neck.

* * *

CHICKEN LIVER

10–12 medium chicken livers, washed, trimmed, and dried
2 tsp butter
2 tsp lemon juice
1 tsp kosher salt
2 large garlic cloves, finely chopped

Dry fry the livers in a cast-iron skillet until cooked through (about 2 minutes per side). Turn off the heat. Add butter, lemon juice, salt, and garlic. Mix for 1 minute. Serve immediately.

This recipe can be paired with mashed potatoes and a cucumber salad.

* * *

That evening when Mother tried to take flight from us forever, my younger brother and I sat on her disheveled, warm bed, gently shaking her shoulders. "Mama?" She looked peaceful, with a faint smile on her chapped lips. "We're hungry. Can we have dinner?" I was five, and my brother was three. Our small fridge was perched on top of a tall cabinet and hard to reach. We were used to Mother's unresponsiveness by then, but she'd always give an annoyed grunt or shift a little when we tried to wake her up. This time she looked different, like an enchanted princess who'd pricked her finger on the spindle of a spinning wheel. In the fairy tale, after the princess falls into deep sleep, fulfilling the curse of an evil fairy, another fairy summons trees and thorny bushes around the castle to protect her from the outside world and let her sleep undisturbed until a prince gives her a life-restoring kiss. In Mother's bedroom, there were no fairies, only the heavy, honey-colored window curtains and that antique piano bought with a bottle of vodka, the carved lions glaring with their mouths open, as if ready to snap. Mother sometimes played on that piano when she was in the right mood, her body swaying, her eyes closed as she keyed the arpeggios in "Für Elise." We'd sit at her feet, mesmerized by the lions and her slippers working the pedals. I don't know if she played well. By the time I would've been able to judge her skills, she'd stopped playing altogether, the ivory keys gathering dust.

When Mother did not wake up, I dressed my brother in wool pants and a winter coat. We trekked through slush across town to our grandparents' house. As we walked holding hands, I prayed we wouldn't get lost. My brother says he has no memory of this event except for one small flashback: that he fell into a mud puddle, that he was scared and disoriented, and that the only thing keeping him from screaming was my hand as I pulled him up from the muck.

In the end, Mother was saved from her flight after being in a coma for a couple of days. She would try to escape again—

next time in a bathroom, hanging herself on a belt from the pipes above the toilet, and a few other times after that. When my brother discovered her dangling from her belt, Grandpa took her down, and off she went to the hospital again.

In between her hospitalizations, always with vodka on her breath, she withdrew from us, reading detective novels or snugging with our new rescue dog on the tiny balcony. The dog's name was Kora, which in Polish means "tree bark"—the color of her fur when Mother and I picked her up from the vet's office moments before she was supposed to be put to death. Kora had had a miscarriage and lost all of her teeth, and her ribs were healing, probably from countless kicks. On our way home with Kora, we saw that she could not keep her tongue inside her mouth and let it drop out one side of her snout, where it swept the ground back and forth as she walked. For months, Kora peed whenever she heard a male voice, even on TV, but Mother and Grandmother nursed her back to health. Eventually, Mother gave Kora away, or so she said when I called her one day from South Carolina. Caring for her was too much work, she said. *Za dużo pracy.* Her *r* rolled off her lips like a machine gun, a sign she was crossing the line between tipsy and wasted.

* * *

What we know about birds held in captivity is that they will often become self-injurious or harm other birds. In eighth grade, I took a bus to the city center to buy a hoodie and instead came back with a couple of zebra finches in a cage. I fell in love with their tiny bright-red beaks and their cute *beep*s and *meep*s as they talked to each other, so I spent Grandma's hoodie money in a pet store instead of the clothing bazaar. But the male finch soon changed his trumpeting song into a quiet *oi oi* and started plucking his own feathers. He died a couple of months later. The female bird followed soon after.

Around that time, I began reading Bruno Schulz. In one of his dreamlike stories, a father takes an interest in ornithology and begins collecting exotic birds, their eggs shipped from European zoos and trading posts in Africa. He withdraws to his room, where the birds live and breed, and he emerges only from time to time to join the family at dinner. "Occasionally forgetting himself," says the narrator-son, "he would rise from his chair at table, wave his arms as if they were wings, and emit a long-drawn-out bird's call while his eyes misted over." When his maid opens the window to get rid of the birds, Father flaps his arms and tries to escape with them. He is an artist, a magician, a godlike creator trying to escape the dull monotony of family life and small-town pettiness by designing an exotic enclave filled with winged creatures, and in the end he becomes a bird, one with his feathered flock.

* * *

The eighth grade was the first time I got drunk. I had tasted homemade wine and *Sovetskoe* "Champagne" at our dinner table, a sip here, a sip there, but never enough to even give me a buzz. That day, I was sitting on a narrow bed in a friend's bedroom, several other teens crammed within its claustrophobic yellow walls, when someone brought in a bottle of vodka. There was no juice to mix it with, only tap water. No ice. Marta, who had invited us to her place earlier that day because her mother had a night shift at a hospital, passed cheap metal shot glasses, the kind people use when they go camping, and poured the liquor. To my left sat a boy I liked, Michał, his knee touching mine, his cigarette breath on my shoulder.

Na zdrowie!

I had seen adults downing shots many times before, moving their arms in a smooth arc, like studious dancers performing their act without a hiccup, punctuating the ritual with a quick jerk of the head backward, slamming their hands on the table and exhaling loudly. I had seen it at family gatherings, at weddings, First Communion celebrations, campsites, and on park benches. I had seen it in Mother's kitchen, a sacrament she performed daily, mostly alone but sometimes with an acolyte—our next-door neighbor who was a pediatrician or one of her boyfriends who never visited empty-handed. So I knew how to position my fingers around the metal, and I knew how to tip it to my lips. But the vodka reeked, and my arm trembled when I smelled the liquor. I shuddered and looked around. Michał was looking right at me, his baby-blue eyes expectant, and I poured *wódka* into my mouth, praying I wouldn't barf. I didn't. I felt my gums burn but soon a warm sensation traveled down my throat and esophagus, landing and dissipating in my stomach. Before I could put the shot glass down on Marta's desk, Michał poured us all another shot. Then another.

I don't remember how I came back home that night. I remember lying on that narrow bed, Michał's body on top of me, his mouth kissing mine. I remember feeling his teeth with my tongue as I was trying to figure out how to kiss a boy properly. I remember Marta's pet parrot shrieking on the other side of the wall, an otherworldly, high-pitched scream.

* * *

In 1939 Thomas R. Henry published the article "Cultivation of the Maternal Instinct" in *The Scientific Monthly.* There, he recounted Dr. Oscar Riddle's experiments with doves. Riddle discovered that when he implanted male doves with progesterone, the female sex hormone, the male doves started sitting on eggs until they hatched and then fed the hatchlings until they were ready to fly away. Henry also reported studies in which male and immature female rats injected with prolactin, a hormone secreted by the pituitary gland, suddenly exhibited "motherly" behaviors toward infant animals. Another study proved that "the mother love of rats was completely destroyed by removing from their diet all the element magnesium."

Is this, perhaps, why Mother was not interested in nurturing me and my brother? Was her aggression toward me as simple as a hormone imbalance, a physiological mechanism rather than deep-seated hatred? If so, can I blame her for suicidal and homicidal attempts? Should I blame her hormones? But aren't hormones parts of *us,* just as the folds of our brain are, just as the shape of our nose or toes influences our own and others' perception of *us*? I want to change my judgment into compassion because that harsh judgment doesn't fit with who I want to be. But doing so will suppress, rather than erase, the wellspring of anger I harbor toward Mother. I somehow doubt increased progesterone or a magnesium supplement would turn Mother into a cooing dove.

Roots

My first vodka was a pure potato spirit called *Luksusowa,* which in Polish means "luxurious," though its metallic aftertaste belied its name. Cheap liquors were prevalent at parties back then, and I suspect the bottle belonged to Marta's mother, who could have gotten it as a thank-you gift from a patient. Bribes and gifts were the rule in hospitals if you wanted to make sure that doctors and nurses gave your family members humane treatment. The most common bribe was liquor.

When the Communist government declared martial law in December 1981, the already precarious food and goods supply collapsed. The only thing we could reliably find in stores was vinegar, which is possibly why we got so good at pickling and fermenting food. When we walked into shops, all we saw was a thick layer of dust on metal shelving. Sometimes a rumor would spread about an upcoming delivery of flour or sugar or meat, and we would join a line outside the store and wait for hours, unsure whether we'd get anything in the end. Grandpa had a military-style collapsible stool he'd take with him to his overnight vigils in front of the store to make sure that we could still get the coffee substitute or the sandpaper-quality toilet paper in the morning. Potato vodka seemed to be abundant.

The rationing cards were made of cheap brown cardboard featuring a grid. On each square there was a product name, plus the allowed amount. The top left corner said *Flour, 1000 g.* Then there was a square for *Sugar, 500 g, Cigarettes, 6 packs, Alcohol, 1 bottle, Fats, 375 g, Bread, 1000 g.* Bingo!

For a while, people could double and triple their allotted amounts by proving that they had children. This meant that those meat lines or sugar lines were noisy affairs. My brother loved them because there were always other kids monkeying around, and he could listen to the older people's stories about the war as they sat on their own collapsible chairs or stomped around in the gray snow. Soon my brother and I joined the legion of *dzieci kolejkowe,* or queue kids, borrowed from day cares by non-family members to prove to the store that they had many mouths to feed. Instead of playing with stacking blocks or singing about hopping bunnies, we were yanked from the nursery and plopped in front of nearby shops with our minders or their sisters or uncles. We all knew to say yes if the lady behind the counter asked if we were related to whoever was holding our hand at the moment. Most of the time we wouldn't even know their names.

* * *

There is a photo of me in front of a small chalkboard with Mother's handwriting: *Agata ma 3 lata.* Agata is three years old. I am holding a tulip and smiling mischievously, two blond ponytails curving away from my face like parentheses. Grandpa is heating up savory *bigos* in Mother's kitchen. He's not in the photo, but the rich smell of mushrooms tickles my nostrils when I look at the black-and-white snapshot. Four days later, Mother will turn on the TV in the morning and listen for the *Teleranek* jingle ending with a shrill *cock-a-doodle-doo,* the sound of a weekend children's show in most Polish homes in the '70s and '80s. Instead of the running rooster on the screen there is a somber man dressed in a military uniform, reading something that makes Mother cover her mouth in a silent scream. I hear the general say, "*Jak długo można czekać na otrzeźwienie*?"—How long can one wait for a sobering up?

"Mama, what's 'sobering up'?"

Mother squeezes my arm to keep me quiet. Tomek is playing with an orange lion in his highchair, babbling quietly and drooling on the hard orange plastic.

"How long will a hand extended for accord meet a fist?" The military man is wearing large glasses on his balding head. He looks like a penguin, his beak-like mouth enunciating words I do not understand. "The nation has reached the border of mental endurance." I move my gaze to Mother, whose body is listening, every neuron trained on the man behind the glass separating his stark office from our sunlit living room.

"I declare that today, the army council of national salvation has been constituted. The council of state, obeying the constitution, declared a state of war at midnight on the territory of Poland."

"*Stan wojenny,*" Mother whispers. Martial law. Minutes later, I hear a *tssssssk* from the kitchen as Mother opens her first beer bottle of the day.

* * *

Almost forty years later, in rural Indiana, I sit in my Subaru with my tween son, idling in a dark alley between a redbrick church and a wooden fence. I am waiting for my daughter to be dismissed from day care, but I cannot turn away from the tiny screen of my iPhone, where the US coup of January 6 is broadcast live. As red-hatted supporters of a petulant businessman-turned-autocrat storm the Capitol, I ask: What kind of a mother will I be to my children? What do I do now? How do I protect them?

The phone's flimsy dust-pink case feels wet in my hand.

I turn around. My tween is in the back seat, quiet and open-mouthed. A child of academics surrounded by Confederate-flag-flying neighbors, he already knows that this moment will weigh heavily on his family, on the family's Black friends, on his Chinese American buddy. I shut my phone.

"We should listen to music," I say in Polish.

"Mama, what's going on?" My son's Polish is already rusty—no trips to Europe during the pandemic—so he speaks English.

"Some people don't want to give up power. There are adults out there who behave like little children who do not want to share their toy truck." Only the consequences of their actions are more dangerous than a playground skirmish, I want to add. Instead, I ask him not to talk about the news to his sister.

At home, after I put my kids to bed, I open a Stella and all of a sudden the *tssssssk* makes me shudder. I drink half the beer and pour the rest over the unwashed dishes in the sink. I click on the blue square with a white *f* on my iPhone and go straight to the group of academic mamas with kids my daughter's age. They are already talking about the coup and the impact it will have on their children, some of whom are Black and Brown, some of whom are raised in single-sex or immigrant households, some of whom are surrounded, like my own kids, by people flying "Fuck Biden" signs from their trucks.

WTF? they say. We feel unsafe, they say. Are you feeling the same fear? Yes. Yes. Yes. Keep your kids close. We will help each other. Just like life-giving fungi providing nutrients to plants, my network of academic mothers gives me hope when I'm numb, reaches out and away, merging, fusing, seeking, working in unison. Our underground network of help makes me thrive among rot and decay, helps me survive the mundane and the traumatic, provides nourishment for my precarious ecosystem.

* * *

In front of my children, I keep quiet. I tell my older one that we are prepared for any emergency and that he is safe in the middle of Indiana cornfields. He says: But you have that sign in front of the house, the one that says "No matter where you're from, we're glad you're our neighbor." At eleven, he already knows that kindness is a political statement that can get us in trouble.

When I say we are prepared, I am telling the truth. Despite my husband's frequent side-eyes and raised eyebrows, I have stocked our basement with rice, beans, freeze-dried veggies, powdered milk, Spam, peanut butter, flashlights, AA batteries, handwarmers, water filters, sleeping bags, a tent, and enough gasoline to get our car to the Canadian border. My husband indulges my preparations but does not fully understand my anxiety.

* * *

By the time I turned three, the Communist regime in the People's Republic of Poland was waning but desperate to hold on to its totalitarian power. My family survived the hunger of two world wars and postwar totalitarian rule, including Stalin's terror. I was three when martial law was declared and tanks rolled out into our streets, and I was eleven when the regime fell. My childhood was dust on empty shelves in grocery shops, queues for butter and meat in frost-sprinkled mornings, drunks sleeping in staircases of our cement Stalinist-style tower blocks, and civilians disappearing from our streets into unmarked vans. I did not have direct experience with the tanks or with the disappearances of opposition activists that intensified during martial law. I do remember, though, the fear in Mother's eyes and her hasty burning of papers in our kitchen sink in December 1981.

I also remember feeling that I alone should protect my toddler brother since Mother was too far gone into the cocoon of booze and drugs. Father was mostly absent. Mothering was

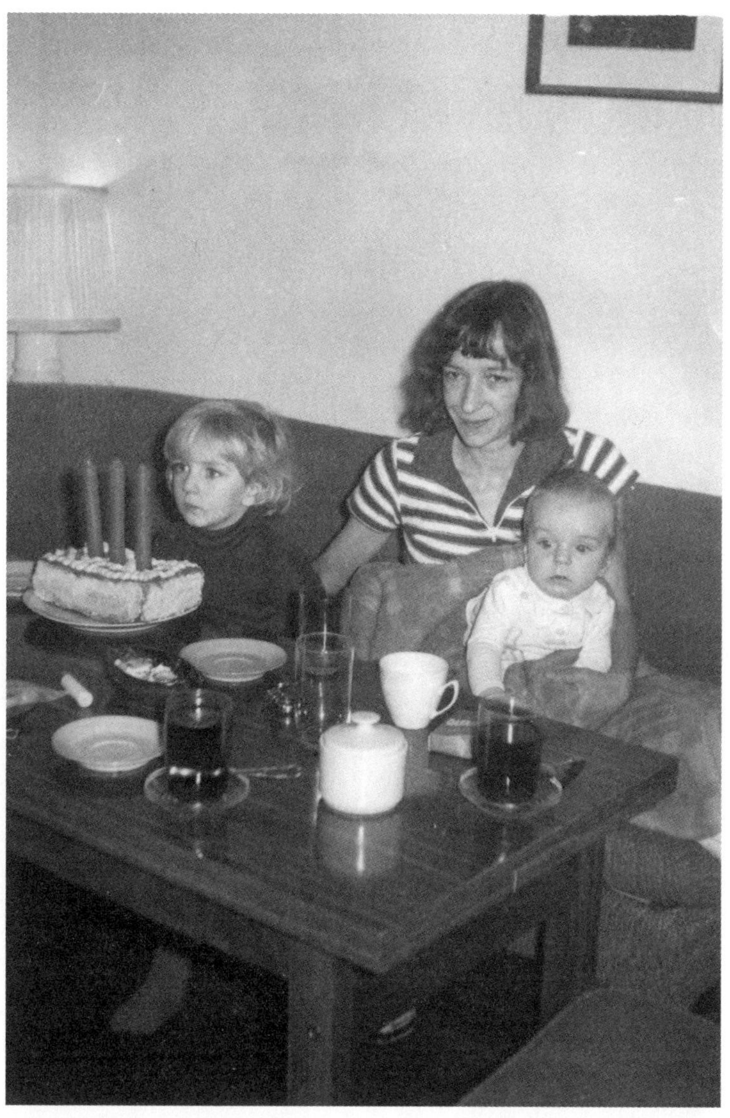

My birthday celebration at home, December 1981. Photo by Ryszard Szczeszak.

what I did most of my childhood—reading books to my toddler brother, later wiping his bloody nose when he got into fights. I also mothered Mother. I begged her to eat, lifted her stringy body from a pool of vomit, woke her up so she could go to work.

* * *

These are my earliest memories of Mother: The penguin man in a military uniform. The sun illuminating her petrified face. Then the *tssssssk* of the beer bottle cap. Her bleary eyes. Her slurred speech. The helplessness of what I now know were several disasters converging on her at the same time: Martial law. Empty shelves in grocery stores. Two kids. An unfaithful husband. Separation. Divorce.

She is fear and anger, sometimes simmering just under the surface and visible only as her pulsating cheekbones and narrowed eyes, heard only in her curt *tak* and *nie,* the *yes* and *no* spat through clenched teeth with gyroscopic precision, sometimes exploding with the firepower of a large-caliber tank gun, the detonation precipitated by alcohol withdrawal. She is a shard of glass aimed at my chest. She is sixty-proof breath and slurred consonants when ethanol mollifies her fury. She is a sleeping beauty on musty bedsheets, a fairy suspended in midair on a leather belt attached to bathroom pipes.

But she is also a woman who sews a gorgeous gown for my ballroom dancing tournaments, the steady *chucka chucka chucka* of the needle and the fluid motions of her foot as she presses the pedal and stretches the bottle-green fabric. She is the pianist swaying her body to "Für Elise." She is a woman who nurses dogs, cats, and rats back to health in our drafty two-bedroom apartment. She is a reader of thrillers and biographies—at least until pills and vodka turn her brain to mush.

* * *

So how do I mother my children? How do I protect them as the world around us seems to crumble?

The morning after the attempted coup of 2021, I hug my kids and send them to school because I want them to continue with their routine. I tell them that Mama has it all planned out, that they are safe, that we will protect them. My three-year-old only half listens because her Elsa doll lost a tiny shoe. My tween nods, pulls his mask up, and hops out of the car. Behind us in the school drop-off is a van. Inside the van, a white woman and a MAGA hat on the dashboard.

* * *

Martial law was the government's response to years of fighting between the totalitarian system and the opposition (mostly Solidarność, but also other pro-democracy groups). Although most Polish people were taken by surprise when it was announced, the government had been planning martial law for over a year, preparing a complete blockade of telephone and postal communication, designating jails that would later hold political prisoners, secretly printing announcements, communicating with the Kremlin about operational details. On December 9, while I was blowing out funeral candles on my coffin-shaped birthday cake, General Jaruzelski, Poland's leader, was making the decision to begin interning political opponents.

Seventy thousand soldiers and thirty thousand policemen took part in massive arrests. Five thousand opposition leaders and activists, intellectuals who refused to follow the Party line in their research and publications, were taken to prisons. Almost 1,800 tanks rolled out into our streets.

Not that Father noticed. The morning of the martial law proclamation he was recovering in bed from a night of drinking at the theater. He had stumbled home from the opposite edge of town in the early morning hours, wondering why the night bus hadn't arrived and why there were so many soldiers in the streets. He even asked one to give him a lift home in his heavy-armored vehicle, but the soldier refused. I guess he didn't arrest Father because he had bigger fish to fry that night—dissidents, insubordinate students and professors, priests. So Father walked. The city seemed more illuminated than ever before. So pretty—lights dancing on icy roads, snow glowing under tall lanterns, and the streets empty except for the silent men in uniform stomping their feet by armored vehicles. Father walked. Maybe he was thinking up an excuse when Mother would confront him about yet another night away from home—"Whoring!" she would scream—until he offered a story, not even a believable one, but an explanation nevertheless, something to hold on to at least for a moment. Or maybe he was too unsteady on his feet to focus on a narrative and simply thought of putting one foot in front of the other, until he unlocked our apartment door and slipped under the warm duvet.

He slept when the penguin man announced war. He slept when Mother stood in front of TV, squeezing my shoulder. He slept when she went to the kitchen and opened a beer with a long *tssssssk*. He slept when she reheated potatoes from the previous night's dinner and served them to us in silence. When he woke up, he left again, this time to "find out what's going on," he said.

* * *

Winter 1982. Mother, Tomek, and I stood in a line snaking up to a tiny kiosk about a block away from our apartment building. The line hadn't moved an inch for more than an hour. The kiosk's transaction window was shut and covered with a thick layer of frost, but we could see that someone had turned on the light inside. The people in front of us breathed out warm air into the early morning. Together we looked like a steam engine readying itself for a long trip.

My brother was bundled up in an oversized snowsuit and a brown knitted hat, squeezed into his tiny stroller. Tugging at Mother's coat, I pointed.

"Mama? Tomek turned into a walrus!"

My brother's snot had frozen in the Polish winter air. Two greenish tusks stuck out of his nostrils, and he was breathing heavily through his mouth.

Mother laughed. Then she checked herself, picked him up, and showed his face to the crowd.

"Won't you let me go first? Look at my son."

When the kiosk lady finally opened the window, Mother was the first one to produce her rationing card. She tore off a little square from its corner and put a jar filled with white powder in her coat pocket. "No toothpaste again. We'll be brushing teeth with baking soda."

* * *

Father straightened the newspaper, murmuring under his mustache, one leg resting on the other knee. Potatoes, the staple of the Polish plate, were under attack again, though who knew whether to trust anything reported by the state media.

"Our plates will be safe only when we destroy the last enemy of the people. The American beetle, aggressive and voracious, is a parasite we will collectively annihilate." Pick up any Polish newspaper from 1950 onward, and they are everywhere: the sneaky little potato fiends.

When the Colorado potato bug attacked Polish potatoes in the 1950s and the press blamed Americans, young Krzysztof Penderecki, future composer and conductor, got into trouble with the local school board. His principal complained to Krzysztof's father that his son, who was among the schoolchildren picking potato bugs in the countryside as part of a "compulsory volunteering opportunity," was too squeamish to do it with his bare hands, like the rest of his classmates. He wore gloves to pick the beetles. "You are raising a bourgeois moocher," said the principal into the receiver.

Food was scarce for several years after the war, and the students who collected high numbers of potato bugs were offered an extra serving of bread for lunch. My parents remember their potato-bug-picking days as a real hoot—they got to leave the city, skip school without getting in trouble, and in their teenage years drink vodka on rickety buses that took them to the fields, where they invented songs comparing the beetle to Stalin. Later the government simply dropped DDT on the infestation, but the bugs quickly became immune to it. By the time I was in school, it was back to the fields.

At first, we did not believe in the potato bug. Like Trotsky, Jews, and the American dollar, potato bugs were standard scapegoats deployed on propaganda posters and in newspapers to explain food shortages. Instead of collecting the insects, some kids would find strawberry fields or cherry orchards nearby and fill their bellies until they puked. When we came back to school the next day, teachers praised us for protecting our precious national resource: potatoes.

"I guess you'll be picking those fuckers again, huh?" Father lowers his newspaper.

"What fuckers?"

"American beetles. Back to square one."

* * *

Alcohol was rationed, but somehow Mother could always get hold of it. When I smelled it on her breath, I braced for what would inevitably follow: a burst of energy during which she

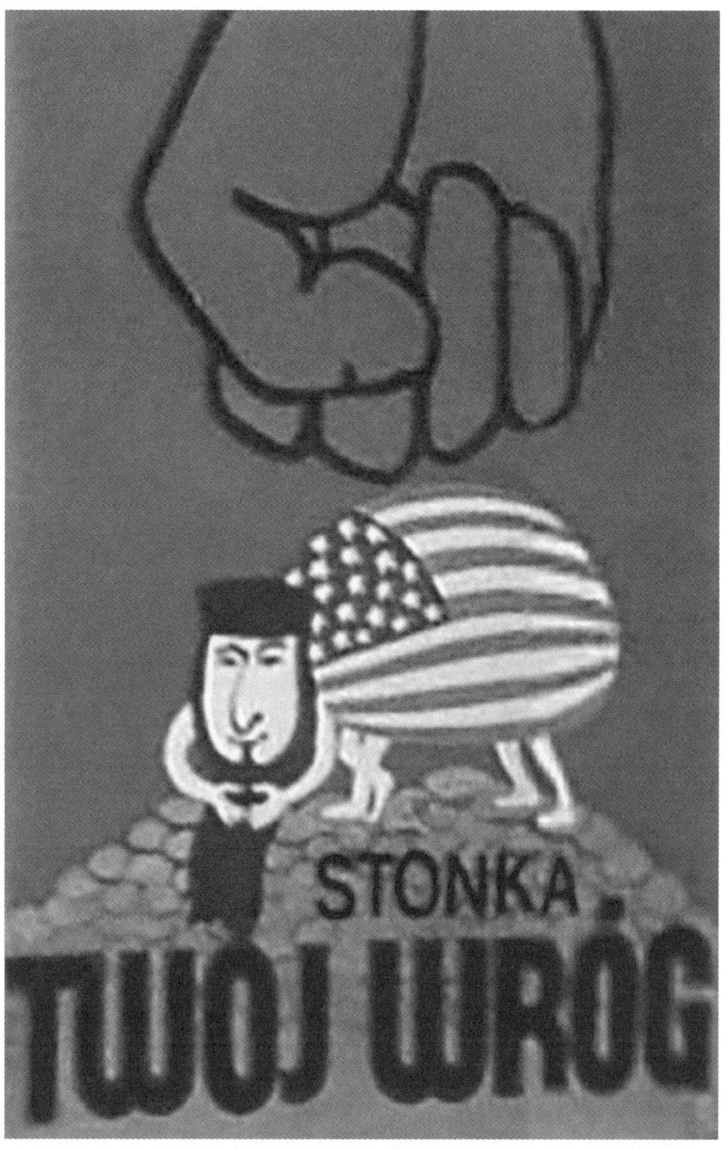

Polish propaganda poster, "Potato Bug—Your Enemy," originally in color.

would scrub every surface in our apartment with vinegar, then slurred singing about peasants or eagles or lovers who died in battles, and finally a collapse, not always into bed, which meant that I had to lift her up onto her fold-out sofa and sometimes clean up her vomit or pee. When she was sober, she was either silent while chain smoking at the kitchen table, or angry. She did not hit us often, but when she did, I marveled at how much power there was in her fragile frame.

My brother and I shared a room—he in his crib with two missing slats, and I in my narrow bed tucked in by the door. Many nights we would try to fall asleep to the loud conversations, laughter, and heated arguments across the wall in my neighbors' apartment, where Mother drank after locking us in. I guess I didn't mind that noise, but I hated the sound I could hear when there was silence across the wall. Our Soviet-style high-rise stood on top of a hill, and the wind howled in the pipes and wall cracks like a forlorn ghoul. I preferred listening to Mother's drunken songs or another guest's slurred cussing against the Communists to the frightful *woooooooo woooooooo woooooooo* of the wind lost in the pipes and concrete cracks.

I nagged Mother to make me a rope ladder long enough to reach the ground from our third-floor window because I was terrified about the prospect of fire in the apartment. Mother was prone to leaving her cigarettes smoldering not just in ashtrays but also on bathroom towels and bedsheets. As we were often unable to unlock the door from inside after she left, the only way out in case of fire would be to jump.

"Don't be silly, Agata. The rope would burn anyway." She told me to climb from our small balcony onto our neighbor's in case of trouble.

When we were a little older, Tomek and I imagined out loud before sleep that we belonged to a different family. Right by our bedroom door was a poster of the German pop duo Modern Talking—Dieter Bohlen with his blond mullet and goofy smile, dressed in a yellow jumpsuit, and Thomas Anders, looking pensively at the camera, his wavy dark hair draping the studded leather of his jacket. They were always there, at the entrance to our room, like guardian angels, ready to burst into a synthesizer-happy song with falsetto choruses.

To know you is to love you
If you call me baby
I'll be always yours.

Thomas Anders was our mother. Dieter Bohlen was our father. Naturally.

* * *

I later learned that most bootlegged vodka at that time was made from potatoes, but people made alcohol at home from just about anything: wheat, pears, tomatoes, sugar, pumpkin, and rose petals. *Bimber,* or homemade vodka, was a common currency on the black market. It was produced mostly in the country, and city dwellers like us made wine or liqueurs in our tiny bedrooms or kitchens. Grandpa had a large glass wine-distilling apparatus in his room, where he made alcohol from cherries and grapes. He stopped once he realized that Mother was stealing his bottles, but until then his room smelled of fermented fruit, and there was always a soothing, steady sound of liquid passing through the siphon hosing into the demijohn. Tomek and I would sit for hours on his bed, rifling through a wooden box filled with his war medals and yellowed documents from his native Horodyszcze, in Belarus.

Grandpa's acquaintances in the country made stronger alcohol. To prepare *bimber,* they peeled and boiled potatoes, mashed them, and boiled them again to free up the starch, which was eventually converted into sugars. They added malted barley and cooked it for at least four more hours. After adding a little yeast, they waited for the fermentation.

Potatoes were not rationed in Communist Poland, and neither were beets, turnips, or other root vegetables, so apart from alcohol, people made soups, salads, pancakes, and casseroles with them, and we pickled them for later, too. In our city, you could buy potatoes from villagers who lined up in front of our empty stores each morning, no matter the weather, pocketing the increasingly useless money with their red fingers.

Our little allotted gardens and makeshift veggie stands also gave us access to lots of rutabagas, beets, and carrots. Those who lived in the country turned sugar beets into sticky sweet syrup that could be used in baking or as a honey substitute. City folk without gardens bought root vegetables on the black market, and out of this limited access to food sources came family recipes for borsht, gazpachos, pickled beets, and root-veggie salads with fermented pickles and apple cubes. The ubiquitous potato gave us *pyzy* (large, round-shaped dumplings, with meat or mushroom stuffing), latkes, and black Silesian *kluski* prepared with raw potatoes and finished with a characteristic indentation into which we drizzled sauce or lard. In the northeastern part of Poland where I grew up, another popular potato dish was the soft, garlicky *kartacze,* which originally came from Lithuania. In the Tatra mountains, we ate *hałuski*—also potato dumplings but torn into small pieces before boiling and often served with spicy, squeaky sheep cheese called *oscypek.* Out of potatoes, eggs, flour, and cottage cheese, we made *leniwe* (or "lazy pierogi"), topped with either sour cream and sugar or with bread crumbs fried in butter. We also made *kopytka* ("little hooves"), parallelogram-shaped dumplings that taste much like gnocchi, often served with mushrooms.

* * *

KOPYTKA (POLISH POTATO DUMPLINGS)
2 pounds potatoes
2 eggs
3.5 cups flour
Salt to taste

Peel and cook potatoes until tender. Push warm potatoes through a sieve or use a food processor to mash them until smooth. Beat in 2 eggs and mix with flour. Salt to taste. Dust a kitchen counter with flour and knead the dough. Divide it into four parts. Roll each part into ropes, half an inch in diameter. (Cover the unused part to avoid drying out the dough.) Slice each rope diagonally into 1-inch dumplings. Cook in a large pot of boiling, salted water. After *kopytka* float to the top, cook for additional 2 minutes. Drain. Serve smothered in melted butter or lard mixed with sautéed onions.

* * *

We ate lots of potatoes and beets once we moved to our grandparents' house. Grandma spent most of her time in the kitchen, sometimes teaching me, too, how to roll the dough for *leniwe,* how to make sure sour cream wouldn't congeal in the beet gazpacho, and how to throw dumplings in the boiling water without burning my hands. Her wrinkly fingers would gently cup mine as I rolled the dough on the Formica kitchen table, rocking it back and forth until we formed a one-inch rope and then cut it up diagonally. As we cooked, I listened to the pigeons' feet scratching on our metal windowsill.

But before Grandma and Grandpa moved to our town to give Tomek and me the stability our mother could not, the only potatoes we ate were the overboiled mush served in day care and the potatoes Mother reheated on a frying pan, often burning them beyond recognition. We would eat the black-ringed slices in silence, the salt crunching between our teeth. Most days her apartment did not smell like food, though. The kitchen was clean and empty, the living room table covered with half-drunk cups of black tea, empty bottles, and ashtrays.

* * *

The night Mother poisoned herself with pills and vodka, there was nothing in the fridge, so we trudged through muddy snow in darkness, my brother's hand in my hand. Grandma and Grandpa had moved into our city by then, about a fifteen-minute walk from our home. My hand held Tomek's, not letting go. I didn't let go even when we finally arrived at our grandparents' door and said: "Mama won't wake up." That same hand, of course, would sometimes slap him in anger when we argued about a plastic horse or our turn at the bathroom sink, but even at three and five, we knew that we would kill to protect each other. That night, Tomek and I sat down at a wobbly table and filled the empty spaces in our coloring books with crayons. I don't remember the pictures. I remember the waxy smell of the pale green color in my hand.

* * *

Mother was a high school English teacher dutifully returning grammar quizzes marked up with red. She knew the correct conjugation of the word *lie*. She still remembered the difference between the present perfect and future perfect tenses. She could explain the conditional verb forms. If she had not been an addict, she might have been able to also say "I love you," in Polish.

On weekends, she drank and slept or worked in our garden.

Because of the food shortage, families got small land allotments from the government where we could grow potatoes, strawberries, black and red currants, wild alpine strawberries, fava beans, peas, and tomatoes. The growing season in northeastern Poland is short, so we harvested and preserved fruits and veggies in glass jars and bottles that lined our basement shelves. In the spring and summer, we made pilgrimages to our garden, a few kilometers away from our house, first by bus, then in Grandpa's tiny burnt-red Fiat. As a child I disliked going there. I was afraid of bees and wasps and mosquitoes coming from a nearby swamp, and I was bored out of my mind by the repetitive tasks of pulling weeds out of the soil or sorting beans. I did love the bonfires right outside the gate to our garden, though. We would first bury potatoes under the wood and twigs, and when the fire burned out, we would dig the tubers out of the ashes, cut them in half, sprinkle them with salt, and then bite right in. The charred crispy skin was bitter, but it was soon followed by the salty, buttery interior.

That garden allotment from the Communist government also became a cemetery for our dead pets. We had a couple of fruit trees there, crabapple and plum, and it was under that plum tree that we buried Aza, our beautiful, furry black mutt with gentle eyes, our traveling dog who always ran happily back home to eat a bowlful of chicken livers. I was at a summer camp when Aza died of food poisoning. Mother and Grandpa buried her under the plum tree the next day, and the family had a morbid satisfaction whenever our teeth sank into plum flesh, as if we were communing with our beloved dog.

* * *

I dig. The shovel's dull shaft presses against my midfoot, loosens ligaments and tendons. Rasp, crunch, slap. Repeat.

I inhale the scent of the horse manure waiting in the plastic Walmart tote I haul from a friend's farm in central Indiana, where I chat with Roosevelt the donkey and their aging horses. As I bend my back to loosen the soil and break stubborn clumps of Indiana clay, so does my grandpa—my *dziadek*—only thirty years before me and in a different universe, one with Communist-allotted gardens and coughing Fiats that take us to them, a universe with currant bushes and wild strawberries and the plum tree where we buried our traveling dog Aza.

Dziadek's love language is buckets of crabapples and a greenhouse filled with bees. His love language is a charred potato hiding in the ashes. You crack it open, blow on your fingers, and inside is buttery, smoky flesh. We sit against a wooden shed and eat in silence. Radishes burst between our teeth. Wild strawberries stain our fingers. We drink *kvas* and wave away the mosquitoes.

In the universe where I teach undergraduate men about iambs, Leopold Bloom, and Marxist theory, I too dig and plant. When I die, I say to my husband, scatter my ashes from a Folgers can right under our apple tree. I don't want to rot under a marble slab. I want to be a morel mushroom or apple or leaf, then deer, then the deer's hunter. Okay, he says, but first, where do you want me to empty the box of horse shit?

* * *

When Polish poet Czesław Miłosz, later exiled to the US, was caught in gunfire on the first day of the Warsaw Uprising in 1944, he saved himself by lying for hours facedown in a muddy potato field. He never let go of a volume of poetry he had been carrying with him at that time—*The Collected Poems of T. S. Eliot*. Later, at Berkeley, Miłosz remembered home not with nostalgia but awareness that his Dantean recollections were not to be trusted. His memories of "potato patches fenced in with barbed wire" dissolve into a mirage:

They played as-if-cards, I smelled as-if-cabbage,
There was as-if-vodka, as-if-dirt, as-if-time.

As-if. I fear that my suppressed memory of Mother's affection—for surely she must have loved us—is damaging and unfair. I search the as-if-kitchens of my childhood, Mother's and Grandma's, for a flutter of her love. There it is—an herb-encrusted pork roast Mother made for my birthday. I search the as-if-apartment in the concrete-paneled high-rise on top of a windy hill. There it is—a firm grip on my shoulder, her lips pressing against my cheek, so hard that I can feel her teeth imprinting themselves on my skin. I search for her as-if-voice on her sober days. There it is—it says "Agusiu," an endearing diminutive for my name, one used only in moments of tenderness.

Is this how she herself searched for evidence of love in the memory of her own mother? In the fragments of Grandma Iza's stories of wartime hunger and survival? In Grandma's as-if-apartment in a prewar working-class Warsaw district? Her escape from the Nazis to a nearby village? Her survival on as-if-soup from potato peels? When Grandma's raised voice lodged itself in Mother's ear more sturdily than the moments of tenderness—which are forgotten more easily than anger—and when Grandma's and then Great-Grandma's war traumas irretrievably changed Mother's own yet-innocent biology, did she search the crevices of her mind for softness and love? It is conceivable that instead she reached for the bottle, again and again, until not reaching for the bottle was no longer an option.

In dire times, when we are starved for sustenance, staying on the surface is easy but futile. Digging deep, searching for the roots, getting ourselves dirty and exhausted and vulnerable opens up possibilities of nurturing. When I first began writing this essay, I wanted to write about Mother. But I could not. I could not will my fingers to tap on the keyboard and form words and sentences about her. Instead, I chose to write about roots. It was a dissociative strategy that so many adult children of alcoholics use, often unconsciously, to avoid the anguish of revisiting traumatic moments. This time, though, this strategy betrayed me, because to write about food, to tease out memories about basic sustenance in times of hunger, is also to write about love, even if it is a difficult, toxic kind of love. Mother loved us, in her own way and as much as her disease allowed her. She probably loved us much more than she loved herself.

They say that trauma gets lodged in our genes and takes root, that it is passed down the generations, influencing our identities, undermining our resilience, betraying us in least expected moments. Grandma's own wartime trauma and the following years of misery in Communist Poland must have influenced Mother and, in turn, must have marked me. Scientists call it the epigenetic inheritance theory. They claim that trauma and other environmental factors like malnutrition switch certain chemical tags on and off and may affect the gene makeup of younger generations. Trauma can produce transgenerational changes in DNA methylation, and this inheritance influences our biology and behavior. This baggage also increases the likelihood of schizophrenia and bipolar disorder in our offspring.

When I look for the roots of my relationship with Mother, for the causes of her alcoholism and, later, her diagnosis with what was then called manic depression, I find a chain reaction going back generations in our war-torn part of Europe. But then something unexpected happens, a revelation. Instead of blaming imperialist Russia, the Nazis and the Communists, the hellish queues for bread and baking soda, and the ubiquitous potatoes, I let these stories turn my simmering anger about Mother's unmotherliness into something else, a liminal space between forgiveness and release. I am finally learning to love her.

* * *

I'm in the allotment cabin, sitting cross-legged on a moth-eaten sofa, *Świat Młodych*—a kids' magazine—on my lap. My hair is in a wind-swept braid. My glasses are too large for my small face. They are heavy, with translucent blue frames. Flies buzz.

The smell of damp wood and potatoes we store in the cellar below me is soothing, but I never climb down the ladder to the deep, dark, spider-infested cavern to reach the potatoes.

I walk out of the cabin. I kneel among sorrel, tear a leaf, stuff it in my mouth. At first it's just grassy pulp, but it soon releases the tangy, sour aftertaste that hits the back sides of my tongue, gives my senses a kick. As I chew, I watch ants marching up a nearby greenhouse stake. I hear Grandpa's footsteps on the gravel path between vegetable and flower beds.

Then I panic because there's a wasp. But he's already here next to me, waving it away and saying in his Russian-inflected Polish, "No need to be scared."

Grandpa built the cabin himself. He is now pulling weeds in our cucumber beds. His hands are large, rough, callused, with dirt permanently embossed in the lines of his palms. Life lines filled with dirt. If I touched his hand now, I would hear a swish of rough skin against my fingers.

* * *

Potatoes are not root vegetables, though they are counted among them in popular imagination because the edible part grows underground. Technically they are tubers—food reserves for the plant above that produce buds from which new plants grow. Like beets, carrots, parsnips, and radishes, they mature in soil that does not have to be extraordinarily rich, and they are quite productive. Potatoes have lots of potassium, magnesium, and vitamins. If you eat the peels, you'll also get some protein and carbohydrates, which you can find right underneath the skin. If Grandma's lore is accurate, people can survive on potato-peel soup for months.

No wonder the government in Communist Poland protected the crop by organizing "volunteer Saturdays" and sending entire schools to pick potato bugs off the plants during an infestation. The tubers were still there, waiting safely underneath the surface of the soil to be harvested, but the leaves were covered with *Leptinotarsa decemlineata,* with their peachy-orange-colored exoskeletons striped with black. If they defoliate the plants before the tubers fully form, the yield is reduced or lost altogether. It is true that the potato bug is not native to Europe. Sometime in 1918, it was carried to the continent from North America, where it is called the Colorado potato beetle. But the Warsaw Pact governments conveniently claimed that the CIA dropped potato bugs from their planes over Poland and other Communist countries to introduce food insecurity and unrest. Newspapers nicknamed the bug "a striped saboteur" and "the enemy of socialism," and the infestation was dubbed an "unspeakable crime by imperialist America."

One day we discovered potato bugs in our own garden. While Grandpa was digging the foundation for his wooden shed, Mother and I walked through our small potato patch and picked the bugs with our bare hands, pinching their smooth ovals and dropping them into soapy water. We worked in silence, but there was comfort in our repetitive movement and even in the smell of raw onion wafting from my skin. The rhythmic rasps of Grandpa's shovel stopped, and we all sat down under the plum tree to drink water and count the bugs in our jars. I don't remember whether there was alcohol on Mother's breath. What I do remember was that she was at peace. Dare I say pleased?

Mushrooms and root vegetables have one thing in common: Their life-sustaining energy is beneath the surface, hidden under forest beds and garden soil. It is this hidden energy, nourishment concealed from view, that I try to access when I think of Mother. I know she must have loved us. But to look for tangible proof of that love feels like reaching through the thick of weeds and leaf debris in search of a parsnip top or beet leaves, wading through woodlands and long-forgotten gardens, stopping from time to time to palpate forest litter and ivy vines and thistles for a sign of nourishment.

Our little garden allotment had a soothing effect on Mother, despite my constant whining about mosquitos and bees. While I was hiding from the heat of the summer in the little log cabin Grandpa had built on his own, while I lay on a portable cot covered with a rough checkered blanket, inhaling the earthy smells wafting from the root cellar beneath me, Mother entered her quiet zone, the zone of contemplation and methodical work. Weeding, composting, or just propping her head against our plum tree, cigarette in hand, she looked almost happy.

My favorite spot on cooler days was the cabin's tiny front porch, where I would sit on a wooden bench and read—usually Tove Jansson's Moomin series, which I knew almost by heart by the time I was a teenager. The small hardcover books with simple black-and-white illustrations inside had belonged to Mother and her brother Sławek when they were growing up in a provincial town of Biskupiec. These books were the first things I packed into my cavernous suitcase when I was getting ready to fly over the Atlantic to go to grad school.

Whenever I hid in my usual "safe" place in Mother's apartment, which was a wood-paneled corner with a large coat rack by the front door, whenever I inhaled the moth balls, trying not to sneeze as Mother's wool winter coat tickled my nose, I imagined I was one of the characters from the Moomin books. In that spot, hidden from Mother's rage, I imagined I was Too-ticky, a quiet, composed, winter-loving creature who always had a solution to a problem. Funny that I never identified with the woodland animal hiding from the dark forces of the world in Too-ticky's cupboard. When I think back to that hallway corner now, I see a scared little girl praying to become invisible. Of course, there was no place to really hide in that two-bedroom apartment. Inevitably, the curtain of coats and robes would be jerked to a side, and a hand would grasp my wrist and yank me from safety into the crimson fury of a woman too sober or too drunk to love.

Lard

I sit in Mother's immaculate kitchen, a spoon in my hand, digging into a large cube of salted butter, letting the fat dissolve on my tongue and the salt tickle my throat as I swallow. In Communist Poland we sometimes got food aid from local churches, including what people called "American butter." I don't know if it really came from America, but it was fun to think that somewhere across the Atlantic Ocean a cow gave her milk to a farmer who then churned it into butter and put it on a ship with our address on the box. When I imagined that farmer, he wore a cowboy hat and a leather lasso attached to his belt. He strutted à la Ben Cartwright across his Ponderosa ranch.

Bonanza premiered on Polish TV in the '70s, and when I visited Grandma, we watched reruns on weekends after the state-censored evening news, my grandparents from their worn-out sofa, and I from the hallway, through a crack in the living room door. The American butter on our table was my direct link to the Cartwright cows.

* * *

The morning sun pours through the uncurtained window, and Mother's apartment is quiet, except for an occasional crash followed by my brother's annoyed grunts when his wooden building blocks collapse in a heap back in our room. Mother has passed out on the living room sofa, cigarette butts smoldering in a shiny black ashtray.

"Want some butter, Tomek? American!"

I hear another crash and then his bare feet on the linoleum floor. *Smack smack smack.*

"No, no, no. Bwed and ward."

Mother's snoring stops after I call Tomek. Did I wake her up?

"Bread is stale. We're out of lard. Should we ask Grandma for more? We could walk there when Mama wakes up."

"She no wake."

"There's prune jam. Want that on bread?"

I hear the living room table squeak. Mother must have propped herself up as she rose from the sofa and would be here any moment. I wrap the butter cube, now more like a snow-covered mountain with a large crater in the middle where my spoon landed, and put it back in the fridge.

"Oh good, you're eating." Mother's voice, though quiet, makes me jump and turn toward the kitchen door.

Did she see how much butter I've already eaten? I scan her bed hair, crumpled face, beads of sweat under the nose, half-closed eyelids. Beer smell, not vodka. This means we can talk to her for a while—beer makes her lethargic but not angry.

Unlike liquor.

"Your father is visiting today. You should get out of your pajamas at some point."

"Will we go to Grandma's for dinner before his train comes?" I realize the fridge is still half-open and push the door to.

"Maybe. I have to lie down."

This time Mother goes into her bedroom and closes the glass door behind her. I hear the metal-on-metal sound of the door handle going up and down. The speed of the door handle often tells me what to expect when Mother emerges from her dark room. The fast movement with the loud spring that follows means that we need to head for my bed or for the corner behind our door. The slow movement of the door handle with a rising pitch is an all-clear, at least until I read her face and smell her clothes, her sweat, her breath.

"Come on," I say to my brother as I unwrap the Cartwright butter again. "Prune jam?"

* * *

There were pigs in *Bonanza,* too, like the ones Billy Pen tries to escape from when he joins the rustlers. We were on state-sponsored vacation in a seaside boarding house, and we were eating our allotted buckwheat with gravy in a cafeteria, Hank Penn's pigs squealing from a boxy TV tucked into a corner, when Mother puffed on her cigarette and we heard through the gray smoke:

"Eat the grated beets, too. We won't leave until they are gone."

It took two episodes for Tomek to clean his plate, and when the third rerun started, with Hoss finding a noose on the ranch and talking a man out of his suicide plans, Mother shot up from her chair and trotted out of the hall.

Later that evening I sat on the balcony railing and watched a boar with three babies a couple meters from the building, searching for food behind park benches. We were told not to approach a sow with her farrow because they had been known to attack. Behind me, Mother entered letters into her crossword puzzle between sips from the bottle. The longer she sipped, the more uneven her As and Hs. I ignored the pain in my butt where the iron railing wedged itself against my still-damp swimsuit and whispered to my brother:

"*Zobacz*!" Look!

Tomek put down his book and turned toward my finger pointing at the boar, and that's when I saw it: His ears were stuffed with grated beets.

* * *

In *Moominland Midwinter,* Moomintroll wakes up from slumber only to discover that his family members are still hibernating and the crippling cold is far from over. He walks up to Moominmamma and tries to wake her up.

He pulled at her ear very cautiously, but she didn't awake.

Moomintroll's house, adorable and inviting during warm months, is now unfamiliar and frightening. Long shadows dance on the walls. Fruit preserves disappear from the pantry. Windswept snow dunes cover downstairs windows, casting the living room in perpetual darkness.

He was so terribly lonely.

"Mother! Wake up!" Moomintroll shouted. "All the world's got lost!" He went back and pulled at her quilt.

But Moominmamma didn't wake up. For a moment her dreams of summer became uneasy and troubled, but she wasn't able to open her eyes. Moomintroll curled up on the rug next to her bed, and the long winter night went on.

* * *

I cover Tomek's feet with a scratchy blanket as we listen to a radio play of *Moomins in Midsummer* and wait for Mother to take us across the neighborhood to Grandma's. The sun's rays have moved from the kitchen to the opposite side of our apartment and, now that the frost is gone from the windows, warm up our living room. I listen to the narrator's soothing voice tell us about floating theaters, rotating floors, bonfires, Filijonks and Hemulens, and I watch specks of dust float in the air. I will ask Grandma for a fat jar of lard this afternoon—bacon, onion, apple, marjoram mixed into the creamy, salty spread.

I devour lard like a starving inmate. I devour books, too: Tove Jansson's Moomin series, Astrid Lindgren's *Bullerbyn*

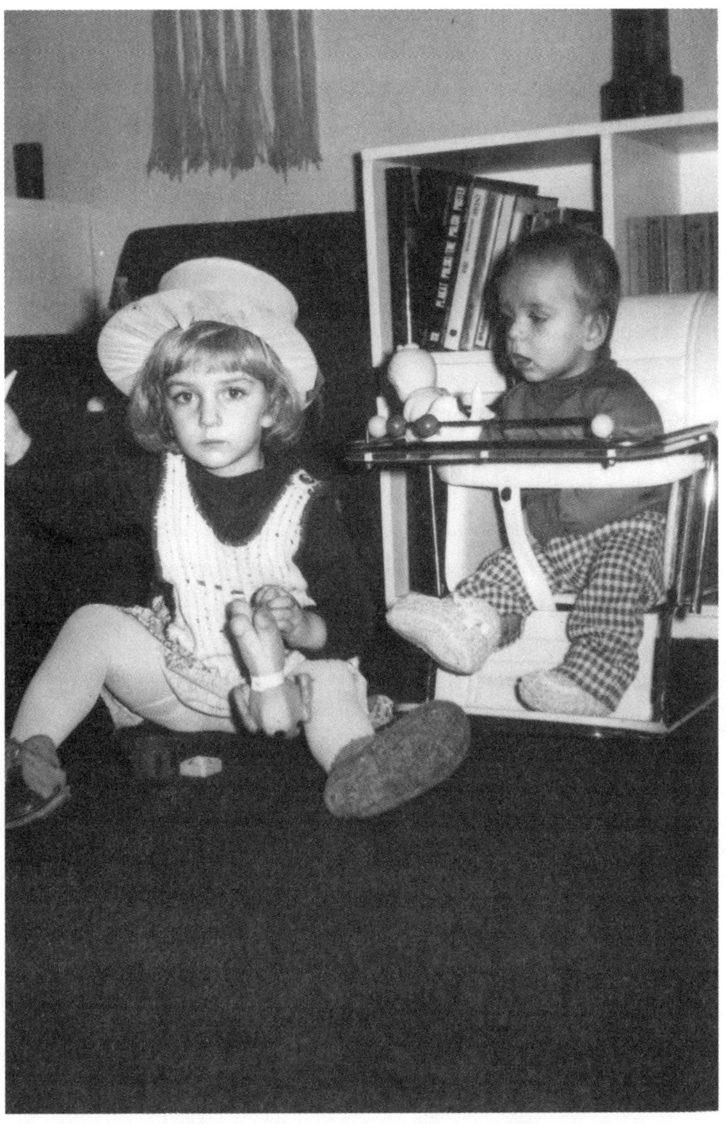

Tomek and I in Mother's living room, 1982. Photo by Ryszard Szczeszak.

Children and *Pippi Longstocking,* and classics like Hans Christian Andersen's tales, especially *The Snow Queen*—all the Finnish and Swedish children's authors that don't shy away from darkness and fear. Despite their occasional gloom, there is comfort in their pages. Denmark's Andersen gives me princesses and beggars, love and death, beauty and haunting ugliness. Lindgren's six Bullerbyn children run feral in the countryside, build tunnels, pretend to be witches, and rescue a dog from the hands of a sadistic shoemaker. Jansson's world has children abandoned by parents, pipe-smoking vagabonds who reject worldly possessions, and lonely monsters inhabiting the same valley as lovable trolls.

Poland in the 1980s was dim, with stinking drunkards sleeping in staircases, long lines for bread in frosty mornings, and generals on our black-and-white TVs. I think I was drawn to Andersen, Jansson, and Lindgren because I intuited honesty in them—about the world, about human relations, about endings that are not always happy. But the stark landscapes on these pages coexisted with the worlds that were simply—though not naively—good.

Take the Moomins, for example. The fuzzy and hippo-like Moominmamma moves between house chores, gardening, and feeding her family with calm certainty. Gardening is not just planting and harvesting; it's also arranging beautiful shells around a tree in a pleasing pattern. She makes intricate boats from tree bark for her son. She paints family portraits on the walls of her house. And she nurtures anyone who cares to be nurtured—family, strangers wandering into her house, orphaned forest creatures.

* * *

I wanted to be like Little My from the Moomin series. I wanted her spirit, her grit, and her courage. A few days after Mother refused to wake up and was taken to the hospital, I challenged myself to slide down the tallest hill in our neighborhood, just as Little My raced down a steep hill on Moominmamma's tea tray. I sat down on my small faux-leather backpack and tried to convince myself that I wasn't afraid, when suddenly someone pushed me from behind and off I went, down the icy hill, toward a school running track covered in dirty snow. I gathered speed and finally turned 180 degrees and reached the bottom, breathless. When I looked up, I saw a group of teenage boys pointing their fingers at me from the top, a gray cement-slab high-rise with tiny balconies behind them, windows lit against the darkening afternoon. Little My would have climbed up and bitten their ankles. I grabbed my backpack and scurried home.

Back at Grandma's, everyone was quiet. We ate bread with lard spread, its smooth comfort sliding gently down my throat, the smell of the sautéed onions and apples Grandma had added to the lard soothing my anxiety. My greasy hands stained the pages of the Moomin books with grayish fingerprints. Mother was still away, though now doctors were saying that she might survive. First, as I learned much later, they gave her little chance to live, since she had swallowed enough sleeping pills to kill a large man. Grandma begged them to save her. "She has two little children," she said to the men and women in white. One of them, a middle-aged female doctor, lost her patience and retorted: "She should have thought about her children before she stuffed handfuls of valium in her mouth and downed a bottle of hard liquor." Grandma asked a priest to see Mother daily, no longer trusting the doctors. When Mother woke up about a week later, Grandma dressed my brother and me in white and dragged us to church. The echo of my boots hitting the marble as I stepped from foot to foot and waited to be allowed to go to the bathroom rang out over Grandma's hushed conversation with the priest.

Moominmamma didn't wake up because she was hibernating, together with the other Moomins. My mother's attempted suicide, this and others afterward (pills, a belt hung from bathroom pipes, gas, a balcony, more pills), was also, I guess, an attempt to retreat from the cold world around her and into the oblivion of sleep. When I sat on Mother's bed and shook her shoulder—"Mama, wake up. Wake up!"—I looked at her gentle profile, beads of sweat still clinging to the little hairs above her right ear, a faint smile. Dare I say she looked happy? She did look happy. In contrast to most days, when she raged or sulked, she seemed at peace. I drew closer to her face and smelled the familiar smell of liquor, but it was mixed with another smell, not entirely unpleasant, one I was not able to identify as a little girl and still cannot identify as a middle-aged woman. Maybe it was the mix of fresh perspiration and laundry detergent, or maybe the valium, chemical sweetness you could almost taste.

* * *

Moomins are imaginary creatures, but most real hibernating animals sleep during winter because they can rely on fat storage. Fat is life. *Sleep* is perhaps not the most fitting word, though. Perhaps *paralysis*? The animals' metabolisms slow down, and their bodies use fat deposits to survive until food becomes available in warmer months. Female polar bears, for example, store enough fat to sustain them and their fetuses while overwintering. There is growing evidence of an evolutionary link between the bears' hibernation and their reproductive timeline, since bears deliver their offspring while hibernating and switch from placental nourishment to mammalian feeding, ensuring adequate supply of life-giving nutrients to both mothers and babies. Brown bears hibernate, too, and so do bats and hedgehogs. Human hearts, however, stop when our body temperature falls below 28 degrees Celsius.

Is it true that you would effectively kill a hibernating animal if you woke it up? In some cases, animals like small rodents would use too much energy to bring up their body temperature, and they wouldn't have easy access to food in the depth of winter. Doctors did wake Mother, and I like to think that the jars of lard Grandma had regularly delivered to our apartment helped her pull through. In any case, that lard reminded me, on days when Mother drank, on days when she slept for hours, on days when she shook and sweated, that my brother and I would be all right. Someone out there delivered greasy jars to our fridge and fresh rolls to our breadbox.

* * *

When rereading the Moomin series as an adult, I think of Grandma whenever I see the black-and-white drawings of the Moomin matriarch fretting over everyone's meals. Moominmamma makes fruit preserves that her son later shares with forest creatures in the winter. Grandma's prune, cherry, gooseberry, and apple preserves lined our dusty shelves in the basement. When she made them, I would sit in her kitchen, breathing in the tangy smell of boiling currant juice and waiting for her to pour some hot preserves into a bowl so I could dip a chunk of bread in it and let the warm juice dribble on my chin like a diabolical goatee. Grandma's kitchen was cluttered. Eggs sat in a basket under the table, next to potatoes, rutabaga, and parsley root. Half-finished tea in clear glasses shared countertop space with sticky spoons and pickle jars. It was a kitchen where things happened.

Butter was scarce but Grandma always had lard in her fridge. Grandpa Wincenty used to visit people in nearby villages as a regional representative of one of the two parties that the ruling Polish United Workers' Party allowed to exist after 1949. The Polish People's Party (PSL) was a social-democratic agrarian organization, populist and Christian in its rhetoric. In 1949 its name changed to United People's Party (ZSL), and it became a de facto satellite organ of the ruling Communist party. Grandpa taught economics in a local high school, and he volunteered as a probation officer for juvenile offenders, all the while maintaining our garden with its potatoes, radishes, beans, cucumbers, tomatoes, strawberries, and currants. As a liaison between the regional office of the ZSL and local farmers, he traveled to the countryside, sometimes bringing back a bottle of homemade vodka (*samogon*) or a cut of fatback. Grandma would melt that cut into fragrant lard. She cut it up into tiny pieces, threw it in the pan with some salt, pepper, and herbs, and made the most delicious spread for our bread. We had different variations of lard: Sometimes we'd add sautéed onions, sometimes sour apple or bacon pieces. To this day when I visit my brother in Poland, this is what he prepares ahead of time: a pot of fragrant lard, served on fresh sourdough bread, with a pickle slice on top.

* * *

LARD SPREAD

3 cups pork fat, rendered
10 slices of bacon, diced
1 large onion
1/2 sour apple, shredded
Salt, pepper, marjoram, and allspice to taste

Heat 2 tablespoons of rendered pork fat and all of the bacon pieces in a cast-iron skillet. Add diced onion and spices and sauté to make the onion soft and golden. Add the remaining pork fat and wait until heated through and well mixed. Turn off the heat. Add the apple. When the spread cools off a little, pour into a jar, close, and store in the fridge for up to a month. It's best when spread on freshly baked sourdough or dark rye bread.

* * *

When things were eerily quiet at Mother's house, and I anticipated an explosion, I read in bed about the Moomins fleeing an angry red comet, or I listened to a radio play based on *Moominsummer Madness,* where the valley is flooded and the Moomins and friends transform a floating theater into a home. Moominmamma's fruity, matter-of-fact voice, the otherworldly setting of theater props and costumes transported me away from the howling pipes in Mother's house and her sterile kitchen smelling like bleach.

* * *

We navigated the silences and explosions of Mother's house with more and more skill, predicting her moods, trying to please her, coaxing her to stay awake and play dominoes with us, and eventually figuring out an escape, if only in our imaginations.

Pleasing her was not easy. We had to catch her in the early stages of drinking to get her attention. As soon as the vodka crossed her blood-brain barrier, she became jovial and energized enough to dust and vacuum and perhaps even read a book or sing a song with us, jumping up whenever her cigarette butt burned her fingers. The longer she drank—and she rarely stopped at one or two shots—the slower she became, and she would finally drop on her bed or the living room carpet and stay asleep for hours. The worst were her withdrawal symptoms: hand tremors, sweating, anxiety. We retreated to our room then and played with our Russian dolls or our modeling-clay zoo. When she was craving alcohol or recovering from last night's binge, she was either volatile or withdrawn, sometimes both. She was a little bit like the Groke in the Moomin series—a scary, ghostlike creature with large eyes, cold and lonely but not exactly evil. The Groke pines for warmth and seeks light, but whatever she touches turns into ice.

* * *

"Agusia!" Mother uses an endearing diminutive, but her guttural *g* betrays her. She's already had at least three drinks, I assess quickly. "I'm so glad you're calling."

I tickle my son's belly as he wiggles on a fuzzy blanket, his hair shiny in the warm Indiana sun, his ribcage visible beneath thin skin above a diaper that seems too large.

"Get the money? Is Western Union open on Saturday in Poland?"

"It was open. Thank you. I'll pay my water bill. But I don't know how I'm going to buy food now."

I want to ask where her modest retirement payment went. I want to ask if she bought the alcohol now circulating in her veins with the dollars I sent her way. But I know what she's going to say: Everything is expensive, and she just can't make ends meet. Tomek moved her from the large two-bedroom apartment we grew up in to a tiny one-bedroom flat in the same district so she could pay the smaller heating bills on time and maybe slow down her drinking without her enabling neighbors around. But she found other enablers. They came over to drink with her and left with Grandma's golden rings or her wedding-day china set or a laundry detergent box while Mother was passed out. They came over and hid stolen electronics in her bedroom for later resale. They came over and left their cats behind. They came over and walked to a nearby store with her so she could buy more alcohol, promising to buy vodka for their next libation.

"So the baby is still sick, and we're scheduled for more tests at the children's hospital. I'm so worried."

"Oh? Well, I've been sick, too, with this cough that won't go away. Hacking, I'm telling you! But I'm not going to a doctor because it's too far, and besides, if I die, I die. What will I do if they say I need to buy medicine? I have no money."

The familiar guilt gnaws at my guts.

"Maybe it's cigarettes? Are you taking your antidepressants? You know you're not supposed to combine them with alcohol."

"I haven't put alcohol to my lips in weeks!"

I recall our last conversation, a week ago, when I hung up on Mother because I couldn't understand her slurred speech. It wasn't just the distorted vowels and throaty consonants. Her train of thought was so disconnected that I simply couldn't follow. I want her to ask about my infant son, who is refusing to nurse and growing weak. I want her to ask how my marriage is surviving the daily stress of caring for an infant in the "failure to thrive" category.

"*No dobra.*" OK, then. "I'm going to take a nap now. Couldn't sleep last night because of the cough. Oh, I may visit you after all! There's this doctor in New York who is looking for a Polish nanny."

* * *

I suppose Mother's mind was preoccupied with getting, drinking, and then recovering from alcohol so much that there was little space left to ask about my life. Like most addicts, her focus was on getting her fix. In those moments, when I had to put down the receiver and refuse to listen to her drunken effusions about her new boyfriend or her cussing about an acquaintance who stole her family gold, I wondered why she was self-medicating and what part of herself alcohol was supposed to regulate. What feelings did she suppress? What pushed her into drinking in the first place, before it became invincible compulsion? Was it low self-esteem? Some kind of trauma she never talked about?

Loneliness after her divorce? Depression? Genetics? Cultural expectations in provincial Communist Poland, where—especially during the martial law—the only diversions were vodka-soaked home parties and books? Mother sent her SOS in empty vodka bottles and smoke signals, and my brother and I were too small and too focused on survival to think about decoding them.

Tomek and I lived in two worlds. After my grandparents moved to our town and started taking us in for longer and longer stretches, our lives became more predictable though polarized in ways that were confusing. Living with Mother, I was always on high alert, anticipating and averting dangers, putting out fires, protecting my brother from her wrath. When I opened Grandma's front door, I could breathe again, curl up on a sofa with my books, sip on homemade cranberry juice, and sometimes even throw a tantrum about a missing school assignment or a pair of sneakers I lost after PE. I could press my cheek against Grandma's, feel her slightly fuzzy and plump skin, and smell her cheap Bulgarian perfume. I could climb into her bed after I wetted mine and have her sing old patriotic songs about soldiers lying in rose-covered shallow graves. I could sit with my brother on Grandpa's bed, listen to the bubbles in his winemaker, and peruse his war medals and old letters from his family in Belarus. I could study a list of natural resources in East Germany for my geography test. I could invite a friend over and not fear that she would hear Mother's drunken ravings. I could explore the neighborhood on a bike or pretend to be an Amazon while running through the thick bushes on a nearby escarpment. I could talk gibberish to people lining up in front of empty grocery stores, pretending I was from England. Grandma and Grandpa fussed over whether we were hungry or cold or sad. They insisted that we finish our homework before going outside. They had homemade cough syrup made from onion juice and sugar when we were sick, and the lard, always the lard, which we devoured in astounding quantities.

Then it was back to Mother's—to the wind howling in the pipes, to the Modern Talking poster in the hallway guarding our bedroom door, to the empty kitchen, and to vodka on Mother's breath.

* * *

My favorite kind of lard was rendered pork fat with ground bacon and sautéed onions, flavored with salt, pepper, and thyme. Rendered pork leaf lard is actually quite tasteless, unlike bacon grease lard, so you can flavor it the way you like it. Baking with lard makes for delicious flaky pie crust and biscuits. We also ate smoked pork fat, paper-thin slices on whole-wheat bread, the Polish peasant's *lardo di colonnata.* Grandma's *faworki* (or "angel wings," deep-fried sugared pastry) were crispy and flaky precisely because she fried them in lard. She made sure the fat came from a sow rather than a male pig because apparently male lard is stinky. Grandma poured a pint of lard into her cast-iron pan and waited for it to be super hot before dropping the wing-shaped dough in.

Lard wasn't actually a bad source of nutrition. Its saturated fat content is around 40 percent, unsaturated a little over 50. Polish lore has it that lard, or pig fat in general, has healing properties. In remote villages, some people still try to fight common colds and even bronchitis with pig fat. They mix lard with ground marshmallow root and hot water, and they eat three spoonfuls a day. Some also use pieces of pig fat placed between a tooth and the gums to get rid of toothache. For arthritis, people used to rub lard on affected areas and wrap them with cheesecloth. Mixed with beeswax, lard is sometimes used to cover open sores and varicose veins. When I was a nursing mother, I also learned that I could prevent mastitis by rubbing lard on my nipples. I never tested this hypothesis.

In modern medicine, some pharmaceuticals use lard as a binding agent. If you see *Adeps suillus* or *Axungia porci* in the ingredients of your ointment, you're rubbing lard on your forehead or sore muscles. Mix lard, flax oil, pine resin, and unclarified beeswax, and you have an ointment for cold and minor burns. Lard has anti-inflammatory and softening properties. Combined with sulfur, it is supposed to alleviate itching.

* * *

After a sweaty and cramped night in a sleeper car on a Szczecin-Kraków train, a compartment my husband Josh and I share with a friend and a family of strangers, we get off at the station and look for a place to eat lunch. We ignore Kraków's Japanese, Mexican, and Indian restaurants, which have sprouted since the fall of Communism like mushrooms after rain, and instead head for a place with outdoor seating, with a thatched sunshade and rustic-looking fence around the beer garden. And there it is—lard. It's the appetizer everyone gets here, like sweet rolls in O'Charley's. A thick slice of fresh rye bread, a bowl of lard, and a pickle.

I spread a generous spoonful of fat on my slice and bite in. It doesn't occur to me that my Jewish friend may not want to have this appetizer on our table. But soon he reaches for lard, too, after seeing bliss on my face as I chew the bacon bits and sautéed onions. I haven't been in Poland for a year now. Life in the middle of Indiana means no lard, unless I make it myself, which I don't because I don't know yet where to buy leaf fat in my small town.

"Slow down!" Warren is clearly amused. "I had no idea such a slim woman would jump on this artery-clogging fat with so much zest."

My husband waits for the menu and nibbles on the bread crust. He used to hunt squirrels as a child but won't touch pork lard.

As I sip on a highly carbonated Żywiec beer, another larded slice in front of me, I am home.

* * *

Lard's unhealthy properties have been recently disputed, but it has at least once been used as a weapon against others. In 1936 the Polish newspaper *Republika* reported that on February 16, passersby on a Warsaw street saw a young man dressed only in a shirt, flailing and screaming for help. A doctor in the ambulance that arrived at the scene recorded serious burns on the man's head, neck, face, chest, legs, and thighs. One third of his body was badly burned. When he briefly regained consciousness at the hospital, he accused his girlfriend of pouring boiling goose lard on him. The fat burned his tissues so thoroughly that the man, named Perec Elenberg, died two days later. Before he died, he identified his killers as his live-in girlfriend, Rywka Junker, her fifteen-year-old daughter, Chaja, and Rywka's brothers, Icek and Chil Szpiro. As it eventually transpired, Perec was planning to move to Palestine, and Rywka asked him to marry her and take her with him. He stubbornly refused. One night, when he was getting ready for bed, the woman's brothers grabbed him and held him down while Rywka poured boiling goose fat all over his body. The men were not charged. Rywka and her daughter Chaja were accused of murder. Chaja maintained that she spilled the lard on Perec by accident. The verdict had not yet been reached upon the publication of the issue in front of me, and I could not find any information about the verdict in later editions. Death by goose fat. A crime mystery without an ending.

National newspapers in Poland reported another lard crime, this time in 2008, when the police in Wieliczka arrested a seventy-year-old man who had been catching dogs and making lard out of them for nearly fifty years. He sold the lard in jars as pig fat. It turns out that killing dogs for lard is a more widespread activity in the south of Poland than I would like to think. Older people praise the healing properties of dog lard and claim that it treats impotence. All you have to do is rub the lard on the affected area every day and voilà! Silesian miners protect themselves against black lung by adding dog lard to a shot of vodka before work. In the Żywiecczyzna region of Poland, older generations tried to treat tuberculosis by adding badger or dog fat to milk or vodka. Some would also wrap the ill person in dogskin.

* * *

We soothe our senses and heal real or imaginary wounds with all kinds of things—pig fat, dog lard, alcohol—so who is to tell us where a boundary lies between morally acceptable remedies and despicable potions? As a dog lover and owner, I shudder at the thought of anyone rubbing dog fat on their arthritic arms or, worse (why worse?), their flaccid penis; yet I reach into my fridge for a jar of pig lard and spread it liberally on a slice of bread, undisturbed by conscience. Until recently I have used makeup foundation containing beef tallow. I laugh at the idea of rubbing pig lard on cracked nipples, but when I nursed my children, I always had a tube of lanolin cream on my bedside table. Animal fat is animal fat is animal fat. My outrage at the death of one species but not the other points to self-serving virtue-signaling rather than a high moral principle.

So who am I to judge Mother, who chose to self-medicate with alcohol until she couldn't choose anymore and then had to drink without respite to dull the pain of addiction? Who am I to judge her desire to die?

* * *

Zbigniew Herbert's poem "Rozmyślania o ojcu" ("Remembering My Father") recalls the speaker's dad, "His face severe in clouds above the waters of childhood / so rarely did he hold my warm head in his hands." And then:

he himself grows in me we eat our defeats
we burst out laughing
when they say how little is needed
to be reconciled.

I don't know much about Herbert's father, but whenever I revisit this poem, it is my own mother I think about, and not the drunk and raging Mother but the sober and silent Mother: her clenched teeth, her tight jaws grinding resentment and anger, chewing air, silent, anxious, unhappy. The shuffling of her house slippers on the linoleum floor, *ssssh . . . ssssh . . . ssssh . . .*— it's how we knew not to cross her path. Her slow, calculated responses to our questions, her crisp and terse yeses, her pithy nos, her sardonic maybes. Her raging was bearable because it proved she was capable of emotion. Her silences were noxious.

But then maybe that's where she was most comfortable dwelling: in silence. When I discovered a few pages that must have been torn off from her diary, they were all covered with her observations about a cat she rescued. The year recorded on these pages was 2008, so Mother wrote this part of her diary six years after I left Poland for the United States on a scholarship that I hoped would allow me as much distance from her as possible, and three years before her run-in with the NYPD. I read the long paragraphs about the kitty's mischief and affection, sentences filled with love and respect for the cat she called Mrusia. I cannot detect any anger in her amused descriptions of Mrusia's destruction of her favorite pillowcase, or her pulling clothes off hangers, or her pooping in the empty drum of the washing machine. Like a scientist in the field observing wild animals from behind a thorn bush, Mother records Mrusia's every move and speculates about its motives. "Now the kitty is sitting next to me, like Buddha, after a joyous rampage and wild frolicking. With her paw, she gently touches the marble ball at the end of my knitting needle. She likes my knitting. With interest she watches my work, touching the yarn, stealing it sometimes, dragging it all the way to the other room. A moment of inattention. Now her evening grooming, methodical licking of her fur after she kneaded a hollow spot in my duvet. She lies down close to me and falls asleep snuggled between my bent knees and my belly."

I can't help it. I'm jealous of the damn cat.

And I regret I didn't show Mother the kind of unconditional interest this kitten gave her.

* * *

I write the scene in which Mother wouldn't wake up while I sit in the quietness of my sunroom right before going to bed. That night, I wake up convinced I am dying. My heart is racing. I am dizzy. I can't breathe. My arms go numb.

The body keeps the score, as they say. When I see my therapist the following day, she urges me to check my heart, but she also says that these are classic symptoms of a panic attack. Revisiting childhood memories triggered my body's defense mechanism, she says. The limbic system influencing emotions and memory affects our endocrines and the autonomic nervous system. When I try to recollect sensory details in that room where Mother almost died, the tiny almond-shaped amygdala fires up to protect me from the imminent threat. So what that the threat is long gone? As I unpack the long-stored sensory memories from that night, they reach the amygdala, which, in turn, prepares me for battle by firing cortisol and norepinephrine. The amygdala also changes my breathing and heart rate. The threat may be imagined or simply remembered from the past. The physical feeling of intense fear is very real.

My therapist tells me to stop writing for a while.

Writing about Mother was supposed to be cathartic, liberating. Instead, I stare with dread at my computer screen, its bluish light penetrating my skull, and I wake up at night to imaginary screams and crashes after an old recurring nightmare revisits my rare sleeping hours, the dream I used to have as a child with surprising regularity. Again, my family is mushroom hunting in a thick forest. Again, we are all walking down a remote road, walls of foliage on either side. Again, Tomek and I are holding hands, skipping ahead of Mother, Grandma, Grandpa, and Uncle—all wearing heavy Wellingtons, large wicker baskets in hand. Again, I see myself and Tomek as if we were facing a camera, our family receding in a blurred shot. Then the adults step quickly into a wall of trees and are gone. Tomek and I turn around, still holding hands, only to see an empty road. That's when I always wake up. The dream ends with a moment of concentrated dread, a fear I can almost touch.

* * *

As a snowdrift on the roof of the Moominhouse slides down and covers most of the windows, Moomintroll winds up all the clocks he can find to cheer himself up. In a picture that follows the scene where Moominmamma doesn't wake up from her hibernation, Moomintroll stands by her bed, scared and lonely and overwhelmed by the dark things around him, his plump body casting a shadow over the floor. All you can see of Moominmamma are the top of her head and her ears sticking out from under her quilt. Moomintroll's sadness turns into anger, and he leaves the house via a chimney-sweep's hatch in the roof. The world he encounters outside is also unfamiliar and hostile, but he meets practical Too-ticky, to whom he confesses his fear of the outside world covered in snow. Too-ticky explains that winter is when all the shy misfits come out of their hiding and can finally be themselves. Other creatures simply want to lead a secret life.

Moomintroll kicked at the table leg and sighed. "I see, I see," he replied. "But I don't want to lead a secret life. Here one comes stumbling into something altogether new and strange, and not a soul even asking one in what kind of a world one has lived before. Not even Little My wants to talk about the real world."

"And how does one tell which one is the real one?" said Too-ticky with her nose pressed against a pane.

Which childhood of mine was real? The one in which Mother races at me with sharp objects or the one in which Grandma rocks me gently to sleep? When friends ask me if I had a happy childhood, I am often at a loss for words. Not because it was so damn traumatizing but because it was not, or not really, not always, not without any respite. It was split between the frigid world of Mother-Groke and Moomingrandma's summer. The Groke seemed scary and different and cold, but we rarely tried to extend our sympathy to her, to love her unconditionally, to think of her as a creature consumed by insatiable longing for light rather than a monster.

* * *

Three weeks after Mother gave birth to me upon disembarking from a train, Poland was hit with what is now called *Zima Stulecia*—Winter of the Century—though winter had already been quite ruthless that year. On New Year's Eve, as I slept in Grandma's bedroom, my perked-up black hair making me look like a swaddled hedgehog, Mother drank *Sovetskoe Szampanskoe* with Father and Grandpa and watched the snow fall gently on the field between the apartment building and a rusty playground.

Snow often softened the sharp edges of the totalitarian poured-concrete world we lived in. It covered the grayness of the Soviet-era high-rises and blurred the brutalist monoliths in our city centers. It made the destitute villages look like romantic post-cards. It obscured the ugly.

But that snow was different. It fell and fell and fell. Strong winds pushed it into enormous drifts. Railroads cracked. Buses stopped. Coal used to heat our homes couldn't be transported. Water pipes broke. Our region was hit with only three feet of snow, but the wind created mountains two or three stories high, and temperatures dropped to –20 degrees Fahrenheit. Everything came to a standstill.

Eventually, city buses started driving through ice tunnels. Local officials resurrected old, 1950s-era vehicles called Autosan because these, unlike the newer ones, could be heated up from underneath to make them work. Father remembers men walking around a bus depot, carrying torches they stuck under the buses.

If this is how Mother's journey through parenting started, with general paralysis of the roads and basic amenities, all the while worrying about Father's infidelities, should I be surprised that she looked for an escape from the world around her and found it in the bottle? Should I condemn her for later lulling herself to weeklong slumber with valium and vodka as Tomek and I waited for dinner?

And yet I cannot help but feel anger when I look back at one afternoon in day care, when Tomek and I waited for Mother to pick us up, our slippers already neatly put away in their cubbies, our boots on, ready to trudge through dirty snow, up the hill and then along a sand-covered sidewalk tunnel dug by the superintendent. We waited as our teachers exchanged pitying looks. We waited as the sky outside turned purple and then pitch black. We waited as I read yet another picture book to my brother. I took off his coat and mine because it was too warm in the dimly lit hallway. We waited as Tomek wet his pants on the hardwood bench and I wiped it off with the sleeve of my coat to spare him embarrassment. We waited.

I don't know how the day care got hold of Mother. Did we have a telephone by then? Phones were hard to come by in the early '80s. Did someone walk over to our apartment and wake her up? When she came through the front door, way past suppertime, her cheeks were dark red and cold, her coat unbuttoned, her gaze unsteady. We walked home in silence, inhaling the alcohol mist Mother puffed into the freezing air.

* * *

Almost two decades after Mother's first attempted suicide I will sit on a wooden bench in front of the library at the University of Sussex and read about an old sow that eats her farrow. Later still, a handsome professor will tell me that it's only domestic pigs that eat their litter, for lack of space, and not wild sows, who can go where they please and don't turn to cannibalization to get nutrients or more space. And then later still, I will visit a large farm in northwestern Indiana, where I will see, from a glass gallery above a large gestation and birth hangar, dozens of mother pigs squeezed into cages, their bodies motionless, spread over the cement floor. Piglets suck, tug, and tear at the swollen nipples. Mother pigs lie there, resigned, still, all function. If I were one of them, and the metal bar pressed against my body lifted for a moment, would I not sink my teeth in one of these piglets' fuzzy flesh? Would I not tear at them with rage? Would I not perhaps sever their arteries to protect them from lying in the same cage and breeding and nursing and breeding and nursing? Would I not rather get slaughtered and turned into lard?

Bread

"*Nie będziesz jadła*?!" You won't eat it?! Mother speaks quietly, unclenching her teeth only for a moment. She is raw menace. Her nostrils flare. Her neck sinews move every time she swallows. I look at these sinews, wondering whether they can break from too much tension, like violin strings that have been tightened too much. Will they make a sound when they snap?

"*Won.*" Scram. Fuck off. Her voice is still quiet. She lights a cigarette and with one hand empties my plate into the trash can. Stale bread and beans in tomato sauce land on top of last night's contents of Mother's heavy ashtray.

I stand in the doorway, not sure what to do—a six-year-old weighing her options. If I apologize, will she explode at the sound of my voice? If I turn around and walk to my bedroom, will she follow me there and hurt not only me but also Tomek?

"*Won.*"

* * *

Earlier that day, Mother went out to the store, leaving us alone for about an hour, maybe two. I rummaged through one of the kitchen drawers, pulled out a screwdriver and a hammer, grabbed my brother, and marched to the living room sofa. There, standing on cushions, we worked. We swung our arms out above our heads and struck the wall above the sofa with enough ferocity to make large chunks of painted cement fall down. I suppose I pretended to be a blacksmith or carpenter or something. Tomek? He just followed my lead. By the time Mother came back, the wall was so pockmarked that it looked as if someone had unleashed a volley of machine-gun bullets in our home.

Mother dropped the net bag on the floor, sour cream and beer bottles jingling against each other. She lurched toward us. The rest is darkness.

In retrospect, I see our pockmarking the wall as a call for attention and affection in a drafty, spooky apartment in which we either had to shield ourselves from Mother's wrath or wonder when the deadly silences would end. Mother's rage was a call for help, too. Where was her village to help raise two small kids and find basic goods to keep them dressed and clean and fed? Who was going to give her love? Increasingly, the answer was the bottle. Sometimes pills. A joint here and there. But mostly vodka and beer.

* * *

My memory picks up at the dinner table. Tomek is napping in our room, and Mother says "*Won*" when I refuse to eat, and after she throws out the bread and beans, I slowly back away toward the wood-paneled hallway.

What happened in between?

* * *

A black-and-white photo clipped from a newspaper. I lean closer and breathe in the moldy air of my grandparents' basement, with its dusty shelves and boxes of photo albums, contraband publications from Stalinist Poland, and my own old geography textbooks featuring flags of Yugoslavia and Czechoslovakia and the Soviet Union. I've already tucked my seventh-grade Russian primer in my coat, hoping I would find space in my luggage for the dog-eared pages filled with smiling Soviet scouts, Karl Marx's beard, and Yuri Gagarin's grinning face inside a helmet that says CCCP. My flight back to Chicago leaves in a couple of days. It's 2016, and the basement is no longer mine, and neither are the books, really, or anything else in the upstairs apartment that now sports a large flat-screen TV and a smart washing machine. I am a visitor passing through.

At my feet is an ancient box filled with photos. The basement shelves to my left used to be lined up with gooseberry jam, black currant syrup, and pickled beets. There are still a few jars in the far corner, with Grandma's handwriting on the labels: *red currant '89, chokeberry syrup '92, cabbage '93*. An empty birdcage hangs above them, the same one in which my zebra finches died, and to its right is a row of old textbooks and banned anti-Communist publications about Soviet gulags where Polish families fried cow manure for dinner. I see an old film projector Mother used to screen slides from fairy tales, on days when she wasn't too drunk to sit upright or too sober to entertain us without blowing up at the slightest inconvenience. The projector's light would flicker off the specks of dust floating in her tiny bedroom as she turned the black knob to advance the film with a soft click.

But the photo. I feel its grainy texture in my fingers. A group of men in shabby raincoats carry a large protest sign in Polish: "CHCEMY CHLEBA!" ("WE WANT BREAD!"). Another man walks ahead of the sign, his hands pressed together either in supplication or anger, his mouth open as if gasping for air. Behind them an old brick tower. *Poznański Czerwiec,* June 1956—the first general strike and street unrest in Communist Poland, trivialized by the official press as an "incident" but in fact threatening enough for the armed state militia to be deployed against the protesters. The unrest started at the Joseph

Stalin Metal Plant in Poznań when men and women quit their jobs and flooded the streets with signs: "WE ARE HUNGRY" and "WE DEMAND HIGHER WAGES." Eventually the movement was crushed by 10,000 People's Army soldiers who killed 57 and wounded over 600 unarmed workers. Soon after, around 250 people were thrown in jail and tortured as a result of the unrest.

I was born more than twenty years after this particular protest, but I remember others like it, with men and women wearing the same shabby blazers and carrying the same old demands: bread, freedom, fewer power outages. Now, crouched over photos in democratic Poland, I cannot recall whether we ever went to a protest when I was a child. It seems we always had bread. When Mother's hands were too shaky to feed me and my younger brother Tomek, we walked to our grandparents' apartment, with its smell of fried eggs, onions, and blood sausage, with its warm radiators and clean sheets, with its mysterious padlocked basement. Labor Day marches, yes, I remember walking in those, white shirted and red tied, waving a flag or a pinwheel. But protests? The only protest I recall attending was after the end of Communism, and it was against animal cruelty, in front of a circus tent, where—soon after we threw paint bombs at the entrance—I was shamed by another protester for wearing leather shoes.

I see more pictures in the box. Yellowed newspaper cutouts, black-and-white photos, postcards, rolled-up posters, pages torn out of magazines. In Communist propaganda photos and posters, bread is abundant. So are wheat bundles and collective harvesting of grains. Here is a procession of horse-drawn carts filled with burlap grain bags, the stern-looking farmers holding an enormous sign that says "WE ARE DELIVERING GRAIN FOR THE PEOPLE OF WARSAW." Here is Władysław Gomułka, a leader of the Party, a dumb anti-Semite, receiving a gift of bread from a radiant blonde dressed in traditional Polish peasant garb during a harvest festival. Here is a makeshift bread store in the middle of a snow-covered village—a rickety bus, really, from which someone is selling loaves of bread to farmers, their faces frozen in the morning air. Against logic, up until the end of the Communist regime in 1989, there were still occasional shortages of bread in the countryside. Like people living in large cities, collectivized and individual farmers stood in bread lines for hours.

Poland—including its vast agrarian areas—was almost entirely destroyed in World War II. The country lost a fifth of its population and sustained the highest material losses of all European countries. Over a quarter of Poland's farms were annihilated and half the arable land was left untilled during the war. Food rationing did not end in 1945, although the allowed amounts of bread, kasha, and salt increased. The rationing was not, as most would expect of a Communist society, equally distributed. The top class—political militia, judges, and apparatchiks—received the most. Factory workers did not belong to the privileged group. And one of the most reviled groups, apart from "bloodsucking Jews" and "capitalist swine," were *kułaks,* or "rich" peasants who employed farmworkers and were, therefore, exploiting others. *Kułaks* were mostly blamed for bread shortages and were objects of theatrical arrests and mock trials for "hoarding" grains. One such trial was against Edmund Szellenbaum, who, in 1951, was accused of hiding over 4,000 kilograms of rye and 2,500 kilograms of oats instead of selling them to the government at regulated prices for further redistribution.

Especially insidious was the common practice of sending city youths to the countryside to check farms for hoarded grains. A photo from February 1951 shows a long line of horse-drawn carriages filled with grains and headed by young men with a sign: "WE ARE GROWING UP AS DEFENDERS OF PEOPLE'S

POLAND." One of the youths holds a red flag. Another sits on a pile of burlap bags, his legs spread in the same triumphant pose you'd see in photos of wild-game hunters and their exotic kill. In effect, a lot of people in the countryside starved during the first two decades after the war.

* * *

I hear Adele's thunderous *doesn't tear you apart* and a door slamming somewhere upstairs. Fourth floor? Third? Who lives there now? My grandparents are dead, and their apartment belongs to my brother. Above him are two floors now occupied by strangers. The basement used to be an excellent hiding place when I was a child—if you were fine with an occasional rat and fleas. It's in this basement that I squeezed myself between the wall and an older, flame-haired girl, Ada, during a game of hide-and-seek, and it's here that she showed me her armpit and pubic hair.

"See? I'm a woman now." She lifted my chin, pity in her eyes. "You know nothing, do you?"

She was right. In the same basement, Grandpa Wincenty stored a couple of sturdy sleighs, some wooden planks, and contraband papers. Our cell was always double padlocked. As a child, I thought the locks were there to keep thieves from taking our fruit preserves and pickled peppers. Later, when Grandpa showed me the shoddily printed magazines about Soviet concentration camps for Polish intelligentsia, it dawned on me that losing a few jars of gooseberry jam was the least of my grandparents' worries.

* * *

Back in my Indiana home, I reach for Ken Forkish's *Flour, Water, Salt, Yeast*—my bread-making bible. His recipes are time-consuming, but the sourdough bread I eventually pull out of the oven tastes just like the bread I remember eating in Poland—dark-brown crust, airy texture, nutty, slightly sour flavor without the vinegary aftertaste so common in commercially sold American sourdough breads. It's his book that helped me perfect the mixing, folding, and shaping techniques to produce an aromatic loaf with complex flavors, right here among the cornfields of the Hoosier State.

Dough fermentation is essential, as is giving the bread time to mature at each stage of its production. Time and temperature are as important in bread making as the quality of flour, which contains natural yeast and "good bacteria" waiting to be released if you let it rest. Forkish reminds his readers that the yeast culture in a homemade starter has "billions of rapidly reproducing, gas-belching, single-celled organisms." He adds: "I like knowing that I can make them do what I want them to do."

* * *

My calves go numb from squatting over the photos, and I shift to the cement stairs outside the basement door. Here the light is stronger, but I have to get up every time the staircase timer goes off with a click and feel my way up to the switch. On this same landing used to be a bag filled with old bread that disappeared once a week.

Grandma Iza never threw bread away. Some Polish people still kiss bread after dropping it on the ground. Others cut a sign of the cross on the crust before thrusting their knives into its airy flesh. We rarely baked bread in my home, but in the late '70s and through the stormy '80s we always managed to buy enough sourdough loaves, rolls, yeast crescents, and heavy whole-wheat bricks to sustain us. We ate them with lard, with pickles, with jam, with dark buckwheat honey. We used stale bread in *kotlety z chleba* ("bread schnitzels," or a mix of bread, milk, onion, and eggs fried in lard or canola oil) and *knedle*. We made breadcrumbs and croutons. We sprinkled stale bread with water to reheat it in the oven. Some families made *kvas.* One of my favorite dishes was *zapiekanka,* a slice of stale bread fried with grated cheese and egg, served with a slice of tomato on top. Finally, if we did end up with stale, hard bread that could not be reused, we put it in a communal bag that hung from a pipe in the staircase of our apartment complex. Once a week, a local farmer would pick it up and feed his horses with it.

One thing you do not do in Poland, to this day, despite the current relative prosperity, is throw bread in a trash can.

In Grandma's wartime stories, a shortage of food, including bread, was ubiquitous. After the collapse of Communism, in the late '80s and '90s, her anxiety about running out of food filled our noisy fridge with more food than we could eat, driving Grandpa to despair. She couldn't help it. She hoarded bread, lard, and pasta. She filled our basement shelves with hundreds of jars of preserves. And even though I do not remember true hunger myself, because I was born during the so-called economic thaw, when food wasn't abundant but people were not necessarily deprived, I inherited this anxiety about lack, to my American husband's mild annoyance. Our fridge is packed with milk, eggs, cheeses, veggies, and jarred leftovers. When I can see an empty corner in that fridge, I panic.

* * *

I have been keeping my own sourdough starter, feeding it rye flour and water once a day, and baking whole-wheat sourdough boules in a weekly ritual. Doing it right is time- and labor-intensive. Is this why I still cannot throw stale bread into the trash? After all, my spacious Indiana kitchen is far removed from the matchbox-sized Polish kitchens of my childhood and youth, when throwing a moldy crust away was an offense against God.

As I bake, I hear a crop duster above, probably heading to a nearby cornfield. I like to imagine the bread starter's origin. I got it from a colleague of mine, a philosopher and bread maker, who in turn got it from someone else. I like to think that the history of this leaven could go back decades or even centuries, though I know it's unlikely. Leaven is, however, often considered a family heirloom and passed from generation to generation, especially in Europe.

So is trauma.

There must be an epigenetic background to my own anxiety about a lack of food. Grandma and her two younger brothers survived World War II first in Warsaw and then in nearby villages, and they did go through periods of food insecurity. Maybe those memories traveled through our genetic wires down to Mother and eventually to me. Is it possible that this intergenerational trauma contributed to Mother's alcohol addiction, like a long-forgotten splinter that gives you a raging infection? To her violent outbursts, hand raised above my head, eyes wild and unseeing? Does it have something to do with my tendency to imagine and fear unspeakable hunger, despite never having experienced it myself? How do we break the chain? When do we decide that the leaven is too moldy and needs to be discarded, that a new starter could make a healthier, more wholesome loaf?

* * *

My flight back to the States takes off in twenty-four hours. I'm in Pułtusk, a small town near Warsaw, visiting cousins and uncles. Jeżyk, one of Grandma Iza's younger brothers—a tall, lean, clean-shaven man—says yes, he can talk to me about the war. Jeżyk's eyes are alert, and he's eager to tell me about my great-grandparents. His speech is fast, punctuated with an endearing tick, as he inserts *panie* (sir) between phrases and sentences.

His parents, Franciszek and Zofia, anticipated the onset of the war in 1939, and for a few months before the Germans entered Warsaw, they had stockpiled food in their apartment in a working-class neighborhood called Wola, on the east bank of the Vistula River, a neighborhood that was home to a sizable Jewish population. Franciszek and Zofia read the news of Hitler's expansionist politics with increasing dread, and they started baking buttered bread rolls to store them dried in their pantry. When the artillery shells dropped on Warsaw, the family had enough dried bread to last them a few weeks. Franciszek joined the army. Zofia and the kids stayed in their top-floor Wola apartment. One day, when Zofia and the kids were hiding in an underground shelter, one of the shells hit their building, and they lost a whole row of five-kilo canvas bags of flour and fruit syrups stockpiled in their house. They also lost—this time to looters—a supply of potatoes, which they stored in a shed outside their building. Only the toasted bread rolls remained intact. Whenever they heard the wailing of the air-raid sirens, Zofia and the kids would stuff these rolls in their pockets and run downstairs.

Then the Germans entered Warsaw on foot. Great-Grandma started smuggling food from the countryside, muttering, "And forgive us our trespasses."

When she was away, Jeżyk roamed the streets of Warsaw, hungry. To make fire, he stole coking coal from a power plant on Bema Street, or parts of a wooden fence. His saving grace and amazing skill was "jumping the cars." On Skierniewicka Street, there was a Nazi headquarters with a huge sentried gate through which coal and bread delivery trucks passed. Jeżyk would hide near the towering hospital, and when one of the trucks slowed down to watch for crossing trams, he would jump on that truck from the back, throw a bunch of loaves on the street, jump off, pick them up, and run away. When a German soldier turned around with his automatic weapon drawn, Jeżyk was already gone.

In 1941 hunger was rampant. News about entire families dying behind the nearby Jewish ghetto walls arrived with warnings of upcoming insurrections and more deaths. Zofia and the kids fled to the countryside to seek shelter with distant relatives. Zofia returned to the city to fetch more belongings and the bags of dry bread in their storage. The children never saw their mother again.

* * *

Now I place a hundred grams of leaven in a large glass bowl and feed it with white and whole-wheat flour, mixing in lukewarm water by hand. I scrape the leaven from the tiny hairs on my hands and arms, but I know I will be finding caked dough on my skin until I shower. I cover the bowl and let it rest for eight hours. The fermentation gas will help the dough rise, and the molecules will give it a mellow acidic flavor.

* * *

Grandma Iza, Jeżyk, and Włodek—ages ten, eight, and three when the war broke out—were city kids, used to running water and electricity, street-smart as they ran around their Wola neighborhood playing marbles, listening to accordion players, or gaping at makeshift magic trick stands, dirty fingers in their mouths. But hiding from the war in the countryside, Jeżyk had to be taught how to feed horses, graze cows, harvest rye and lupin with a scythe, thresh the grain, tie hay into bundles, lift fifty-to-eighty-kilo bags of rye, and till the land with the other young people working on the farm. The farmer he lodged with was an older man, injured in the head in World War I. Jeżyk often stared with amazement at the sunken part of the farmer's skull until he was chased out into the field.

Grandma Iza also worked, for the butcher in another village. She cleaned the blood and guts after the animals were processed, scrubbed the machines, floors, and walls. She helped in the butcher's house, polishing kitchen floors and grating potatoes for pancakes. She was also mothering little Włodek, who cried for his mama at night. She smoothed his unkempt hair and sang the same songs she'd later sing to me when I couldn't fall asleep, about patriotic boys marching to war, Baba Yagas in huts made of butter, or angels watching over our sleeping bodies.

"*Ale nas zbaw ode złego. Amen.*" And deliver us from evil. She used to kiss the top of my head before turning off the light. Did she kiss Włodek's?

My great-grandmother's decision to move the kids to the countryside saved them from the slaughter back in the city. By 1943 most of the Jews in the Warsaw ghetto were already dead, most sent to Treblinka with only one goal—extermination. In 1944 the Wola district of Warsaw witnessed more Nazi atrocities, especially during the Warsaw Uprising. In early August, following Hitler's direct order to destroy the city and kill all its inhabitants, SS commandos murdered 20,000 civilians in what is now known as *Rzeź Woli,* or the Wola Slaughter. Men, women, and children were executed at random in their apartments, basements, bomb shelters, orphanages, factories, tram cars, and in the streets. Mass executions, rape, and pillage lasted for days.

Iza, Jeżyk, and Włodek would learn of the atrocities much later. If they ever wondered whether their mother was still alive and hiding in some cellar in Wola, the news of *Rzeź Woli* and the near destruction of Warsaw put their hopes to sleep.

* * *

About eight hours after feeding the leaven, I autolyze 90 grams of white flour and 710 grams of whole-wheat flour by adding lukewarm water, mixing by hand, and letting the mixture rest for twenty minutes. I use a large, round tub, and I have to stand on a stepstool to be able to reach into its cavernous bottom when it sits on my kitchen countertop. Finally, it's time to mix the final dough. I sprinkle salt and a little bit of yeast on top of the dough, add the leaven and water, and fold it all using the pincer method my French historian friend taught me years ago. Forkish recommends two to three additional folds applied within the first two hours of mixing the dough, which helps develop gluten and gives the bread strength and volume. I flip the dough after folding to help it hold tension.

Sticking my hands in the tub, I reach underneath the dough, stretch a part of it, careful not to break the gluten strands, and fold it on top. I repeat the same action with the two opposite sides and finally flip the whole thing, seam down, and cover the tub. Baking good sourdough bread requires focus. I can't do it when I'm in a hurry. I can't do it when my mind is racing. I can't do it in between email dings from my students or with my kids' tiny hands pulling at my skirt. So I create a quiet space at least once a month. Kneading, pinching, folding—it's all tactile, sensory, repetitive experience, and I think it slows down my heartbeat and soothes my spirit more than prayer ever did.

* * *

Back there on the cement staircase in northeastern Poland, I hear footsteps and tense. They are slow and muffled. Slippers? When I turn around, I see my brother, a bouquet of shiny keys dangling from his hooked finger.

"Remember when we used to hide here from Waldek?" Tomek peers into one of the corners.

Waldek was a neighbor who walked the streets all day yelling one question, "*Gdzie była*?"—Where was she?—over and over again. *Gdzie była*? We never heard him say anything else. Where was she? His shirt was always stained with drool, but his pants were clean and pressed.

"Yeah. Where was she? We always wondered who she was and where she went. You said he was abandoned by his mother."

"Nah, someone took care of him. You said a frying pan fell on his head. And that the 'she' was his sister, a KGB spy somewhere in America."

"I must have made it up."

Gdzie była? echoed among the cement high-rises and rusty playgrounds, and it filled us with unspecified dread. Hence the basement hideout.

"Are you sure you want to go through everything before you leave?"

"Yes," I reply. "Don't you?"

Tomek looks down. "No, I don't think so. I prefer to stay in the present."

I'm about to tell him to go upstairs and let me sit here on my own when I feel the first sting. Then another.

"What is it, mosquitoes?"

"Shit." Tomek grabs the box and carries it upstairs. "Bedbugs."

This is the moment I should realize, before I start writing about Mother, that the journey back in time will not be easy or as cathartic as some memoirists suggest. As I scratch my arms until they bleed, sipping my tea at Tomek's kitchen table, I look through the photos in search of a clue. I want to know what made Mother drink. I want to dig until I unearth a clear-cut explanation of her disease and her anger. I want to touch the invisible hunger that drove her away from us, feel its jagged edges, know where it begins and where it ends.

* * *

When the Germans started retreating from the Soviets in 1944 and 1945, rumor had it that they took cows and horses with them. Uncle Jeżyk had to hide all the cows in a nearby forest. He didn't know, however, that the Germans would stay in the village an entire week. As it turns out, the village was lucky. Instead of breezing through and burning it down, the soldiers stayed with the chair of the village council, who got them all drunk with *bimber* and sent them off with a large supply of spirits. They left the village intact. During that week of libations, Jeżyk lived in the forest with the cows, in the rain, without food, wearing a thin tweed jacket. Over the distant Russian artillery sounds, he could hear the cows moo louder and louder because they had not been milked. He was afraid their bellowing would attract the Germans or Russians to his hiding spot, so on the second day he found a German helmet in the bushes and milked the cows into that helmet. When they started spreading around, he made halters from straw and tied them to trees at night. He also found a wreck of a Russian plane, so he used pieces of aluminum from the machine as a frying pan, on which he cooked some saffron milk caps. He drank brown water from ditches and tried to catch loach there, but they were too agile.

In 1946 two aunts found the siblings in their villages and took them to their home in Pomiechówek, another village in east-central Poland. There, hunger began anew. Initially, there were care packages from the United States: clothes, tinned meat, powdered eggs in a burgundy box with a white CARE sign in all caps, an acronym for Cooperative for American Remittances to Europe. Sometimes the food came in a box stamped with UNRRA (United Nations Relief and Rehabilitation Administration), a delivery colloquially known as *ciocia unra* (Auntie Unrra). Humanitarian groups sent Uncle Ben's rice, Franklin cane sugar, Jersey condensed milk cans, and Plymouth Rock canned veal and gravy to war-torn Europe, including Poland. When the relations between the US and Stalin worsened in 1948, the packages stopped coming.

When their aunt cut bread into slices and gave it to everyone, she'd mark the spot where she stopped cutting it so nobody would secretly take more. But sometimes the youngest, Włodek, was so hungry that he cut a thin slice for himself and marked the new spot in the same way. Scavenging for food in local forests and farms was out of the question because land mines still littered the area.

* * *

Five hours after mixing and folding the dough, I sprinkle the countertop with flour, tip the tub, and gently ease the dough out, careful to keep the gas bubbles intact, savoring the earthy, slightly acidic smell. Once the dough is divided in half, I shape the pieces into two loaves, gently pulling, stretching, and patting each surface. Cupping my hands around the back of each loaf, I pull it gently toward me and turn it, tightening it up a little so the ball holds its shape before I place it in a wicker proofing basket. Covered with a cloth, it will sit in the fridge overnight.

The air bubbles count. When you bake bread, the air pockets are as crucial as the gluten strands. The nothing that fills spaces between molecules, the invisible gas making the visible loaf delightful and divine and whole. Bread making is paying as much attention to what's not there as to the tactile and the tangible. The nothing is almost holy. The emptiness doesn't want to be filled, doesn't wait to become something. It just is.

Yet I long to fill the blank spots in my memory as I grope for substance with the anxiety of a writer who wants to create a linear, logical narrative from the fragments, fissures, and absences that refuse to cohere. My memory of childhood and my teenage years is pockmarked like the living room wall I destroyed, filled with dark spots, amnesiac, as if it were a stream of passing out and waking, passing out and waking. I fear that the story that could fill the nothing is now gone forever, and this inability to access parts of my memory erases my sense of self instead of making it whole. I want to think that this hole-riddled story of who I was and therefore who I am creates a gourmet product, one I can hold up to light and say, "See? I don't need to know what happened during Mother's assault on me in that dark hallway. The nothing that is in place of this story will make my narrative even more scrumptious, even more delectable, rare." But deep down I know that these erasures need to be recovered for the story to make sense. For myself to make sense. Otherwise, I am a fraud, or—at best—a sloppy storyteller.

* * *

Grandma Iza, Uncle Włodek, and Uncle Jeżyk got a message from the Red Cross: "Franciszek Kosewski is searching for his family." Their father wrote a letter from England: "Please write that at least one of you survived the war and I will rush back to Poland." When he came back, the children barely recognized him. Włodek, the youngest, had been three when his father left to fight in the war, and he was eleven when Franciszek came back from England. Włodek called his father *pan* (sir), which in Poland is reserved for people outside the family. After being admonished, he switched to *wujku* (uncle).

Since nothing remained from their apartment in Warsaw, they went north to *ziemie odzyskane,* or reclaimed land, that had been Prussian territory before the war. There they found an abandoned three-bedroom apartment, and Jeżyk started looting deserted German mansions. He climbed balconies and used bedsheets to carry away pillows, plates, and silver spoons.

* * *

My great-grandfather Franciszek once put together a Volkswagen with parts taken from an old military car, together with a German mechanic named Hessmann or maybe Hussmann. They labored shoulder to shoulder, whistling old tunes, and not talking much. One day, as they were leaning against a different car, a polished black *wołga* that Franciszek drove for a local Communist Party dignitary, they started listing the places where they fought during the war, and they realized that they both fought at Monte Cassino: Franciszek on the side of the Alliance, and the mechanic for the Germans. There was a long silence as they stared at the rusty-colored poplars ahead of them. Hessmann or maybe Hussmann pulled out a pack of filterless cigarettes and offered one to Franciszek without averting his gaze from the trees.

There's bonding aided by fermentation, and there's bonding aided by amnesia. We tend to think of remembering the past as something inherently good—for individuals and for societies. We're encouraged to talk through trauma in order to heal and grow. But what if all the bubbling and frothing that's supposed to break down sugars to create energy leads to a breakdown of relationships? A souring of existing bonds between two men who smelled each other's sweat as they leaned over a fuel tap and adjusted the front brake drum, who felt the warmth of each other's hands as one handed the other a rusty pedal shaft?

Then again, why should they keep their silent friendship? The friendly exterior of the Volkswagen, its smiley front and beetle-like profile, concealed the difficult history of the car and the people who used it in World War II. The company employed thousands of forced laborers—including prisoners shipped from Auschwitz, Jews, Poles, Russians—mostly in production of land mines and rockets that were later fired on British cities. These workers subsisted on meager food portions allocated according to their ethnicity.

Volkswagen collaborated with the Nazis. Hessmann or maybe Hussmann fought for the Nazis. This ugly truth must have changed the two men's relationship. Once uttered, was there any going back to comfortable silence?

A newsreel from Monte Cassino, 1944. On the screen, bloodied soldiers, prisoners of war, an abbey in ruins, empty shells of a nearby town. In that town, an old toothless woman, head covered with a wrinkled hood, sinks her gums into a chunk of bread. Her chin is propped on a walking cane. In front of her a metal bucket. Behind her gutted buildings and crowds of aimless people. The upbeat voice of the anchor proclaims an Allied victory to the accompaniment of a military march.

* * *

Grandma Iza and Grandpa Wincenty met after the war, after he moved to the same town, decorated with medals for bravery in the Battle of Berlin. Their marriage was turbulent but loving. Whenever I hear the "Do You Love Me?" song from *Fiddler on the Roof,* I think of them—bickering, annoyed with one another, and yet unable to live apart, unable to hide the depths of care they harbored for each other.

One time Grandma left a bowl of gingerbread dough unattended on a kitchen stool. She had mixed melted butter, honey, allspice, ginger, nutmeg, ground cloves, and cinnamon in a large pot. I smelled the bittersweet, earthy aroma of the root spices, put down my guitar, and wandered into the kitchen. Grandma added flour and stirred. The wet, chocolate-brown dough sat in a plastic bowl on top of a kitchen chair because the tiny table was covered with spices, flour, oil, and eggs. Grandpa had just finished helping Tomek with his math homework and came to the kitchen to relax and watch Grandma's baking ritual. He sat down with the deep sigh of a man who had survived explaining the hypotenuse to a tween boy claiming that math existed for the sole purpose of oppressing him, and he propped his head against the wall. A minute later, he asked Grandma what she was looking for, eager to help. She told him she had a big bowl of gingerbread dough somewhere, but it seemed to have evaporated. Grandpa stood up to help her look. And that's when the bowl unstuck from his bottom and fell on the floor. To this day I'm not sure how he didn't feel that his buttocks were squeezed into a plastic container filled with goo. I guess that math session must have been really exhausting.

I retreated to my guitar practice, anticipating an explosion. Instead, I heard laughter. When I came back to the kitchen, they were both laughing so hard that tears streamed down their faces. Grandpa was propping himself against the table. Grandma was scraping off the dough from his trousers, wiping her eyes and trying to catch her breath.

Mother is not in this memory because she was in detox, something my grandparents forced her to do after particularly intense drinking bouts, usually when she became so aggressive that we walked around bruised or after she became so suicidal that we had to hide her psychotropic pills and give her only the prescribed daily doses. Mother never willingly sought help. She was always dragged by a team of nurses and doctors into an ambulance and taken to the psych ward when she became belligerent and dangerous.

The day before Grandpa's gingerbread-dough mishap, Mother punched him so hard that he took a few unsteady steps back, licked the blood off his upper lip, and called an ambulance. Kicking and screaming, Mother was carried downstairs by two large men. I imagined our neighbors peeking from behind curtains at yet another front-lawn spectacle, shaking their heads, labeling our family as *margines*—literally "a margin," a word equivalent in Polish to *trash*—or, even worse, pitying us. I vowed never to show my face outside the apartment again. I vowed to stay in my room until I died. But the next morning, Grandma made me an egg sandwich and sent me off to school as if nothing had happened.

I took a bus to my high school but didn't get off at my usual stop. I stayed on it until the morning crowds thinned out and the bus passed a theater, a cemetery, and then the psychiatric hospital, ending its route by a community cultural center. I wandered around in the park behind the center, taking a path I hadn't followed before, wishing my backpack were lighter. After about an hour, I took the bus back to the city center and sat on a railroad bridge overlooking a fourteenth-century castle where Copernicus once calculated the equinox. I was sixteen. I couldn't care less about the equinox. I was waiting for my punk friends to gather in the castle's empty moat and open the first bottle of *jabol*—cheap local wine reeking of sulfur.

* * *

Before hopping on the plane back to the States, I visit Grandma Iza's youngest sibling, Włodek, in his tiny apartment in northeastern Poland. My aunt, *ciocia* Zosia, is making *barszcz*. When I start recording our interview, Włodek's first words are: "We can't talk while you're hungry. Bring yourself a piece of cake, and then we can start."

The cake waiting for me in the kitchen is homemade *szarlotka*—an apple pie Slavs have been making since the Middle Ages. Its buttery, flaky crust hides a bounty of apples stewed with cinnamon and cloves. When I come back, already licking my spoon clean, Włodek is reading a book about a Jewish woman in the Warsaw Ghetto, and he shows me the book's photos of a *Kennkarte,* a Nazi ID card with fingerprints, and an *Ausweis,* an employment card. Włodek tells me without looking up from the volume that at the beginning of the war, one kilo of onion cost one *złoty,* but after four years of war, twenty-five *złoty*. "Most people couldn't afford this onion," Włodek lifts his head. "But once we got out of Warsaw, there was food."

"How far from Warsaw was Jabłonna?" I ask, trying and failing to compose a seamless narrative out of the sometimes contradictory fragments I've collected from Grandma's brothers.

"Not far," he says, "because during the Warsaw Uprising, I remember that *gospodarz,* the farmer, woke me up at night and carried me outside and pointed at the huge red glare on the horizon and said: 'Look! Warsaw is burning!'"

Włodek lowers his head again, and I see a tear splash against the cover of his book. Then another. I imagine a small boy secretly hoping that his mother was alive somewhere in the big city, despite everyone else's judgment, and waiting for her return every waking hour only to be thrust in the middle of the night in front of an angry red horizon, where Warsaw used to be.

"Stupid memories," he whispers. "My eyes are not well, and they tear up a lot." He turns off the light.

We sit in silence until *ciocia* Zosia brings a pot of blood-red steaming *barszcz.*

* * *

Grandma sometimes mentioned eating *żurek* during the war. Even when she was weakened by cancer and barely walking, she would make *żurek* in her tiny kitchen and ask my college friends to join us at the table. This sour rye soup is a traditional Easter dish, but Poles eat it year round, with or without bacon and kiełbasa. Its potent taste and smell repels some people, including my husband, but for me it's comfort food. Grandma didn't add a whole lot of horseradish to hers, probably because Tomek and I wouldn't like it too spicy, but I do now, and I love the combination of the sour, the doughy, and the sharp followed by a bite of a hard-boiled egg.

ŻUREK (FERMENTED RYE SOUP)

4 pints of vegetable or beef broth
20 oz (or less) thin sourdough starter
1/2 lb kiełbasa
1/2 lb bacon

1 medium onion
1 garlic clove
2 Tbs horseradish
2 Tbs sour cream
2 Tbs dry marjoram
Salt and pepper to taste
1 hard-boiled egg per bowl (to serve)

In a heavy skillet, heat diced bacon pieces and add thinly cubed onion and kiełbasa. Stir until the onion turns golden yellow. Add broth and simmer for 45 minutes. Add a crushed garlic clove, sourdough starter, marjoram, salt, pepper, and horseradish. Mix well and simmer for 10 more minutes.

Pour 1/4 cup of the hot soup into a mug and mix in the sour cream until no bumps remain. Pour this mixture back into the pot. Serve by pouring the soup over a quartered hard-boiled egg. The soup tastes great with a side of larded bread.

* * *

I wake up from an uneasy dream and kick off my damp cover sheet. Indiana birds are already singing. The dough has been proofing in the fridge for twelve hours. I heat up a Dutch oven with its lid on and transfer the first loaf into it. Forty-five minutes later, the bread is ready. My hands have shaped the loaf, and the loaf has shaped me. Baking bread on a weekday morning in a quiet house is therapy—letting my hands sink in the dough, feeling it slip between my fingers, shaping the loaves into medium-tight boules, taking the bread out of the oven and hearing its gentle song as it cools on the counter.

In some ways, shaping the story of hunger and longing in postwar Poland is less predictable, the ingredients not always within my reach. There's no leaven to start the process, no yeast to help the story grow. I gather snippets of narrative from family and friends. I spend hours in basements and archives and libraries. I reread the only diary I did not burn as a teenager, searching for—what? Clarity? Reassurance? Evidence? Against the odds, I pull together a collage of sepia photos, yellowed documents, and recorded voices of those who will soon pass away. At first my goal was to simply understand why Mother drank, why she neglected us, why she never apologized, even when Tomek and I became adults. But this search soon turned into something larger. I want to know how hunger and trauma several generations ago shaped Mother's attitude toward nurturing, and how my family history and the history of my home country has shaped me. I want to break the cycle of children hungry for food and for love. So I make this imperfect loaf without a recipe and with limited ingredients. It will have to suffice.

Blood

Tomek and I sit on the kitchen table in Mother's apartment, our feet dangling in the air. I'm six or seven, so Tomek must be around four years old. The only sound is the loud humming of the fridge, like a dying sheep. Behind us a large window and a cold night, another Soviet-style prefab high-rise, just like ours, with lights flickering through driving snow. Tomek and I are busy competing. We want to see who will peel more skin off our hands.

I start with my thumb. I pinch the thin, ribbed flap of the skin adjacent to the nail and slowly detach it from the flesh. It doesn't hurt. The skin on the edges of the patch I pull on is thinner than the middle, translucent, letting through the white light that pours from the bare bulb above me. The skin tears off at my knuckle, and I lift it up for both of us to see.

"It looks like boom," Tomek says with awe.

"Lightning? *Nie.*" I shake my head and flip the skin patch upside down. "It's East Germany."

"What's Germany?"

I don't answer because Tomek is already winning. He's been pulling at his skin patch as well, and he still hasn't stopped. The tip of his thumb looks raw, like the insides of a chicken liver, and I see more and more red as he pulls the skin almost all the way to the wrist.

"I win!" He places the skin on the palm of his other hand, a paper-thin malnutrition trophy. The Most Impressive Epidermis Peel in Communist Poland.

That winter our bodies are pale and thin and dry, our nails white and brittle, but we do not starve. Tomek gets regular meals in preschool, and I line up each day for a full meal at my school's cafeteria, often buckwheat with gravy and a side of beets. I guess we eat dinners, too, though I cannot recall supper at Mother's apartment. I suppose the oranges we get once a year for Christmas are not enough to supply the vitamins our growing bodies need to thrive, and the bread, cheese, and sour cream Mother stands for in interminable lines are not enough to prevent cavities and scoliosis. Or peeling skin.

There is a free dentist at every school, where we get our regular fluoride rinses and checkups as well as drilling without anesthesia. Once, a hygienist says in front of my class: "Agata has teeth like pearls—in each one a hole."

* * *

Unlike Mother, who spent all day teaching high school and all evening recovering from the indignities of living in a totalitarian state with the help of a bottle of vodka, Grandma Iza had time to make potato pancakes, pierogi, *kiszka*—spiced potato pie—and sometimes meat, which Tomek and I often rejected, to her horror.

As a child I turned my nose up at a chicken thigh or meatballs but devoured blood sausage without blinking. I didn't care about its grainy texture, not even the mysterious unchewable bits I either spat out or swallowed. When fried to crispness, blood sausage was like a present: There was a thin crunchy casing hiding a rich interior—salty, pungent, filling. Mixed with the sweetness of sautéed onions and maybe some ketchup, the taste lingered on my tongue long after I got up from the table.

* * *

Friends from grad school are visiting our Indiana home. Mike and Mandy drive down from Wisconsin with their kids, and they come bearing gifts—blood sausage from a Polish store and rich, dark beer. A decade after graduation, we are all more weathered, our faces more wrinkled, our eyes less eager. I grab the still-frozen meat package from Mike and put it in the fridge. His wife is vegetarian. My husband doesn't eat blood sausage. More *kaszanka* for Mike and me.

"It will be perfect tomorrow. Let's grill it."

But the next day I pull out the package and make a rookie mistake: I read the list of ingredients. In the Poland of my childhood, the sausage would come from a butcher's or from a village smokehouse, wrapped in bloody paper, no ingredients. Now I see them. Now I cannot pretend that the sausage miraculously appeared on the sizzling grill grate without slaughter.

* * *

My first published book was on James Joyce and Joseph Conrad. I read and reread passages about Leopold Bloom, who "ate with relish the inner organs of beasts and fowls" and who "liked thick giblet soup, nutty gizzards, a stuffed roast heart, liverslices fried with crustcrumbs, fried hencods' roes. Most of all he liked grilled mutton kidneys which gave to his palate a fine tang of faintly scented urine." Bloom was my guy. I, too, loved kidneys and tripe soup. I, too, relished the inner organs of beasts and fowl.

In Ireland, England, Poland, the Philippines—everywhere, really—there is always a part of cuisine that "outsiders" find unpalatable or barbaric. Masai people drink fermented milk mixed with cow blood. Swedes have their *blodplättar*—pancake batter mixed with molasses and blood. The British have their black pudding. The Irish their *drisheen.* In Italy, you will find *biroldo,* and in Spain *morcilla.* In the Philippines, blood soup with chili is called *dinuguan.* In Vietnam, you can order "snake blood," which is vodka mixed with, yes, blood of a snake. Poles have *kaszanka, czernina, kadrel, czarny salceson,* and more fresh-blood dishes. But come to think of it, all meat dishes are bloody, have bloody history, are the result of bloody animal slaughter. So why is *kaszanka* (blood sausage) or *czernina* (blood soup) more repulsive to some than a medium-rare steak?

Kaszanka takes its name from *kasza,* or kasha, the grains added to enhance its texture, but the other two ingredients are less appetizing: offal and fresh blood. All this is stuffed into a stomach or bladder lining. I loved *kaszanka* as a girl but refused to eat *flaki,* a tripe soup in which swam gray and bumpy pieces of skin, chunks of intestines, and whole kernels of black pepper (as if the soup needed additional unpleasant surprises). Now, in the absence of Polish restaurants in Indiana, I order menudo from a local Mexican restaurant, which is spicier and less peppery than *flaki,* but it will do.

Old Polish recipes include a dish called fried blood, or *krew smażona,* which includes onion, pork lard, and fresh pork blood, unstirred so it would congeal and form a solid block, which cooks serve cubed with a side of bread. *Czarny salceson*—a type of cold cut that resembles blood pudding—is made with jowl, herbs, and fresh blood. On rare days when we had access to fresh beef, Grandma would make *tatar,* or steak tartar—raw, ground sirloin meat which she served with raw egg yolk, onions, pickles, salt, and pepper. I devoured *tatar* with savage glee, more readily than, say, *myśliwska kiełbasa* smelling of juniper, garlic, and pine needles.

* * *

Grandma never made *czernina,* blood soup, but some Poles eat it regularly. To make *czernina,* you have to cut the head off a duck, tip the duck upside down like a jug, duck heart still pumping, and pour the blood into a bottle or a jar. You mix in vinegar so the blood doesn't congeal. This will render about twenty to thirty milliliters. If you live in a city, you simply go to a fresh market to the babushka who sells ducks and geese and eggs. The duck is already plucked, and the gizzards are inside. And the babushka gives you duck blood in upcycled bottles labeled "mineral water" or "milk."

You bring this bottle home. You cook broth with the insides of the duck—neck, wings—and with carrots and other sweet vegetables. After cooking the broth, you cut up the heart and kidneys into tiny pieces, add a little salt and pepper, and then pour the blood through a strainer until the soup thickens. You can add a little sour cream and chili flakes. Some people add sugar. Others serve it with prunes.

Apparently, the soup is very filling. No bread necessary. I imagine there is probably a lot of iron in there.

Did I mention that I never had the courage to taste it?

* * *

Czernina used to be made with goose, duck, hare, deer, or even pigeon blood and served with *kluski* (dumplings) or potatoes. Traditionally, this was the soup served to a bachelor who asked for a girl's hand whenever the parents refused to grant his proposal. Instead of having to say no, they invited him to share a meal and served *czernina.* No words were necessary. Blood soup meant rejection.

The closest I ever got to consuming blood in liquid form was when I was fifteen. I was in love with a boy who loved the Doors. He wasn't really interested in me, but he did lend me his pirated VHS tape with Oliver Stone's movie about Jim Morrison. When I returned it, he asked me about the blood ritual scene, the one in which Val Kilmer and Kathleen Quinlan snort coke and fuck and drink blood and dance to "Carmina Burana." At that time, I didn't know that the lyrics of "Carmina Burana" extolled the pleasures of drinking, gluttony, and sex. Carl Orff's unpredictable meter and rhythm in that scene, the frequent caesuras, the timpani and snare drums contributing to the escalating tension, the emotion of the choral crescendo, it all made a brilliant background to Jim Morrison and Patricia Kennealy's blood union and Wiccan frolicking, and I wanted to be like them, wild and carefree and in love and far away from the cement staircase smelling of urine where I returned the tape to the boy I loved and where he asked me if I liked the blood scene.

"You know, we could try it."

"Try what?" I leaned my head against the metal mailboxes attached to the wall, hoping this position would make me more attractive, pensive-like.

"The blood thing."

"Oh."

Robert spat in the corner, right on the cement floor. So manly, I thought.

"Hey, let's go kayaking on Długie. Been on the water there?"

"Just the beach." I knew Długie Lake quite well but only from the side of its public beach, with playgrounds and docks, ice cream booths and cotton candy stands, its vandalized volleyball court. "I've never been to the side with yachts and canoes. Is that where you want to drink blood?"

"No, silly. We'll rent kayaks and spend the day on the lake. I don't know about the blood."

That was our first and last date. We took a city bus to the yacht club, stuffed our lunch bags into our one-person kayaks (bummer!), and off we rowed, exploring the coves in the mile-long lake. All this time I was hoping he'd invite me over to his apartment afterward and we'd dance to "Carmina Burana." He was in front of me most of the time, so all I could see were his shoulders moving the paddle and the small ponytail moving left and right as he looked at storks and kingfishers.

"Let's pull up here! We can swim and eat our sandwiches," he yelled without really looking at me.

We rowed toward a little cove with a grassy beach amid oaks and poplars. I was nervous about undressing to my bathing suit, thinking about stretch marks on my upper thighs.

"Shit!!! Oh fuck!" Robert started rowing backward. He then turned around.

I looked at the shore and saw a middle-aged man, his white hairy torso glistening in the sun, his flabby penis dangling, his feet in the water. Then I saw another naked man. And another.

"Fucking nudists." Robert rowed too fast for me to catch up, but I still heard him. "Let's pick another cove."

In the end, we didn't swim. We ate our lunches in a hurry, in our separate kayaks, parked under a large poplar. There was no blood ritual, no dancing. Only a memory of white flabby flesh covered with hair.

* * *

Nowadays, in capitalist Poland, you can buy *czernina* in restaurants, served sweet or spicy, depending on the region. The soup of the peasants became a trendy item on the menu in fancy venues mostly inaccessible to an everyday Pole. Like sushi or Brazilian steak, *czernina* is photographed and uploaded to the Instagram accounts of Polish influencers dropping loads of cash in trendy bars and night clubs.

Blood soup is not uniquely Polish. Ancient Spartan black broth, or *melas zomos,* which Greeks looked down on as barbaric and uncultured, was made from fresh blood, but it included boiled pigs' legs and olive oil. The soup was often served to the Spartan soldiers to keep them strong and healthy. No wonder the soup was reportedly praised by Benjamin Rush and Adolf Hitler (the latter before he turned vegetarian in his later years).

* * *

Mother pulls out an ointment from her fake-fur-covered cosmetic bag and unscrews the top with one hand. The other hand is holding a rat. My rat.

Earlier that day I went to *fosa,* a remnant of a moat surrounding the fourteenth-century castle in my town where punks and anarchists gathered to drink cheap wine, fight, and listen to music. There, an acquaintance handed me a cage with a rat and asked me to take good care of it while he was in prison. Okay, I said, and shuddered as I noticed bloody pustules on the rat's fur. I took a bus home, the rat with a mysterious skin condition on my lap, sniffing through the cage bars. I named her Chlorencja. When I walked through the front door, Mother stopped in her tracks and took in the scene. Then she told me she'd help me with the pustules.

"This will make her skin less itchy, so she won't make the sores worse with her scratching." Mother dabs the ointment all over the rat's skin. Then she strokes her tiny head and touches her translucent ear. "Don't worry. We'll make you all better."

We do. Mother puts all kinds of concoctions on Chlorencja. She starts taking her out of the cage, and the rat travels across the apartment perched on Mother's shoulder, chattering into her ear. I never see the rat's previous owner again, so she becomes ours. Mother's.

Years later I will write a paper for a conference in Pasadena in which I will quote Leopold Bloom's words about rats: "One of those chaps would make short work of a fellow. Pick the bones clean no matter who it was. Ordinary meat for them. A corpse is meat gone bad." I will talk about Glasnevin Cemetery's "maggoty beds" in the same breath as Molly Bloom's warm marital bed, a place of verbal and bloody profusions. I will remember my rat—Mother's rat—but I will not mention it to the audience of bespectacled scholars who couldn't care less about Mother nursing a rat back to health. And it will not occur to me then that Mother's own bed and her flesh will eventually lodge themselves in my memory.

* * *

My husband is flipping the meats—the blood sausage, some chicken breasts, burgers—and portobello mushrooms while reminiscing with Mike about grad school in South Carolina.

"Remember when Agata took Jim's challenge to drink vodka?" Josh puts the tongs down.

Mike is stretched out on the deck chair, beer propped on his belly.

"She drank him under the table. Jim barfed all over Todd's apartment, and Agata was like, really? You can't handle a quarter liter?"

Josh is proud. Mike is snickering. Their heads nod in approval.

"Never challenge a Pole to a vodka drinking contest."

"I'm going to check on Mandy and the kids." I go inside.

* * *

The moment I knew I was pregnant with my first child, I made a vow to myself, one I haven't broken, that my children would never see me drunk. When I was sitting on the toilet, the smooth white plastic of the pregnancy test against my thumb and pointer finger, I hoped for a path different from Mother's.

"Josh? Come to the bathroom. I want you to see something."

"What?" My husband's eyes were still closed, his head half-buried in our comforter.

"Something beautiful."

If alcoholism was in my blood, if Mother's addiction made it more likely that I would develop one, too, I would not drink more than a couple of beers at cookouts and birthday parties, I decided right then and there. God knows I could drink more without slurring my speech. If Mother's inability or unwillingness to nurture offspring was in my blood, I would beat the odds and nurture my children. I would love them, damn it, whether I knew how to or not.

So the next thing I did was buy a stack of books: *What to Expect When You're Expecting, What to Expect: The First Year, The Attachment Parenting Book, The Happiest Baby on the Block, The Happiest Toddler on the Block, 1-2-3 Magic,* and later *The Whole-Brain Child, No-Drama Discipline, Raising Your Spirited Child,* and so many more. Behind the purchasing and reading frenzy was fear. Fear that I would be like my mother. Fear that I would not know how to love my children. Fear that being unmotherly was in my blood.

Mother must have been stretched beyond her limits. I want to know whether I can simply blame the circumstances of her birth, the nauseating grayness of Communist Poland, the constant food shortages, and the disease of alcoholism in addition to other forms of mental illness when I think back to her veins pulsating with anger, her clenched teeth, her cold eyes, her lack of interest in our lives. Is it possible that if she had been transplanted into another world, perhaps one similar to my current relative comfort of regular bill payments, a fully stocked fridge, a small savings account for travel and movie nights, she would have managed her illness? Would she have loved us more?

* * *

I turn to Sarah LaChance Adams's book *Mad Mothers, Bad Mothers,* a reflection on the ethics of care, on the meaning of "feminine" and "maternal," on the common experience of "maternal ambivalence"—mothers' "desires to nurture and violently reject their children" at the same time. Here Adams validates conflicts between mothers' and children's needs. She points out that popular culture portrays maternal rage as "either a result of postpartum hormones, the product of a more pervasive pathology, or the consequence of living in a racist, heterosexist, and classist patriarchy that idealizes the nuclear family." She agrees that such diagnoses fulfill an important role in uncovering hard facts about women's position in the world, especially women of color, and that we need such accounts in order to empathize with their experiences and change these circumstances. "However," she adds, "to begin the inquiry in this way invites us to *diagnose* maternal ambivalence" as an "atypical problem to be overcome." So instead of leading to our profound understanding of the structures that produce maternal ambivalence—in order to, I hope, change them—we medicalize maternal rage and dismiss it as pathological.

But there is this nagging feeling in me, nothing but a hunch, maybe a grudge, a petulant finger-pointing drive, that my own mother was just not cut out for motherhood. In another universe, she could have been an inspiring teacher, a journalist, a musician, a lover, a free spirit. But not a mother. How much of my own resentment and hurt hides in this guess?

Some women seem to have nurturing in their blood. Others (am I one of them?) internalize society's injunction to bear children and love them. We see good mothers on TV, or in other people's homes, we read about them in books and magazines, and we learn. And then there is a whole universe of women who are simply not interested in childbearing, who happily admit to themselves and the world that they would not be good mothers. Or that they don't want to be mothers. They fulfill their ambitions elsewhere, and of course this elsewhere is equally valuable (or perhaps more so than breeding in this increasingly unstable world?). If my own mother had lived in an environment that encouraged her independence, her self-development outside of the patriarchal institutions and injunctions, perhaps she would have made different decisions, and I would not be writing this book.

Adams says that it is much harder to "shake the dependence of others upon oneself" than to conceal our own dependence on others, as examples of men successfully denying their dependence on women's labor or rich countries denying their dependence on exploited countries prove. Mothers want to believe that their goals and ambitions outside the institution of motherhood can still be fulfilled without interruptions, but anyone who's tried to finish a simple email while little hands pull at a laptop screen knows that this is an illusion. This illusion of independence is interrupted constantly. These interruptions, even when temporary, "inspire ire because they impose needs on us far greater than what we can fulfill, even if we gave them everything we have. They force us to confront our own perpetual ethical failure."

I turn a blind eye to the cruel mechanisms of animal slaughter because I cannot risk obliterating my sense of integrity every time I put bacon on my toast. I eat my steak well-done because I don't want to be reminded that in front of me is the blood and tissue of an animal that once lived, an animal who would still be grazing on succulent grass if it weren't for me, an animal who can feel pain just as much as I do. And, although I love my children and know I would die to save them from danger, although the most cherished moments of my day are hugs and snuggles after school, although I miss them dearly whenever I spend more than eight hours at work, I do have fleeting moments of recognition that some kind of exchange took place when I decided to have them, one whose terms I did not clearly understand at the moment. I push these thoughts aside when we're together and pour my affection on them, at times too much perhaps, maybe the better to dull the nagging thought that I relinquished independence and freedom in order to mother them with love.

Maybe my own mother could not, did not know how to suppress her interruptions. What exactly did she trade in for having children? What ambitions and dreams did we make impossible?

Adams brings up Beauvoir, who claims that "when freely chosen, motherhood is a vital commitment to care for another and, moreover, that a person's ethical standing is indicated by how she negotiates the ambiguity between her independence and her responsibility to others. Motherhood heightens the possibilities for 'existential evil,' since it provides the opportunities to dominate a vulnerable person and/or escape one's freedom in devotion to another."

I think of Beauvoir when I lie awake in my bedroom, listening to my daughter's gentle snores, her body pressed to mine, the only position in which she's been able to sleep for longer than an hour ever since she was born. My Velcro Baby. Attached. Always. This of course means that I cannot sleep comfortably myself, that I cannot change positions through the night, scratch an itch, stretch my restless legs, lest I wake her. My older son slept in his own bed unless sick, but he, too, has demanded that I be available at all hours, regardless of my own needs, and I give myself to his well-being. He, too, has been seeking sensory input from me, so I have always been touched and hugged, and I touched and hugged in return. And yet. There are days and nights when I cannot bear another demand on my body, when my whole being revolts against my skin being in contact with anything except my clothing, when I want to fight for a sliver of autonomy, a shred of independence. I get the whole maternal ambivalence thing. I, too, feel it.

* * *

It's a snowy Sunday in Indiana, and I'm heaving book stacks and potted plants out of my sunroom, which is my writing space, because on Wednesday a contractor will change out our nasty 1970s carpet for vinyl planks. The last items in the room to go are the sofa and my writing chair, and I hesitate because I know that once they are gone, I won't sit back down to my laptop for a while. So I pour myself cinnamon tea, grab a blanket, and sit on the sofa with a book. It's Adrienne Rich's *Of Woman Born.* My son is playing Minecraft somewhere downstairs, and my daughter is building Elsa's castle in her room. The snow picks up speed. I begin reading where I last stopped when it was time to make lunch for my kids:

. . . I remember a cycle. It began when I had picked up a book or began trying to write a letter, or even found myself on the telephone with someone toward whom my voice betrayed eagerness, a rush of sympathetic energy. The child (or children) might be absorbed in business, in his own dreamworld; but as soon as he felt me gliding into a world which did not include him, he would come to pull at my hand, ask for help . . .

"Maaaaaamaaaaa!" I hear from the front of the house. "Heeeeeeeeelp!"

No fucking way. What are the odds? I think. And then the answer comes readily: high, very high.

"Just a moment!"

I keep reading, hoping against experience that whatever problem made my daughter scream will resolve itself. So back to Rich:

. . . ask for help, punch at the typewriter keys. And I would feel his wants at such a moment as fraudulent, as an attempt moreover to defraud me . . .

"Maaaaaamaaaaaa!"

. . . defraud me of living even for fifteen minutes as myself. My anger would rise; I would feel the futility of any attempt to sal-

vage myself, and also the inequality between us: my needs always balanced against those of a child, and always losing.

I put a bookmark in between the pages and listen. Maybe I can squeeze in another sentence?

I could love so much better, I told myself, after even—

"Maaaaamaaaaa! Heeeeeelp!"

I slam the book shut with a snap. I breathe, taking in the white world outside.

When I walk into my daughter's room, she tells me that the throne she built for Elsa is too small. Elsa can't sit in it.

"See?" My daughter pushes the Lego figurine into the throne, and the back pops off.

For her, this is a real emergency. To me, it's an annoyance, an interruption, a reminder that her minor problems loom large in her yet-underdeveloped brain, that Elsa's throne is a matter of life and death at this very moment, and that Adrienne Rich cannot compete with the Throne Disaster. I take a deep breath.

"Let's see how we can solve this problem. It seems we need to make the throne deeper."

I know that I should ask her to think of solutions, to try and fail, to come up with the answers herself, with my guidance. But I'm being impatient. I want to go back to my book and my blanket. So I quickly build a bigger throne and leave. But I hear her footsteps behind me.

"Can we play together?"

She is holding two Elsas now, one bigger than the other. In her other fist are clear-blue Lego pieces.

"Mama, they have to find and fix these gems. They have to!"

"Sweetie, you'll have to wait until I'm done with what I'm doing now. I'm reading a book. I need ten more minutes of quiet."

"But if they don't find and fix the gems, the world will be

broken!" She changes the pitch of her voice to imitate one of the Elsas' voice: "Where are the elements of harmony? Where?"

We walk to the sunroom and play with the two Elsas and their gems of harmony on top of my book.

Resentment grows inside me like a weed. You can shove these gems of harmony up your ass, I think. Then guilt. And more resentment. More guilt.

My daughter must know. She scoots up closer and says: "Mama, hug?"

I feel her little body pressed against my chest, her bottom nestled on my lap, her ear against my check, and I let myself be carried away from anger, away from *should have*s and *I'd rather*s, away from my need to be alone and toward my need to be close to her, to love and be loved. It's a good feeling. I feel whole. I feel generous. I am the snow that keeps falling on the dry asparagus fronds and zinnia stalks in my withered garden, on the wooden fence, on the backyard sloping toward our little lake, on the crooked dock. Underneath that snow is rot and secret underground life—bugs waiting out the winter, a network of mycelia that will soon produce mushrooms, tree roots, chipmunks and squirrels in their dens.

* * *

Cheryl Meyer estimates in *Mothers Who Kill Their Children* that a mother kills her child every third day—and that's just in the United States. There is no one predictor for maternal aggression. Instead, it is a complex continuum, sometimes involving mental illness, but not always, sometimes with socioeconomic difficulties at play, often after a mother is stretched beyond endurance.

Mother love, maternal instinct, mother hen. We're supposed to have motherhood in our veins. Not so.

In the end, I got lucky. Unlike Mother, I had my children after I attained basic financial stability. I didn't have to queue for hours on freezing mornings just to get some toothpaste or butter or formula. My marriage was relatively stable. Our house was large enough for each of us to find solitude when desperately needed. Unlike many parents, I could afford therapy, and I found a professional who approached my childhood experiences with empathy and expertise. Perhaps the gene responsible for addiction skipped a generation.

* * *

"I love you all and sundry."

I'm reading a Christmas card from Mother. This year she wrote it in English. She must have found a template in an old textbook, a template for signing off with affection. I haven't seen her since the NYPD incident last Easter. My son is now more verbal. He says he remembers *babcia,* his Polish grandma.

I love you all and sundry.

* * *

Josh is still at the grill, and Mike is still in the lawn chair. All the windows are closed, but I smell the barbecued meat inside the house. Two decades ago, I'd relish the smell of grilled *kaszanka.* Now I have to stay inside to avoid retching. Me, who just a couple years ago took a neighbor to a tasting of "midwestern oysters"—deep-fried bulls' testicles.

* * *

In Pasadena, dressed in a dark-gray suit that is one size too big, I tell the audience of Joyce scholars that *Ulysses* exposes Ireland's fear of the unclean, assertive, and sexually aggressive woman. I talk at length about Joyce's inclusion of menstrual blood and "bloodred wombs" of soon-to-be mothers. I am composed. Caffeinated. My gestures and my words are rehearsed, conforming neatly to the prescribed mold of academia. The chair of my department in a midwestern college tells me that my tenure is certain. And yet, I feel like a fraud.

What I want to say is that I don't really care about James Joyce. That reading and writing about *Ulysses* is just an escape from a nagging pain, from loss, from distance. I dress up my thoughts about Molly Bloom's menstruation and infidelities in the barely comprehensible phrases of literary criticism, passing yet another test on the way to inclusion in an esoteric group of academics who will pat each other on the back at the end of the conference. They are kind people, most of them. Yet I have this suspicion that we're engaged in some strangely choreographed dance, a masked play.

Back in the hotel room, I think of my first menstruation, which happened at a summer dance camp. Beautiful new undies, white with a bouquet of violets on the front, narrow purple lace on top. I pulled them down when I was peeing into a bucket in our cabin, and I saw blood. Shit. I knew what it was, though I don't recall who told me about menstruation. Father, maybe? He's the only one who ever talked to me about sex and relationships ("Don't marry before you check whether he's good in bed"), so perhaps he also told me about periods? But I was still unprepared and embarrassed. So I did the only thing I thought was reasonable: I threw my undies out of the window, and they landed on a low-hanging branch of a nearby tree. I stuffed my shorts with toilet paper and went out to look for my friend Paula, who was in the same dance group and summer camp, and who had already gotten her period a few months before me.

"I need a pad," I whispered when I found her on a dock as she was getting ready for a swim.

"Uh-oh."

She slipped back into her shorts. We went to one of the filthy public toilets, where I promptly peeled off the strip and secured the pad, upside down.

"Your first one, no? Any pains?" Paula clearly enjoyed playing the role of a mentor at that moment, telling me all about cramps and clots and heavy days.

"No pain, except the pulling on my pubes," I replied after a while from behind the stall door. "Is the pad supposed to yank my hair like this?"

"No, dumbass. You probably put it in glue side up."

Paula listened patiently as I yelled "*Kurrrrrrrrrwa*!" with each tug at the pad. She also covered up for me when our camp counselor showed up at the cabin door with my bloody undies dangling from a stick.

"Who threw these on the tree?"

Paula knew they were mine. I had lusted after the undies with violets for months before Grandma bought them for me. Still, she said nothing. All six of us sharing the cabin looked perplexed and disgusted.

"Eeeeeeewwwww." I screwed up my face and went back to my bunk bed.

* * *

It's a school night again, and Mother is singing songs about hungering cities, blood, and peasants avenging burned villages.

My ze spalonych wsi
My z głodujących miast
Za głód za krew
Za lata łez
Już zemsty nadszedł czas.

The song, I will later learn, is "Marsz Gwardii Ludowej" —"People's Guard March," sometimes called "The Partisan's Song," written by a female Communist poet in 1942. The People's Guard was an underground Communist militia, armed and aided by the Red Army but also collaborating with Jewish partisans in Poland, smuggling weapons inside the Warsaw Ghetto. They engaged in sabotage and guerilla warfare but also mass atrocities, like the one in the village of Ludmiłówka on December 6, 1942, during which members of the Guard killed dozens of Jews. But such stories were hushed in totalitarian Poland and only uncovered much later.

We're from the torched villages
We're from starving towns
For the hunger, for the blood,
For years of tears
It's time for revenge now.

Mother sings. She sways. Her eyes are closed. This is the song she sings most often when she's drunk.

When she sings the song with her eyes open, they are either glazed or angry, as if she were geared up by centuries of peasant oppression, readying herself for battle with the Nazis or the Cossacks or the Tsarist army. Or her unfaithful husband. Or . . . us? Occasionally, there'd be a fist on the table, for emphasis. Then a suck on a cigarette, a wistful glance at the blocks of cement outside our kitchen window, and back to the song.

* * *

Mother's singing voice wasn't conventionally pretty, but I liked its scratchiness, the smoky darkness of her low tones and the wistful shaking of her high notes. It was different from Grandma's voice, which was clearer, softer, undulating slowly, as if a sudden change of pitch could hurt the listener. Grandma also sang about blood, spilled by Polish soldiers on the fields of Monte Cassino, where the poppies on the hills drank Polish blood instead of dew after the battle, the same battle where my great-grandpa Franciszek fought against his future car-mechanic friend. Grandma sang about gray infantry marching to battle through Polish villages, admired by girls who peeked from across their fences and saluted by trees lining dirt roads. But my favorite song was "Czarna Madonna"—"The Black Madonna."

Madonno, Czarna Madonno,
Jak dobrze Twym dzieckiem być!
O, pozwól, Czarna Madonno,
W ramiona Twoje się skryć!

The song is about a painting of the Virgin Mary called *The Black Madonna,* which hangs in a cathedral in Częstochowa. The painting is a popular pilgrimage destination, and there's a legend behind two "scars" on Mary's face in that painting. The painting's history is disputed, and stories abound. It is possible that it was discovered in the year 326 and then improperly restored in medieval times by Polish church officials after it was slashed during a raid. The legend goes that as a knight slashed the face of Black Madonna, the face started bleeding.

As a child, I believed the legend and often sang the song in bed when I couldn't fall asleep in Mother's apartment.

* * *

Grandma strokes my hair and sings about Mary's concerned eyes, "as if She wanted to ask you / To surrender to Her motherly care." The refrain's minor key gives me goosebumps. "Madonna, Black Madonna / How good it is to be Your child / Oh please, Black Madonna / Let me hide in Your arms."

Grandma shifts on my bed, and I hear the crinkling of the tarp she always puts under my sheet because I am a hopeless bedwetter. That's why she's in my bed so late at night. She had to change the wet sheets. Again.

Today, with turbulence around us
Where can we seek shelter
Where shall we go
If not to our Mother
Who'll give us consolation?

Grandma's hands are plump and a little scratchy. Her face smells of her lily-scented night cream, a soothing smell like a meadow or a garden where you can stretch on a patch of grass and close your eyes. Grandma sings.

* * *

Grandma prayed to the Virgin Mary daily. She was a devout Catholic, carrying in her purse a rosary blessed by Pope John Paul II. She pulled that rosary in grocery store lines or in waiting rooms at the local clinic, on buses, and in our little Fiat. She helped me and my brother write a song about the Virgin Mary looking over us as we slept, a song that won a competition at our parish, a song for which we got a gypsum statue of Mary surrounded by doves.

Once Grandma went on a pilgrimage to a shrine in Gietrzwałd, where—she and many other Catholics believed—in 1877 two local girls saw an image of the Virgin Mary on a maple tree. Mary spoke to the girls in Polish, Grandma told me with pride. Polish was forbidden at that time, as the land belonged to Prussia.

From that pilgrimage, Grandma brought back a light-blue plastic bottle shaped like Mary, whose yellow cap looked like a crown.

"In this bottle," Grandma told me, "is holy water from the Gietrzwałd stream. It has healing powers because it was blessed by Virgin Mary."

“Is this why you brought it back home? To heal Mama?”

No healing came. On occasion, Grandma would pull the bottle from its special place high on a bookshelf and give us a drop or two when we had a stomachache or when we got hurt playing at a nearby construction site. She’d promptly replace the cap and put the bottle back in its place.

Later, in my teenage years, I came to her home from one particularly wild party, still drunk and parched, reeking of cigarettes. I tiptoed to my bed and closed the door as quietly as I could. As far as I knew, nobody had woken up. Grandma and Mother were sleeping in the living room. Grandpa in his little bedroom. Tomek in his bed on the opposite side of our room. I crawled into my bed and tried to steady the spinning inside my brain. I really, really had to have a sip of water. If I opened the door and went out to the bathroom or kitchen, I’d wake up Grandma, who was a light sleeper, and she’d smell the alcohol and cigarettes on my breath and my clothes.

I reached up to the tallest bookshelf above my bed, unsteady on my feet. My hand felt the dusty book spines, the shelf, and—yes!—the blue bottle shaped like the Virgin Mary. I uncapped it and drank until it was empty.

The next morning, remorse gnawing at my chest, I filled the bottle with tap water and replaced it on the shelf. For months, whenever Grandma tried to give me or Tomek a “drop of holy water” for stomachache, I’d be seized with pangs of conscience. Did she still give the water to Mother? Was she certain then that this water still had magical properties? What if—hear me out—what if the water really could heal her, but I ruined it with my drunken irreverence?

* * *

“Where you ever hungry, Dad? During Communism?”

We're in a car. He is driving me to Pułtusk so I can interview Uncle Jeżyk. Big band jazz is playing in the CD deck. The road is bumpy.

"Not really, no." His eyes are trained on the potholes. "I was born in 1950, so too late to remember Stalinism. When I was a child, I ate a lot of *zupa nic*."

I chuckle because I immediately think of a photo I've seen of a jubilant restaurant owner hanging up a banner on her Ukrainian restaurant in Washington, DC, right after Stalin's death. The banner says

FREE BORSHT
In celebration of
STALIN'S DEATH

Zupa nic literally means "soup nothing": milk, egg yolk, sugar. You beat raw yolks with sugar and then add this to boiling milk to thicken and sweeten it. Some families serve it with rice, others with sweet rolls. Those in Ukraine who survived starvation (the Holodomor) in the 1930s and Stalin's executions probably knew the taste of soup nothing.

"It filled my stomach fast. And tomato soup, cucumber soup, pea soup. Lots of soup. Sometimes meat. Pierogi. My grandma made amazing *gołąbki*. She soaked that cabbage in vinegar first. That's why they were so soft. Rice and meat. Lviv cuisine."

"She was from Lviv?"

"She was born there."

I think back to a literary party I attended as a grad student, after interviewing Nobel Prize winner Derek Walcott for a journal, after Walcott invited me upstairs to his hotel room, and after I refused. Instead of joining the guests, he sat with me in the garden by a brick wall and asked me to read Adam Zagajewski's poem "Going to Lviv" in the Polish original. I read this and other poems, but sensing hostile looks from other guests for hogging too much of Walcott's attention, I soon snuck out.

* * *

It's early morning. I sit down in my quiet kitchen in Indiana with a cup of coffee and turn on my phone. I see a photo in the *New York Times* that makes me think of my great-grandmother leaving Lviv. A bird's-eye view of an ashen evening in Kyiv, gray except for the glaring red taillights of cars fleeing west toward the Polish border. A major highway lit up, bloodred, families escaping the Russian shelling. Red like the ribbon I wore around my neck at May Day parades, where I sang, "Пусть всегда будет солнце." Let there always be sunshine.

A crawling procession of cars fleeing Kyiv. Putin's bombs buzzing down on the breadbasket of Europe like locusts. Now the unreal, distant Lviv Zagajewski's poem yearns for washes over me:

> *Jeżeli Lwów istnieje, pod*
> *pokrowcami granic i nie tylko w moim*
> *nowym paszporcie.*
>
> *But only if Lviv exists,*
> *if it is to be found within the frontiers and not just*
> *in my new passport.*

If the Lviv of Zagajewski's childhood is but a mirage replaced by a new, otherworldly polis, is it really Lviv he is returning to? The poem always struck me as a meditation on the impossibility of returning to places we know only from family lore, from legend, from history books, from the food on our plate. From soup nothing.

Zagajewski dedicates this poem to his parents, both Lviv

natives, who, like my great-grandmother, were told after the war to leave their city of learning and culture, of cobblestone streets between cathedrals and Orthodox churches. Zagajewski was both born in and banished from Lviv in 1945, the same year my great-grandmother boarded a train with a one-way ticket, sent even farther west after the Polish border shifted, as it had many times before, and left her behind.

Every time that border shifted, with every tyrant who came to power, others were told to leave: Ukrainians, Poles, Jews, Armenians. Still others perished in Ukrainian pogroms and in the Holocaust. The culture of Lviv changed with each exile, with every life lost; it is not one thing but an amalgam of many peoples, a child of human migratory paths and constantly shifting borders. So is its history, its language. As Adam Kirsch reminds us in *The Odessa Review,* "in the course of the 20th century, a resident of the city now known as Lviv would have lived in five different countries without ever leaving home": the Austro-Hungarian Empire, Poland, Germany, the Soviet Union, and finally Ukraine. The list of names for the city itself is migratory: Львів, Lviv, Lvov, Lwów, Lemberg.

My great-grandmother must have felt, after spending the war in Lviv, that she was being relocated to a foreign land, even though she technically traveled to new Poland on that slow train. She and her husband didn't know anyone west of Lviv. My great-grandfather picked a train station in Inowrocław, most likely at random. Both of his granddads had worked in the train business, so getting off at a large train hub was a logical choice. As logical as any other.

The forced expulsions that followed World War II—of ethnic Poles from the eastern edges of what used to be Poland, of Ukrainians "back" to their "homeland"—affected more than a million people. It was Stalin's policy, but Churchill and Roosevelt agreed to it, first in Tehran and then in Yalta. Autocrats love euphemisms, so these expulsions were called "repatriations." Putin calls his 2022 invasion of Ukraine a "peacekeeping mission."

Peacekeeping—a word I want to wrap around my shivering body as I scroll through endless images of gutted buildings in Kyiv and Kharkiv. Peacekeeping—two long, lulling *e* sounds that drag out as I avert my eyes from an image of a six-year-old girl killed by a Russian bomb.

Do not panic, people in Ukraine heard from an autocrat abroad. Do not panic, they heard from pundits. Do not panic, they heard from priests. Do not panic, they heard from strangers at the bus stop on their way to work.

War, like Zagajewski's Lviv, is unimaginable until our fingers touch its scorched stones. Until our eyes see its lightning. Until our ears hear the silence it makes of our church bells. Until our feet feel the trembling of the earth.

There was too much of Lviv, and now
there isn't any, it grew relentlessly
and the scissors cut it, chilly gardeners
as always in May, without mercy,
without love.

War is unreal until we feel the cold, precise metal cutting, as Zagajewski once had it, "diligently, as in a child's cutout / along the dotted line of a roe deer or a swan." From the fire and metal falling through the sky, the people of Kyiv, Lviv, Kharkiv, Odessa hide—in subway tunnels, in basements, in cars along roads that can no longer guide them to safety. They hide from a nightmare that always starts the same way: with an air-raid alarm, announcing that the once powerful Soviet project, collapsed in disgrace, has been resurrected by Putin's tanks, bombs, and cyberattacks and returns to lay claim to truth and memory.

Zagajewski asks in "To Go to Lviv":

dlaczego każde miasto
musi stać się Jerozolimą i każdy
człowiek Żydem i teraz tylko w pośpiechu
pakować się, zawsze, codziennie
i jechać bez tchu, jechać do Lwowa, przecież
istnieje, spokojny i czysty jak
brzoskwinia. Lwów jest wszędzie.

why must every city
become Jerusalem and every man a Jew,
and now in a hurry just
pack, always, each day,
and go breathless, go to Lviv, after all
it exists, quiet and pure as
a peach. It is everywhere.

Lviv is everywhere. War is everywhere. Unreal until you can touch it.

* * *

"Dad, isn't it your grandma I'm with in that photo from my first birthday? There's another, older woman next to your mom. She's holding me in her arms."

"Maybe. I don't recall the photo." Father's eyes are fixed ahead.

We drive off the bumpy country road and onto a fast, new highway sponsored by the European Union. We pass neon signs and billboards, fancy gas stations offering shower cabins and KFC, and I realize how unrecognizable Poland is to me now. Or, rather, too recognizable. Those billboards, the yellow-and-red plastic of McDonald's, the Happy Meals, the soda dispensers, even the smooth off-ramps—they all look generic, not much different from any road in Germany or France or the United States. The irresistible urgency of the giant exclamation marks reaches out to us from billboards, screening out the rolling hills behind. I don't want to romanticize the pothole-riddled roads of Communism, the poverty of the villages, the dilapidated grayness of roadside bars, but with the influx of money came a loss. Loss of authenticity. Loss of creativity. Loss of difference.

"Dad, where are the babushkas selling mushrooms and berries by the side of the road? Is it still a chanterelle season?"

"Where would you stop if you spotted them? We're going too fast."

Grandma, in her rare moments of anger, would sometimes tell me that if I didn't start taking school seriously, I'd end up selling parsley in front of a store or by the side of the road. Sitting in a ditch with cheaply priced produce was my fate if I didn't do my math homework, she'd say, wagging her finger.

"What about your philharmonic tours in the '70s, out West? You must have eaten well then, Dad."

"Oooohohoho . . . Yes, but you know what? I remember a tour in Italy, where we were treated with beautiful-looking cold cuts, ham, I think, and you know what? The ham had no taste. Sure, you could buy it easily, but it had no taste. It turned out that the sausages we took with us from Poland, the ones we bought fresh and then dried on radiators in our apartments, those sausages were much tastier than that Western food."

"Huh. Maybe they tasted better because it was harder to get them? You probably had to line up for hours."

"You could taste the juniper and garlic, smell it from the radiators. They really were delicious."

"So you didn't stand in line for them?"

"Always. I remember one evening your mother and I heard that there was going to be meat in the store across the street.

The ration cards didn't list the kinds of meat available, just categories."

"What do you mean?" Poultry? Pork? Beef?

"Category one was good meat, then two was worse, three was the worst—scraps. At that time, it was martial law, so gathering was forbidden. Our staircase was the closest one to the entrance of the store. We could see the entrance from a landing window."

The landings with the trash chute were the spots where we arranged doll picnics, played cards, smoked our first cigarettes. Those chutes were crawling with roaches and stinky, but the landings were safer than some of our homes. There were drunken rows behind many doors in our staircase. Or family members tiptoeing around a sleeping drunk. I was not the only child there with an alcoholic mother. If one of us heard our name roaring from a cracked door, we could retreat either downstairs or upstairs. If you climbed up, beyond the eighth floor, you entered the attic, where some tenants dried their laundry. If you climbed down, you had the basement to hide in. And both the attic and the basement connected you with the neighboring staircase if you wanted to create an even larger distance between yourself and the roaring drunk.

"During martial law, the landings were safe spots from the police. Gatherings were forbidden. We would stand in line anyway, writing down the names of people who came after us, keeping the 'queue list' updated. When we saw the *milicja* approaching, we ran to our door and hid there in the staircase, looking out through the window to see if the *milicja* were gone and to make sure other people were not taking our own place in line."

"And you kept your place on the list?"

"Most of us did. I was often the list keeper."

Father is tall. Formidable. His glance can communicate a

threat. Mother, on the other hand, resorted to sabotage in her interactions with other adults. When a neighbor who lived directly above us continued drilling in walls after quiet hours despite her pleas, she one day crept upstairs with a rare bottle of canola oil. She knew the neighbor kept his shoes outside his front door. She poured oil into both shoes and went back to her apartment. An hour or so later, we heard a loud "*Kurrrwa*!" and a door slammed shut. The drilling continued.

* * *

I am four. It's the weekend when Father visits, and I'm hanging upside down, nose scraping the red carpet, blood pooling down which is up which is down, my ankles in his grip. I want to hang like an overripe apple forever, swing left and right, nose stroking the carpet. Because at the end of the swinging and hanging comes the strike. Then another. Then another. A hit. My butt. My thighs. A hit. A slap. A spank.

* * *

After I give my kids loaded nachos for dinner—Mama, I don't want beef on mine! Mama, I want a burger, not nachos! Mama, ketchup! Mama, fork! Mama, it's too hot!—I sit down with a cup of tea, and little hands immediately reach for me. Then my phone rings. I put it on speaker because I'm balancing my daughter on one leg and my son on the other.

"Hey, I really need to scream. And cry. I need to talk to somebody before I go crazy." A friend from a Facebook group of academic mamas is single-parenting four children today. It's Sunday evening, and she's stretched too far. She's breaking.

I switch from loudspeaker and send my kids away from the room. My husband closes the door.

"Do you know what I just did? I stabbed a banana with a knife, several times, and broke the fucking knife."

I can't stop myself from laughing even though I know she's in trouble.

"Well, I'm glad it was just a banana," I say. "Can you leave the kids with a sitter and go somewhere on your own?"

"Where? This fucking pandemic made me friendless. I suck at making friends anyway. I'll be okay, I just need to vent, and I need someone to listen or else I may explode. I stabbed a fucking banana."

Whatever isolation and demands on my time and body my own children brought to my life is multiplied in hers. I have no answers and no advice. I listen. I nod. My *uh-hmmms* are genuine expressions of empathy. I know why she stabbed the fucking banana.

"I love my children," she says. "I just need to get rid of this anger. Somewhere. That's why I went to the kitchen. I didn't want them to see me angry."

I think back to Adrienne Rich: "Degradation of anger. Anger at a child. How shall I learn to absorb the violence and make explicit only the caring?" And this: "Perhaps one is a monster—an anti-woman—something driven and without recourse to the normal and appealing consolations of love, motherhood, joy in others." When she showed her journal entries from early motherhood to her adult son, he responded: "You seemed to feel you ought to love us all the time. But there is no human relationship where you love the other person at every moment."

* * *

The year after I get a teaching position at an all-male college in Indiana, my male department chair puts me on the "entertainment" committee and suggests I bake cookies for a poetry-sharing event with students. The following semester I will rebel, but now I'm still timid. I don't bake, though. I grab a bunch of Oreos from Kroger and several jugs of skim milk.

At the event, I read Anna Świr's poem "Maternity," from her 1970 collection *Wind*:

Urodziłam życie.
Wyszło krzycząc z moich wnętrzności
i żąda ode mnie ofiary z mojego życia
jak bóstwo Azteków.

Like an Aztec deity, the newborn demands a sacrifice. I twist my tongue to conform it to the procession of Polish consonants, and I wonder whether my audience knows how unromantic the speaker's memory of birth and motherhood looms in these words. It's a battle for the self, not a smarmy embrace, motherhood.

—Nie zwyciężysz mnie—mówię.
Nie będę jajkiem, które rozbijesz
wybiegając na świat,
kładką, po której przejdziesz do własnego życia.
Będę się bronić.

I will not be a fragile egg you can crack or a footbridge, she says. I will fight, she declares. My voice rises, and I'm with her, ready to take up arms. Although still childless, I feel her exhaustion and defiance.

Pochylam się nad małą kukiełką,
spostrzegam
drobny ruch drobnego paluszka,
który jeszcze tak niedawno był we mnie,
w którym płynie pod cienką skórą
moja własna krew.
I oto zalewa mnie

wysoka, jasna fala
pokory.
Bezsilna, tonę

This is where my voice cracks. She leans over the puppet-baby and the sight of the tiny finger

which a little while ago was still in me,
in which, under a thin skin,
my own blood flows

floods her with a wave of humility, a tall and luminous wave, and her powerless body goes under.

After I read the translation, the room is silent save for a grunt from another male professor. My mind wanders back to Mother's living room, her white hanging bookshelves, and on one of them a book with a naked female body on the cover. It was Anna Świr's poetry collection *I Am a Woman.* In fragmented scenes, Świr presented raw and unadorned lives of women—their ecstasies and betrayals, bowel movements and beautifully sculpted thighs. The economy of her poetic miniatures contradicts the abundance of feelings and experiences of girls, women, mothers, daughters, adored lovers and rejected wives. I didn't understand these poems as a child, even though the words on the page seemed clear. There was something forbidden in that little volume, a taboo I knew I should not break, so I opened it only when Mother was too far gone to notice.

* * *

After showing Josh two red stripes on the first pregnancy test, I call Mother. She's sober this time, maybe just a little tipsy. She sounds genuinely happy, elated even, and she launches into a series of tips:

"If you smoke, you need to limit the number of cigarettes now. Just a couple a day. That's what I did. I smoked much less."

"Mom, I don't s—"

"And remember, limit your alcohol, too. A beer or two won't hurt, but I made this mistake with you: I had way more than that at my birthday party, and I was big then, you were supposed to be born in January. So I had one too many at my party and got on a train to see my parents the next day, and you know what happened . . . My water broke! Right into my winter boots! I was panting . . . shit . . . so much pain . . . water everywhere . . . But your uncle and I waited until our station and went straight to the hospital. And you popped right out."

"Mom, I know this story. It's okay. I don't smoke. I'm good."

"Have you thought of names? Maybe something we can all pronounce in Poland?"

In the end, both of my kids will have Polish first names, ones that their teachers and friends will have trouble pronouncing correctly, and I will cringe each time my tween asks me and others to use the English equivalent. Another moment of betrayal. No pierogi, no *bigos,* no *żurek,* and now a name change. I use my students' preferred names and pronouns but sulk when my son chooses an easier, Americanized first name for himself.

"They say now that nursing is best. I nursed you a little but didn't nurse Tomek because he bit. He would latch on and bite me hard, even before his teeth came in. I had bloody nipples."

Bloody nipples. My own, smothered in lanolin, when I nursed my babies. My mother's. Grandma Iza's.

I see Grandma's bloody nipple clearly, in sharp relief, after one of the violent fights at home, probably about alcohol. I normally cowered in the bedroom and listened intently for a slap, a thump, a scream that would be my cue. Then I'd rush out to help. This day Mother and Grandma are shouting and I wait, steadying my breath by the door, until I hear Grandma's yelp and then "Jezus Maria! Look what you did, you scum."

As I rush out of the room, I hear the front door slam and see Grandma alone, shirt up, bra down, her tears dripping on the bunched-up blue cotton above her breasts. And then blood around her right nipple.

"She bit me."

Later that night, when Mother comes back unsteady on her feet but still feisty, she'll get a bloody lip from Grandpa. I will not rush to defend her. I want her to get hurt. I want her to die.

* * *

What poison flows in my arteries, capillaries, and veins, I wonder as I stroke my swelling belly. My firstborn, my son. A tsunami of affection washes over me for the fetus inside, for the iridescent outline of the head and toes and fingers on the ultrasound pictures. Who are you, baby? Who am I?

Until now, I've been a neglected child, a loved grandchild, a ballroom dancer, a guitar player, a chorus girl, a wild and inconsiderate teen, vodka-imbibing, pot-smoking, cocaine- and speed-inhaling club fiend, a studious college student, an undocumented barmaid in a working-class London neighborhood, a toilet scrubber, a lover oscillating between too much investment and total withdrawal, a girlfriend with too much commitment, a girlfriend with too little commitment, a scholar traveling the world to archives and conferences, a writer, a flawed wife, a deeply flawed human. Now I will be a mother. What kind of mother will I be?

As I stroke my taut skin around the swollen belly button, I imagine blood vessels in my son's (my? our?) umbilical cord carrying nutrients and oxygen to his organs, carbon dioxide and waste away from his tiny body, sustaining his life. His and my circulation work in tandem, with the help of the placenta, which also does the work of breathing for him until he can use his lungs outside my body. We are one, and yet we are not. Where does my body end and his begin?

During delivery, I will refuse all medications in fear of poisoning my baby. I will be exhausted from hours of pushing, severely dehydrated, and shocked at the amount of blood and shit on the birthing bed. Finally in a moment of defeat an anesthesiologist will shoot epidural into my spine, and I will almost code from the loss of blood pressure.

When they clamp his umbilical cord at birth, my son will no longer breathe my oxygen or eat my food. My blood will no longer be his blood. Will it? They will sew me up and send me home with post-caesarian painkillers that I refuse to take for fear of poisoning my nursing baby. I will set my teeth against the pain in my abdomen and nurse him around the clock like a somnambulist returning to the same spot over and over: his tiny, helpless body.

Two weeks after his birth, I will cradle him on the patio in the spring breeze and feel warm wetness spread across my abdomen and my lap, and I will think: pee. My son peed on me. But no, when I stand up, I see a growing expanse of red on my dress that already sticks to my skin, blood soaking me and my son, and I will think: Please no, please no. Let it not be his blood.

After a doctor stiches me up again, he will tell me to stay in bed. Let other people take care of the house, take care of the baby. But who? My family is across the Atlantic. Josh's sister has already returned home to Oklahoma after doing laundry, washing dishes, and vacuuming for us for days. Josh is working because his boss already docked his pay for attending the birth of his son and then threatened him with salary reduction if he missed more classes. So I will let the house go. I will spend days, weeks, in dirty sheets, nursing and napping, nursing and napping, like a wild animal.

***

A Sunday evening. I'm doing fifth-grade geography homework on the living room carpet. It's dark outside, and Mother is sewing tulle ruffles onto my dark-green ballroom dancing gown. She made the gown for my tournament on a bulky sewing machine with a pedal. She found dark-green cloth in a downtown textile shop that would look beautiful against my skin, she said. Now she is adding sequin ornaments and tulle fringes by hand.

Everything is quiet. My brother is already asleep. Mother is working the needle with precision. Down and up, down and up. Stretch. Down and up, down and up. Stretch.

"Ouch!" She jerks her finger and sticks it in her mouth. There is probably blood. I'm too squeamish to look.

Soon I will be dancing the waltz and foxtrot and quickstep in a gorgeous, undulating, ankle-length dress. I will not give a second thought to the endless evenings when Mother's sewing machine played a staccato rhythm in our living room, to the hand-sewn tulle fringes, to blood on her finger.

Carp

I lean over an iron bathtub and touch the slimy scales on Bolek. The carp shudders and swims away, but there is nowhere to go, really. He—or is it she?—turns around, swishes his tail, and resorts to making laps in the water littered with black ribbons of his poop. The smell of laundry detergent mixes with the smell of swamp. My cheek rests on the cool bathtub ledge. I lean back to sit against the door to Grandma's tiny bathroom, and that's when I see it: a loose tile under the sink. I remove it quietly and see a tiny bottle with red lettering: *Wyborowa.*

In Poland we call shot-glass-sized liquor bottles *małpki,* little monkeys. Is it because they make people loud and unruly after they sneak them to work, dry family gatherings, hospitals? I twist the cap and pour the vodka into the sink. Then I put it back inside the drywall hiding spot and replace the tile. Suddenly, I feel tired.

Earlier that month, Mother came back from one of her stays in the psych ward. This time the hospital added rehab to her menu, but she went back to drinking a week after checking herself out. Much later, in my Indiana home, I will open an email from my brother with Mother's medical history he received from the hospital. All in all, she ended up in that psych ward twelve times, mostly with deep depression, sometimes after suicide attempts, sometimes entering reluctantly but with consent, sometimes forced by Grandpa, who was the only one in the family strong enough to keep her arms and legs down as she lashed out and kicked and screamed. Her first visit to this particular psych ward was in 1986. Her last was in 2013.

It's Christmas Eve, hence the carp in the bathtub. In most Polish homes, there is at least one swimming in circles in murky bath water, waiting to be butchered and fried, encased in aspic, placed on white tablecloth already covered in dishes—there have to be thirteen, according to tradition—and prune juice jugs. Kids all over the country lean over bathtubs and touch their carp's slimy scales. They—we—name the fish, talk to it, and watch the water turn greenish. Maybe some of them also find *małpka* behind a loose tile.

Then someone drains the water and kills Bolek or Jan or Sebastian.

My family's Christmas Eve gatherings, with aromatic traditional dishes like pierogi with sauerkraut and mushrooms, pickled herring, *kutia* (noodles with poppyseed and honey), *ryba w galarecie* (fish aspic), *sałatka* (root-vegetable salad), or prune compote, started with prayer and often culminated in physical fights and drunken rows. Mother's suicide threats intensified during holidays. But before the fights, Christmas Eve festivities would bring our family to the table for at least ten hours. People would come and go, plates would be exchanged, washed, and returned to the table, and despite all the food shortage in the country, on Christmas Eve we would have enough food not only for us but also for a lonely neighbor next door, a friend of mine or Tomek's, an unexpected guest. Somehow, also, there would be a ton of presents under the tree, a cornucopia of plastic toys made in China, Soviet dolls, beautifully illustrated children's books, real coffee and tea, oranges.

In nervous anticipation of the holidays, I spent hours in the bathroom, away from family, watching the carp. I didn't make the connection between the live fish and its cooked flesh suspended in Jell-O until I was a teenager. As a child, I simply accepted that the fish appeared in our apartment and then a couple of days later disappeared. Similarly, when we visited relatives on Zaduszki, or All Saints Day, I played with Uncle Włodek's caged rabbits for hours and did not realize that one of the rabbits ended up as a roast at our great-uncle's feast. The Zaduszki dinner gave us energy for that evening's visit to a cemetery where my great-grandfather Franciszek was buried. We spent hours among the candlelight and incense, praying, catching up on gossip with old friends, arranging flowers on marble slabs, wiping down crosses and plaques, blowing our noses in November drizzle.

Now as an adult I make a connection between the silence about the carp and the rabbits and the silence about alcoholism. Everyone knew the dark secret, felt its shame, yet remained suspended in silence and fear. I didn't realize back then how much effort went into not revealing the dysfunction. Our bodies, of course, paid the price for that silence.

My family has never been emotionally sober. The actual drunk was Mother, but we were all drunk in other ways—living in denial, constant cover-up and shame, reeling from one intense emotion to another. Adult children of alcoholics (ACOAs) suffer from cumulative trauma and PTSD, a long-lasting shock engraved in our bodies. We are more likely to become alcoholics ourselves. We engage in other compulsive behaviors, too: drugging ourselves with toxins, overeating, overworking, engaging in unsafe sex, spending, gambling, and more. We are often hypervigilant. When Mother was not being violent or unconscious, she would often smirk. To this day when I see a person close to me smirking, I get flushed and shaky. Smirking is the prelude to violence.

Psychologist Tian Dayton compares living with an alcoholic

to driving at night without headlights on, constantly and nervously squinting to see better, to anticipate danger. Children of alcoholics are trained to interpret signs and moods, a skill we retain long after we leave our homes.

Then there is the amnesia about some parts of our childhood and adolescence. I pore over hospital records and diaries, and I realize that I will never be able to assemble a coherent narrative about my life because I cannot rely on my memory. It's as if I were half-conscious, drunk, dissociated from reality when I was near Mother. Some of my most vivid memories end abruptly, or they come from intense and recurring nightmares that may or may not be rooted in truth.

I think I spent so much time with the carp in the bathtub because I sensed a kindred soul in the fish trapped within the iron walls, getting enough oxygen to stay alive—but barely—and swimming, swimming in circles, without direction, with only one goal in mind: to survive.

* * *

When people think of Polish cuisine, they often mention pierogi or pork, but salt- and freshwater fish have been quite prominent on Polish tables for centuries, and especially since War World II. After the war, the Communist government confiscated livestock and consolidated private farms into collective state-run *kołchozy,* and hunting was dangerous because of mines, so people went fishing in streams, rivers, and lakes and on the Baltic Sea. Even little channels in turf had an abundance of crucians that could be ground—bones and all—and made into fish balls.

As a boy scout, my brother used to wrap perch in toilet paper, soak it in water, and then put it on embers. The paper would burn away, and the fish was nicely baked inside. Later, after our grandparents' death, Tomek took over the ritual of butchering the bathtub carp on Christmas Eve.

* * *

Grandpa Wincenty died in an oncology ward on the outskirts of the city. I took long bus rides to get there, walked along a quiet wooded path, and entered the bleached building, careful not to come close to the other part of the complex that was devoted to TB patients. By the time Grandpa went to a specialist to deal with his persistent cough, the tumor in his lungs was the size of an orange. The man who bought me my first guitar from a Russian peddler, who taught my brother to shave, who unveiled for us the magic of complex fractions, who volunteered as a mentor and court advocate for troubled youth, who tirelessly tilled, planted, and harvested now looked as thin as an asparagus stalk. His unfocused gaze no longer lingered on our faces.

Grandma Iza followed a few years later. By then I was in a master's program in Wrocław, about eight hours southwest by train from my hometown. One evening, my roommate was out, celebrating Valentine's Day with her boyfriend, so I was happy to have the solitude to work on my thesis. I put in a floppy disk and stared at the blue screen, then out my twelfth-floor window at the ice-covered roads—white and red lights snaking to and from the market square with its elegant townhouses—at the Oder River dissected by bridges, and at Ostrów Tumski—an island between river branches, with gorgeous iron bridges across which I walked to my classes every day, inhaling smoke from the nuns' courtyard and incense from the cathedral. I finally returned to the screen and typed up a few lines about Joseph Conrad's *Secret Agent* and his Professor moving through London crowds with a bomb in his pocket.

Mother was still in Olsztyn. She was now taking care of Grandma, who had been diagnosed with lymphoma. I traveled back home to see Grandma about once a month, each time embracing her weakening and shrinking body and praying for a miracle. Grandma now subsisted on ice pops, after radiation damaged her esophagus. On Christmas Eve, she had a sip of advocaat at the family table, probably the most nutritious thing she had had for a while, but she shuddered, unused to alcohol. I skipped the January trip back to Olsztyn, preoccupied with classes, with a theater production where I played Emilia, Desdemona's maid, with men and rave parties at Wrocław clubs. I'll go next week, I repeated every Friday.

Then, as my fingers hovered over the keyboard to type up another quotation from Conrad, the power went out.

Shit. When did I last hit Save? Do we have any candles?

But before I could move, I heard a phone ring. I could still see a little because the city below was brightly lit, so I walked around the computer table and picked up the receiver.

"Agata? I'm so sorry." Mother's voice. Quiet.

Then she sobbed.

That night, I could not fall asleep, but when I finally did, I dreamed. In the dream, just as the sun's rays hit our windows, Grandma walks into my studio apartment and sits on my mattress, stroking my hair. She says nothing, only moves her wrinkled hand across my head slowly, rhythmically. I sit up, and she gives me a hug. I feel her flesh against my thin nightgown. We sit like this for a long time.

I awoke covered with tears.

* * *

How much heart-wrenching and back-breaking work did Mother do around Grandma Iza as she lay on her death bed? How many evenings did Mother spend washing her dying mother's body with wet wipes, calling nurses with questions, administering morphine while I drank Red Bull and vodka and danced to techno music among strobe lights?

* * *

While Grandma was still alive, she sometimes bought smoked mackerel or eel from the neighborhood fishmonger. I ate the eel, its buttery and smoky flesh melting against the roof of my mouth, while she put away the other groceries and fussed about queues. Paired with a toasted sourdough slice, eel is the taste of comfort. When I moved to Wrocław to study English literature, I missed this taste, unable to afford much food beyond rice, buckwheat, and beets. Although education in Poland was and still is free, I had to rent a shared studio apartment, and I spent most of the money I earned from private tutoring on parties and books. Years later, I would find a Russian deli tucked in between a Goodwill and a Thai restaurant in Indianapolis, and I would eat smoked eel again, remembering Grandma's steamy kitchen, warm slippers on my bare feet, and the peace that came with her presence.

* * *

FISH ASPIC

1 large carp, fresh
1 small onion
1 slice of stale bread, soaked in water
1 egg
1/2 cup raisins
1/2 cup shaved almonds
8 potatoes
1 small celery root
4 carrots
32 oz vegetable broth
3 tsp gelatin
1/2 tsp of each: turmeric, allspice, rosemary, parsley

1 bay leaf
Salt and pepper to taste
1 lemon

Filet the carp, keeping skin intact. Grind the carp meat with onion, soaked bread slice, raw egg, salt, and pepper. Add a handful of raisins and shaved almonds. Stuff the ground carp meat into the skin and sew the skin's edges together.

Place carp in a pot. Simmer for 30 minutes with cubed potatoes, celery root, and carrot together with discarded fish parts in vegetable or chicken broth, adding turmeric, allspice, rosemary, parsley, bay leaf, salt, and pepper.

Gently take out the carp and place in a serving bowl. Strain the broth and add gelatin. Pour over the carp. Serve with fresh parsley and lemon wedges once the gelatin sets.

* * *

An eel lives her life in a stream or brook or pond, hiding in the mud or slimy green detritus until night comes, when she slithers out and strikes her prey, only to return to her murky home. But one day the eel feels the urge to move. She just knows she has to go. She stops eating and starts to grow reproductive organs. She swims downstream to another waterway, then another and another, all the while her body transforming. She emerges in the sea, maybe the Baltic, and from there she eventually crosses into the Atlantic Ocean, where she knows exactly where to swim—to the Sargasso Sea, the only place on earth where she can reproduce. After she makes eel eggs, she dies. Her offspring swim across the Atlantic Ocean, first as tiny larvae, then as willow leaf–like shapes, perhaps toward Europe, via seas and streams and rivers.

* * *

I got into college by reciting W. B. Yeats's "The Two Trees" and Jim Morrison's "The End." I didn't get into the top programs in Poland because my grades were not high enough. Although I had As in English, Polish, and biology, I barely passed math and chemistry, mostly because I so rarely attended these classes that my teachers sent me greetings through my classmates. Frankly, in my early twenties, I still didn't know what to do with myself. Teach high school English like Mother? Join a rock band? Emigrate to London and work in a pub for a decent wage far surpassing what I would earn as a teacher in Poland?

I started the English program at a local university while drifting between binge-drinking and jerkily moving about dance floors to techno music on some nights, and on others writing essays and reading *Beowulf* and *The Fall of the House of Usher*, aided by Turkish coffee. I rarely slept. I crammed English, German, and Latin vocabulary. I plastered flash cards all over my bedroom, bathroom, and kitchen. I couldn't stand being alone with my own thoughts. So it was either a party or repeating *unheimlich* or *vernacular* or *bellum bella bello* in front of a dirty mirror as I brushed my teeth. Anything but silence. Anything but self-reflection.

Then, already in my master's program, away from Olsztyn, I got the phone call about Grandma's death. I knew at that moment that I had to move farther away. With both grandparents gone, I wanted to turn my back on everything I knew and start over. With the arrogance of a twenty-three-year-old who thought she knew the world because she'd read *Ulysses* and spent three months in England, I applied for scholarships that could facilitate my flight. One of these scholarships asked on its form where I wanted to study. Without thinking, I listed five

Anglophone countries at a safe distance from Mother: Australia, New Zealand, South Africa, the United States, and Ireland. Several months later, a kind, bearded Rotarian said to me: "You got the scholarship. You're going to South Carolina. Now stock up on some tapes with American English so you don't get lost there with your Queen's accent."

* * *

Away. Put as many miles between Mother and myself as possible. Away from vodka on her breath, in her sweat, in her eyes. Away from the sterile kitchen with its Formica table. Away from picking her up from sidewalks as neighbors' kitchen curtains part and close. Away from rifling through Mother's purse, her closet, her bedsheets. Away from loose bathroom tiles and toilet tanks hiding tiny liquor bottles. Away from the prospect of one day being picked up from the gutter by my own child.

* * *

I sit at a large table with five other volunteers training to become CASAs—court appointed special advocates. It's late, but the spring sun still lingers, casting a warm striped glow through the window shades of the Youth Service Bureau building in my Indiana town. In a few weeks, I will be sworn in by a judge to advocate in court for neglected and abused children. I will get my first case: two boys whose parents are addicted to meth. But right now I'm still learning, even though it means leaving my own kids with my husband two evenings a week and missing their goodnight kisses. Our teacher is showing a movie about adverse childhood experiences.

Experts talk about attachment, survival, brain mirroring, and resilience. I'm good at listening to lectures, taking notes, regurgitating new information. I'm an academic.

But I'm not prepared for what video enactments of child

abuse will do to my recovering brain, to my body. A scene unfolds in front of me: a thin, blond-haired girl, maybe seven or eight years old, serious and intense, shields her younger brother against a blow from a drunk parent. She grabs the boy's hand, and they run away from their trailer and hide from violence. I don't know how the story ends because my body has frozen. I can't breathe. I can no longer hear or see anyone, and when I come to, my face is covered with tears, and the class leader asks me if I need to take a break. I cannot respond. I open and close my fish mouth.

Vodka

Places I drank alcohol as a teen: tiny bedrooms where boys forced my mouth open with their tongues; barns on the outskirts of my city, with MC Hammer chanting "You can't touch this" as I engaged in exploratory petting on prickly straw; *fosa,* the castle moat, where I chugged sulfury wine with other punks, our anarchy pendants swinging when we reached for a joint; abandoned bus stops where I chugged vodka straight from the bottle, its fire burning my insides; a riverbank where I was told by another punk that I was *zimna,* cold like an ice queen, when I didn't want to kiss him; lakeshores, by campfires, with guitar in hand, singing about prisoners in dark cells who long for their girlfriends, where I bit into the charred flesh of sausages and wiped my greasy face before taking another swig of beer; in community center basements, before, during, and after practice for my punk band (Omen) and after practice for my rock opera band (Enola Gay); the music school cloakroom, on the countertop, unlit cigarette between my teeth, waiting for my guitar lesson that sometimes turned into a fuck-fest; dive bars where I talked to refrigerators and once befriended and took home a runaway teen girl, tiny like a bird, who later stole my red jeans and studded leather boots and chased me around town with two large-breasted women; techno and house clubs where I fancied myself sophisticated and worldly after sniffing meth off my student bus pass, until an older man came up to me and said, "You dance like a tart"; disco clubs where a US Marine from California stationed in Poland once told me he was a Baptist, and I thought that this had something to do with Voltaire; rock concerts where a Chicago guitarist once played "Purple Rain" with his teeth and told me that he "hates fucking Marines"; Jatki, a club in Wrocław, where I stumbled into a flooded bathroom stall and found Salman Rushdie's *East, West* in Polish translation and tucked it in behind my tight jeans and took it home; a Best Western lobby, where another American said, "I'd like you to meet my brother Jake. He's upstairs," and I did go upstairs only to discover that Jake was a pile of ash in a plastic urn; salsa clubs in Brighton, UK, where I attended summer school at nineteen and wrote clichéd papers about Virginia Woolf's depression; the rocks jutting into the Adriatic, during my first trip abroad (Italy!) with thirty other teens and an aging alcoholic actor who used to sing in children's TV shows about cucumbers and bunnies; playgrounds and parks at midday, where I once blacked out only to be collected by a retired nurse and taken home in a taxi and put in bed, where I'd pee and wake up as the sun set, with my family sitting by my side, Grandma and Grandpa sobbing; behind a storage shed near my high school, where together with a friend I drank a bottle of wine before class, after which I fell off a chair and told my teacher that she was fat; the steps of a movie theater before seeing *Fearless,* about a plane crash survivor; a cemetery, where I stumbled over graves, groping in darkness for a dropped box full of cream-yellow, round-shaped Relanium, the night blacker and blacker, the odor of freshly mowed grass mixing with the smell of cheap wine; the steps of the Philharmonic building before singing Mozart's *Requiem*; a wedding reception for my guitar teacher's friend during which he, my teacher, told me that my breasts were beautiful and I was lovely and he loved me and then asked why I was only sixteen.

* * *

"You didn't put your doll on the shelf. No doll." Mother grabs my red-haired Russian doll, the fancy one that cries when I tip her over and closes her eyes when I put her down to sleep, the one in a beautiful, flowery red dress hemmed with delicate white lace, the one I can make walk if I stand behind her and push her forward by the shoulders. I run after Mother. The rest of my toys have already gone down the trash chute. All the shelves in my room are empty. Mother saved Dorota the doll for the last act, knowing just how much I love her.

Mother runs to the staircase landing, two steps at a time, and opens the chute. But the doll is too large. So she presses the elevator button, determined to take Dorota down to the dumpster herself. When the elevator stops on our floor with a loud clack, out comes Grandpa.

"What are you doing?" He sees my tears and Mother's clenched teeth.

"I'm throwing out Agata's toys. She didn't clean up her room."

"But they are not your toys to throw out. I bought most of them." Grandpa pushes Mother away from the elevator with his body. He grabs the doll and marches inside the apartment and into my room. He looks at the dusty shelves, then grabs my hand and down we go to the dumpster. While I watch with Dorota in my embrace, Grandma climbs into the stinky metal container in his good clothes and throws whatever toys he spots onto the cement floor. Out comes my yellow penguin, my plastic sailboat, my stuffed dogs, including the black and orange poodle I got when I was in the children's hospital. I scoop them up, dropping some as I go.

* * *

During Communism, Poland became one of the drunkest

nations in the world. In the '70s, 5 million people (out of the total population of around 32 million) had problems with alcohol, and 900,000 were registered addicts. Among them, 10 percent were women. Workplace drunkenness was commonplace. An average Pole spent the equivalent of one month's salary a year on alcohol. Each day there were 350 car accidents caused by drunk drivers or drunk pedestrians.

Totalitarianism was conducive to the society's turn toward escapism through alcohol and sometimes pot or heroin. Lack led to excess. When people could not satisfy their basic needs, when they were not allowed to complain publicly about these unmet needs, they turned to vodka. About three quarters of Polish alcohol consumption was vodka—pure vodka, not mixed drinks. People notoriously came to work drunk or got wasted at work. How else would you have endured the cement-gray existence among neighbors who could be spies, the store shelves that gathered dust, in a country where words could be missiles and truth a noose, where *milicja* could make you disappear from a sidewalk, where political prisoners rotted in jail without trial or on made-up charges, where queuing up in front of empty shops was a national pastime, where coffee was made without coffee beans, chocolate without cocoa? After a few shots you could forget that your fridge was empty, that your spouse was sleeping with another woman, that you were not allowed to get a passport or complain about the government too loudly, that you couldn't buy shoelaces for your children, that there were stacks of cut-up newspapers on the toilet floor because you hadn't seen toilet paper in months. During the deepening economic crisis of the second half of the 1970s, vodka transported many through the looking glass and allowed them to live in a more colorful world free of ideology.

* * *

It's Christmas Eve. I am visiting Poland, just for a week. I left my son with my brother and hopped on a bus to see Mother. The bus is not crowded because it's going from the outskirts of the city toward the center. The buses coming from the opposite direction are packed with red-faced shoppers, splashes of pink or red or yellow scarves behind large, fogged-up windows. After the fall of Communism, stores filled with more goods than we could have imagined before—name-brand jeans, colorful hoodies, expensive perfumes, Swiss watches, French wines, Dutch beers, Coca-Cola—so people spent less time queuing in front of empty shops and more time in their cubicles so they could afford imported candy bars. Now, right before Christmas, I see Levi's bags and plastic totes filled with toys, food, and wrapping paper rolls. The lights outside twinkle against the dirty snow.

The closest stop to Mother's apartment is by a brand-new supermarket, Carrefour. From its bowels crawls a line of cars, some old Fiats, some fancy Volvos and Citroëns and Toyotas. I walk through dusk, holding my large canvas bag. Soon, I think as I breathe out steam, I will sit down and share *opłatek* with Mother. I will give her the books and sweets I bought for her, and we will sing a carol.

But when I ring the doorbell, nobody answers. Then a shuffle. Metal shifting against metal. The door opens. Mother's eyes are half-closed, her breath foul.

"Oh." She says. "Agatka."

She hugs me, and I can smell that she hasn't bathed in a while. Her tiny apartment smells of sleep and cigarettes. I start unloading my presents and groceries only to discover that the fridge is not working.

"Mom, I can call someone to fix this. I'll pay for it."

"I don't need a fridge."

"Have you eaten today?"

"Yes." Her half smile—a smirk?—doesn't give away whether she's telling the truth.

"I have fish here, herring, and salad and poppyseed cake."

"I'm not hungry. Bartek cooked for me this morning."

Her new boyfriend. I'm glad she's not alone, but I also know they drink together. He brings other people with him, all thirsty, all trying to figure out how to buy or steal another bottle.

"Where would you like these books?" I didn't wrap my gifts, but the bookstore paper bag looks festive, with red ribbons on a dark-green background. One of my gifts is Michael Cunningham's novel *The Hours*. "*Wesołych Świąt,* Mama."

"There." She points with her chin to the bedroom the size of a closet. I drop the bag on the carpet.

"What's that? Did you buy it for Tomek?" On the floor is a brand-new Xbox. Other electronics, too.

"It's not mine."

* * *

A *melina* is an apartment where drunks imbibe homemade or store-bought vodka. *Melina* used to mean a place in which criminals hid from the police, where they stored stolen goods, where men could bring a prostitute or a lover. But after 1945, as Polish society got increasingly drunk, the word acquired a more specific meaning related to the illegal sale and consumption of alcohol. These apartments were often open 24/7 and only for trusted clients. They were mostly run by alcoholics for other alcoholics, though some were operated by sober people with business ambitions. They were the speakeasys of the Eastern Bloc. Customers either drank *bimber* on the spot, with a bite of pickle or *kiełbasa,* or took a bottle home. Even after the fall of Communism, street sales of *bimber* flourished, this time peddled by Russian and Ukrainian visitors lugging their wares in checkered bags. In my town, we called these bags *przemytniczka*—the smuggler.

At the same time, after the war, alcohol became a currency with which one could buy more sugar than the ration cards allowed, American cigarettes and other smuggled goods, a tool stolen from a state-run factory, a dog, a piano . . . Alcohol also ensured an early spot on a surgery roll, a numbing shot at a dentist's. Some people remodeled their apartments by paying for materials and labor with the currency of half a liter of vodka. Want tiles in your bathroom? Three bottles for the materials stolen from the factory and two for labor. Want an extra cut of meat at the store? Slip a bottle into the checkout lady's pocket. *Półlitrówka,* or half a liter of vodka, was a currency much more stable than our złoty.

* * *

It's 1 a.m. in Indiana. I slip out of the bedroom and rummage through a desk in my home office. In one of the drawers, I find the only diary from my teen years that remains intact, probably because its blue leather covers would be harder to tear up or burn in rage than the plain notebooks I destroyed as a teen. The year recorded in sloppy cursive is 1995, then 1996. I turned sixteen two months before the first entry. On most pages—shame and anger about Mother's drinking. References to skipping school and watching trains from the top of the historic viaduct. Lots of entries about staying up late, until 4 a.m., outside the house, drinking and smoking. One bad poem.

February 18, 1995

I left for my Music Theory class at 7 a.m. and came back at noon. Tomek met me at the front door and said that he and grandparents couldn't wake Mother up, that she tried to commit suicide by swallowing her pills, but she didn't have enough, so she is fine but sleeping in my bed and I can't go into my room. She stayed in my bed, like a limp rag, the entire day. I was planning to invite Gosia but can't now because even if we stay in the living room, Mother may wake up and Gosia will see what's happening. So I went out to see Chopin, and we smoked Don Pedro cigarettes outside his home.

* * *

It's early morning, still dark except streetlamps and an occasional lighted rectangle in the high-rises flanking the street. I'm in eighth grade, no longer a straight-A student. Fuck school, I say more and more often, except when I'm at Grandma's and I'm forced to sit at my desk and write that overdue essay for my Polish class or to climb a hundred steps to the top office in our city's observatory so I can be tutored in physics by a stiff, disdainful man whose breath smells like onions. Teachers sign me up for math, geography, and literature Olympiads, mostly out of habit, but I no longer prepare for anything, so my results are dismal. Mother does take me to the library once so I can study Czesław Miłosz, and we make some photocopies in the lobby, but I never really read them when I come back home. Instead, I go out seeking excitement.

I sit still at the window. Earlier that night, after drinking some vodka at a friend's apartment, we got magic mushrooms from her older brother. We sat on a lawn between our building and the street, waiting for Marta to finish peeing, and suddenly I saw the tall apartment buildings in front of me sway and bend, sway and bend. They were alive. They were exchanging messages. They spoke in whispers, and I hushed Marta's singing so I could hear them.

Now there is silence. I'm too far to hear.

* * *

Psilocybin, the active ingredient in magic mushrooms, may be able to reset the brain in people suffering from PTSD or severe depression by destroying and then forming new pathways between brain cells and activating serotonin receptors. A study published in the *Proceedings of the National Academy of Sciences of the USA* helped "explain the functional effects of specific serotoninergic receptor (5-HT_{2A}R) stimulation with psilocybin in healthy humans. Longer term, this could provide a better understanding of why psilocybin is showing considerable promise as a therapeutic intervention for neuropsychiatric disorders including depression, anxiety, and addiction." Mushrooms soften the edges of human experience and open up new cognitive pathways. Does alcohol?

Mushrooms are everywhere. Yeasts grow on our skin, in our gastrointestinal tract, and elsewhere in our bodies. And there would be no alcohol without fungi: We use fungus in brewing and baking. Yeasts transform sugar into alcohol. Claude Lévi-Strauss claimed that yeasts—in particular the ones facilitating the production of mead as well as beer and bread making—spurred cultural transformations within human societies, that is, the transition from hunting and gathering to cultivating land. Merlin Sheldrake reminds us that humans feed yeast before they feed themselves. And he adds: "Alcohol and inebriation are some of the oldest magics. An invisible force conjures wine from fruit, beer from grain, mead from nectar. These liquids alter our minds and have been enfolded within human cultures in many ways: from ritual feasting and statecraft, to a means to pay for labor. For just as long, they have been responsible for dissolving our senses, for wildness and ecstasy." Even animals get drunk—"birds eat inebriating berries, lemurs lick millipedes, most drink the nectar of psychoactive flowers—and it is likely that we have been using mind altering drugs for longer than we have been human."

Fungi transform a solid log into soil, flour into bread, grain into alcohol. Honey becomes mead, fruit juice becomes wine. Even LSD was originally developed from fungi. But how do these processes alter human consciousness? What happens inside our brains?

Alcohol enters our bloodstream through the lining in the stomach. It spreads across our tissues and reaches our brain within five minutes. Most of us know that alcohol affects the parts of the brain responsible for judgment, memory, speech, and balance. Those who drink regularly in large quantities will eventually feel the results of shrinking neurons inside their brains. Especially vulnerable to neuron alterations are adolescent drinkers.

I watched Mother transform from a functional alcoholic, someone who could teach, read difficult novels, and solve impossible crossword puzzles despite her addiction, into a vegetative slurring vulgar drunk incapable of understanding the plot of TV soaps. The transition was gradual, but it accelerated when she retired. Having no anchor in reality, no schedule, no deadlines, she gave herself wholly to drinking.

It's not entirely true that the trauma of living with Mother is the only thing to blame for my fragmented and pockmarked memories from childhood and adolescence. Starting in eighth grade, I drank, too. I experimented with drugs—shrooms, pot, and later cocaine and meth. I was lucky that none of these experimentations ended in addiction. My grandparents' interest in me and Tomek, the constant reminders that I had to protect my brother from Mother's wrath and neglect, and finally—I suppose—an unlikely win in the genetic roulette, protected me from becoming a lifelong alcoholic and drug addict.

Still, until I reached my twenties, my drinking was often

uncontrollable. It wasn't just one beer or one shot of vodka. When at a party or concert, or visiting a friend, I often drank until I blacked out. I drank to numb. I drank to forget. I drank to chase dopamine. I drank to impress.

And then I stopped. There was no decision or resolution or health scare. I got bored, I guess. By the time I finished my master's, binge-drinking didn't excite me at all. I'd have an occasional mulled wine on a blustery night after a walk from a theater, or a pint of fizzy beer at the market square when my boyfriend visited me on a spring Saturday, but the need to numb, escape, pass out, was gone. I was also away from Mother, over 500 kilometers removed from her suicide threats and attempts, her drinking, her aggression, her sadness and disappointment, in a city where I could remake myself, start over, plot an escape even farther away.

And when I escaped, to South Carolina on a Rotary scholarship, I went back to binge-drinking at parties because almost everyone in my grad school cohort drank—a lot. There was the party when I drank the baddest drunk under the table, to everyone's approval, it seemed. There were pub crawls where I drank to fit in, dance clubs where I chugged Red Bull and vodka to shed inhibitions and dance. But gradually, drinking became boring again. Writing became a more exciting escape—academic papers, essays, short stories, a novel I never published, all offered a world with more pathways, mazes, and universes than a buzz or blackout could ever offer.

Something bizarre happened when I got pregnant with my first child: Even the smell of liquor would make me retch. After my son was born, I felt no desire to drink. An occasional beer or glass of wine—fine. Bingeing? So far, I have kept the promise that my baby would never see me drunk. Chemoreceptors somewhere in my brain decided for me that the smell and taste of hard liquor would trigger nausea. I wish I could boast of a superior willpower or saintlike self-sacrifice, but anyone who has seen me open a new sleeve of Thin Mints and devour it in one sitting can attest to the opposite.

A lot of people with drinking histories similar to mine have developed addiction. Why was it so easy and stress-free to stop in my case? I turn to the National Institute on Drug Abuse to seek the answer. I read that addiction has nothing to do with moral principles, good intentions, or willpower. Whether someone will become addicted to drugs, including alcohol, is determined by a number of factors, including genes, other mental disorders, stress, development, and environment. So I keep digging.

I read papers with titles like "Early Life Adversity Potentiates Expression of Addiction-Related Traits" and "Genetic Background and Epigenetic Modifications in the Core of the Nucleus Accumbens Predict Addiction-Like Behavior in a Rat Model," and I still don't have the answer. There must be an off switch in my brain that some people who develop addictions don't have. Maybe my adverse childhood experiences were less adverse than those of others. These comparisons are not helpful, though.

One answer pops up in my head again and again: Grandma. As a teen, I hated her nagging, her nosiness about my affairs, her double-checking whether my homework was done, her breath checks after I came back from an evening out with friends, her insistence that I spend time with her and Grandpa at the garden allotment among bees and mosquitoes. But she—together with Grandpa—was the one constant in my life, the role model I could follow. Scientists say that plants sharing "a network with others grow more quickly and survive better than neighboring plants that are excluded from the common network." The fungal mycelia under the forest floor help plants communicate and nourish each other. I think I learned to thrive because, despite the adversities, I had my network.

* * *

I am alone on the dance floor at a student club, dressed in a baggy bohemian tunic and suede shoes, swirling and swirling to Jim Morrison's deep crooning and Robby Krieger's gothic, sitar-like guitar. Ride the highway west, babe. The cymbals dictate my steps. The guitar riffs snake into my brain, lift me up the floor, drop me down. I'm holding a cigarette, and when the tempo increases, I drop it and swirl even faster, faster, faster, hands flailing, eyes closed, free. The end of laughter and soft lies. The end of nights we tried to die. When the song slows down and stops, I open my eyes to look for Gosia and Ola, who came here with me, but the wooden benches are empty. Then the DJ says:

"Agata Szczeszak. Agata Szczeszak. Your grandfather is here to take you home."

I hear Gosia and Ola explode into laughter as they walk back from the bathroom. There are only a few people in the club, sipping beer at the bar, but they all look in my direction.

Fuck.

Gosia, Ola, and I squeeze into Grandpa's Fiat, which promptly fills with cigarette and beer fumes. Grandpa says nothing. After about fifteen minutes, we stumble out of the car only to hear Grandma screech from her kitchen window:

"Look at you three! Eleven p.m. on a school night!"

I go straight to bed. The next morning, Grandma wakes me up and sends me out to the bus stop so I don't miss school. Before I enter the school building, I throw up in the bushes—first all beer, then all bile. I don't know if my math teacher smells me or sees my droopy eyes, but she asks me a question about trigonometry ratios, then repeats it to Gosia. And then:

"You don't know. Of course you don't know. Gosia, I see your future. You don't need high school to be a nanny. And Agata?

You don't need high school to mow lawns for a living. Why are you here?"

* * *

Recently there has been an increase in studies and publications about magic mushrooms—psilocybin in particular—having a positive impact in treating alcohol use disorders. Apparently, psilocybin helps repair the parts of the brain responsible for alcohol cravings. Even in the 1950s, researchers had a hunch that magic mushrooms might be one way to address alcoholism, as 40 percent of patients who received psilocybin reported no relapse a year later. It repairs glutamate receptor function damaged by alcohol. Researchers suggest that it could also help treat depression, anxiety, and PTSD. Could it be that the cure for Mother's unrelenting addiction and debilitating depression was just within reach?

On the other hand, some people respond to magic mushrooms with paranoia. Hieronymus Bosch is rumored to have had mushroom-induced hallucinations that influenced his horror-filled paintings. His macabre hellish landscapes materialized on oak wood after a catastrophic fire he witnessed as a boy but also possibly due to ergot mushroom ingestion. Then again, Jessica Cale says that "Bosch's monsters have been attributed to mushrooms, rancid rye bread, alchemy, Freudian theory, and even a mystical sex cult, but the truth was probably more mundane. It was the middle ages. Monsters were everywhere."

* * *

A photo. Mother, five-month-old Tomek, and I are sitting on a sofa. In front of us is a brick of a cake with three large lit candles, the kind we used in church ceremonies and at cemeteries. I look at them cross-eyed, my brows furrowed. Mother is holding Tomek and looking at the camera with misty eyes—the unmistakable look of inebriation I learned to recognize quickly. I will soon blow out the candles. A few days later, soldiers will be warming their hands over burning trash cans in the streets of Poland, and countless censored papers will smolder in kitchen sinks, bonfires, and fireplaces.

* * *

Melina was the place where people got their bottles after stores closed down. For many, after *melina* came *Izba Wytrzeźwień,* a sober-up clinic, a unique institution created by the government in 1957, different from alcohol addiction wards at psychiatric hospitals. By 1989 there were fifty-six such places within Poland. They served as both clinics—where heavily intoxicated people could be seen by a doctor or nurse—and prisons. By 1980 over 317,000 people a year were scooped up from gutters and *melinas* and transferred to *Izba Wytrzeźwień,* hosed down in windowless cement cells, and left to sober up wherever they collapsed. Most were working-class men, but a fifth of all the patient-inmates were underage drinkers. In 1976, 50 percent of fourteen-year-olds declared regular alcohol consumption. Among fifteen-to-eighteen-year-olds, that percentage was 80.

Krzysztof Mętrak's 1982 entry from diaries published posthumously describes *Izba Wytrzeźwień* this way: "Psychologist, deposit—personal items, the most expensive worker lodging in the capital. Drunk doctor; naked sleep, barred windows. The male nurse is elite, master—he leads you to your destination with a series of kicks. You'll get belted—the whole belt theory, eight hard beds screwed into the floor, doors without handles, peephole, metal mesh. No place to hang yourself, to drink, to smoke, to piss."

In the short story "One Day," Edward Stachura's character says: "In the twentieth century the only two options are to fight for peace or to get regularly drunk. I chose the second option because I have free will." But another Polish writer of the Communist era, Marek Hłasko, says in "Noose": "Vodka is the truth which one understands always too late." In the 1980s, the number of people suffering from alcohol-induced psychosis admitted to psychiatric hospitals was 38 per 100,000. Twenty-five percent of those in psychiatric hospitals were alcoholics. A report listed 1.5 million children growing up in pathological families.

In Communist Poland, 10 to 15 percent of the national budget came from alcohol, whose sale was limited to state monopoly. In the USSR, the percentage was even higher, about 25. The Polish government launched a series of anti-alcohol campaigns with posters and infomercials, but historians admit that the income from the sale of alcohol was higher than the losses from workplace drunkenness. Nevertheless, on fences and storefronts popped up large images of an emaciated man in sunglasses, walking feebly with a cane, the caption underneath: "*Bimber przyczyną ślepoty*"—"Homemade vodka causes blindness." *Bimber,* or *samogon,* became even more popular when the state started limiting production of vodka, citing alcoholism as a national plague. In 1982 the government uncovered and closed down 14,000 illegal productions of vodka, mostly in the country, but some were discovered in cities. Most homemade vodka was distilled from beets, wheat, or potatoes. Some had toxic amounts of methanol.

Former Communist leaders claim to this day that the system fell because of the toilet paper shortage or, alternatively, because of the sugar shortage, which they blame on *bimber* production in forests and on farms. A documentary maker once discovered that on average Communist Poland could allot seven rolls of toilet paper per person for a whole year. Meanwhile, legally produced vodka was made in a nationalized company named

Polish propaganda poster, "Bimber przyczyną ślepoty" ("Homemade vodka causes blindness"), originally in color. Author Włodzimierz Zakrzewski.

Polmos, and its sales reached 10 percent of the nation's annual budget.

***

Feb 25, 1995

I'm such a coward. A moment ago Grandpa came in and said that if I have some time, he'd like to "book a reservation for a chat." I tensed and asked what he wanted to talk about. He replied that both he and Grandma are old, and the family has a lot of problems, and he wanted to talk to me about them. I said I was busy. I wasn't. I'm just afraid to talk to him about their death, about Mother's drinking. . . . Yesterday, for example, Grandma found an empty bottle of vodka behind the toilet. Mother can't stop drinking even under supervision. Earlier she would at least pretend and drink at a neighbor's home or when she was alone. Now she can't even wait until her visit at Grandma's is over.

On Thursday we played a concert at Music School to a crowded audience. Recently I've been practically living in Music School because I can't stand being in the house, with its non-stop tension and rows, most often because of Mother's drinking.

***

Music school gave me something to do. Every day after high school classes, I shlepped with my guitar to the cement building housing both the philharmonic orchestra and classrooms. As I walked near it, leaving the oppressive redbrick behemoth of my high school with its dark hallways and stern men looking at me from portraits, the air became lighter, the edges of the rowhouses softened. I loved hearing the first notes from the practice rooms, especially in the spring when the windows were open and trumpets mingled with xylophones and pianos and flutes. Soon I would discover another comfort in that building: a teacher who took a special interest in me, who asked me whether I'd eaten, whether I had time to practice and why not, and whether I wanted to join his band on their trip to a concert next weekend. We made love in his house, in practice rooms, in vans taking us to or from concerts, in his Volvo, on the floor of a dingy community center.

* * *

May 4, 1995

Shit. Mother totally drunk again. Grandma told me that while I was away, Mother tried to cut her wrists and after that she tried to hang herself in the bathroom. I'm so glad I wasn't home then.

May 5, 1995

Holy Fucking Shit. Another row. Mother and grandparents shrieking. I hope they all kill each other. Sometimes I look at Mother and wish she were dead. One day, when she grabbed three pill boxes off the bathroom shelf and closed the door to one of the bedrooms behind her, I hoped she did it to poison herself, and I hoped she'd succeed. I didn't say a word about what I saw to anyone. But Grandma checked on her after a couple minutes and took the pills away from Mother. Mother once said, while drunk, that she regrets having me and Tomek. She's been drinking for at least 17 years. At least she doesn't beat me anymore (because she's afraid I will beat her back), but she's torturing me in other ways. She laughs when I am clumsy. She says I am not very intelligent. I'm the spitting image of my father.

* * *

Why do we condemn intoxication? Why do we find it desirable? Evolution helped humans develop a highly efficient enzyme, ADH4, that helps our bodies detoxify from alcohol. Sheldrake, in his *Entangled Life,* mentions the "'drunken monkey hypothesis,' proposed by the biologist Robert Dudley to explain the origins of humans' fondness for alcohol. In this view, humans are tempted by alcohol because our primate ancestors were. The scent of alcohol produced by yeast was a reliable way to find ripe fruit on the ground. Both our human attraction to alcohol and the entire ecology of gods and goddesses that oversee fermentation and intoxication are remnants of a much more ancient fascination."

What's in this bottle that makes people go nuts? What magic hides in the shot glass that is potent enough to drag a mother from her children? I don't know why Mother reached for a drink and continued reaching for it until she could not survive without a shot of vodka or a bottle of cheap beer. But I can think back to my own early drinking days, at fifteen and sixteen, and say with confidence that for me, it was curiosity. It was also, as is the case with most teen drinkers, a desire to impress and to fit in, yes, but there was more, so much more when I first felt the burning in my throat, after I shuddered. A drink felt like a warm embrace, love surrounding and entering my body, a promise that things would work out. And if that feeling was followed by a blackout, an oblivion, even better.

As *wpadka,* a birth-control accident, I will never know whether I was wanted. I will never know whether I was the reason Mother drank. I will never know whether her violence and drinking are in my genes. But I do know that Mother wasn't alone in her struggle with booze.

By 1986 five million Poles abused alcohol. One million were registered alcoholics. One million homes, often with children whose lives were permanently affected by this epidemic because with alcohol abuse, of course, came violence and neglect. In the last decade of Communism, over 200,000 children were under the supervision of the court, almost all because of alcoholism at home. So Tomek and I were not the only ones yearning for love from someone who was too far gone into the Technicolor world of alcohol and drugs to register that yearning and to offer love.

* * *

Tomek wakes up with a jerk in the middle of the night. A bad dream? A noise? He shifts in bed but cannot go back to sleep. Then he smells gas.

Mother stayed up late watching TV. Earlier that evening, Tomek had told her not to drink in front of his daughter or she'd have to move out. Her response was a smirk and a retreat to the living room, where she had been staying while her own apartment was rented out for income. It's a good financial arrangement. A horrible arrangement for my brother's emotional health. She must have been watching something, because later Tomek will tell me that he heard voices from behind the wall before he fell asleep with his toddler and his wife.

As he opens the door to his bedroom, he squints against light. Hallway lights, bathroom lights, kitchen lights. He finally sees all four of the gas burners turned to their highest settings. No flame. Just a hiss.

After turning off the stove top and flinging the windows open, he marches to Mother's room. She sits in her bed, calm. The smirk is still on her face.

Her previous suicide attempts—her "mushroom poisoning," wrist cutting, pills and more pills, the noose—did not directly endanger the rest of the family. This time, my brother's daughter, his whole family, perhaps even neighbors, could have died. This moment marked Tomek's separation from Mother. I was already in the States, working on my dissertation, but he was entangled in her life, living and reliving a nightmare. But after kicking her out, he would still check in on her on occasion, bring her to the psych ward when she needed detox, drop off a pack of cigarettes as she sat at a barred window, dressed in white, numb. Even that was too much, I now know. Even that prevented him from starting to heal.

* * *

There's a question that keeps nagging at me as I write about Mother: Where was Father? Where was he when we trudged through dirty snow to tell our grandparents that Mommy would not wake up? Where was he when Mother ran at me with a large shard of glass? Where was he when we stood in the middle of a cold room, dressed in thin pajamas, shaking with fear?

As a teen, I had Mother at my fingertips, ready to blame for all the ills and failures, for my mood swings and my own drinking, for sneaking out after dark. It didn't occur to me to blame Father and his absence. By the time I was fifteen, he visited less often because both Tomek and I had our own lives filled with friends, bonfires, music, ballroom dancing (me), tennis lessons (Tomek), homework, and truant explorations of the city. We were no longer interested in hiking through local forests with Father. We didn't know him well. Talking to him felt awkward. Once Tomek asked him if he could move to Gdańsk where Father now lived, away from Mother. Father refused. I don't think he refused because he didn't love us. He just didn't know what to do with us—never did. And he was lucky that drink did not take over his own life. If he drank too much, he didn't drink more than an average Pole at that time. He has always been a social drinker, someone whose life did not fall apart due to addiction. Genes? Perseverance? I don't know why he and I are not wrestling with the bottle the way other family members have.

***

A memory not recorded in my diary: I'm fourteen, maybe fifteen. Mother sits in her usual spot, on a stool between the kitchen table and a mostly unused rotisserie oven, barely upright, smelling of liquor and sweat.

I hit her head with my hand, hard. An open palm landing with a thud above her ear. She bursts into tears, saliva dripping from her mouth, her hair sticky and wet. She wails.

Despite the snow outside, the window is cracked open. The kitchen is cold.

I am pure rage.

"You fucking drunk! You ruin everything! I hate you."

***

Who am I to judge Mother when I, too, drank? My first drink was vodka. I became the cliché of a Polish teen getting drunk on cheap liquor in friends' bedrooms, behind bus stops and sheds, on lakeshores, in staircases, behind gates, under bridges, on park benches, and even in school bathrooms. I drank vodka, cheap wine we called *jabol* (with exotic brand names like Arizona or Apacz), beer from cans and bottles and tumblers, *ajerkoniak* (Polish egg liqueur), Soviet sparkling wine, *winiak* (Polish brandy), *wiśniówka* (cherry cordial), and homemade currant or cherry wine from Grandpa's basement collection.

"Fermentation is domesticated decomposition—rot rehoused," says Sheldrake. Grandpa made his own wine from red and black currants, from grapes, from any fruit we grew in our allotment. For him, it was a hobby. He distilled the wine in a large glass container called a *gąsior,* or a gander. Whenever I sat reading on his bed or took a nap in his room, the regular *blub blub blub* of the air bubbles escaping upward soothed me.

Homemade or store-bought wine of low quality had many

slang names in Poland: *jabol, bełt, siara, alpaga.* What connected the store-bought *jabol* was bad quality fruit plus sulfur dioxide. Grandpa's wine was made from freshly picked fruit, but it still had an acidic, sulfury aftertaste.

Poles often passed down recipes for *jabol* or *bimber* from generation to generation, especially in the countryside, where city folk sometimes traveled to buy alcohol. Trains were rarely on time, mainly due to the poor state of the tracks, but also because they stopped in the middle of nowhere to allow people, including the train drivers, to buy *bimber* from local villagers.

Then there were other alcohol substitutes reserved for the poorest: *denaturat* (denatured ethanol) filtered through potato mush, *autowidol* (liquid for washing windshields), salicylic alcohol, *woda brzozowa* (birch lotion). I suppose these, too, dulled the pain, eased helplessness and guilt, and fed the never-ending craving for drink.

I never saw Mother drink birch lotion or denatured ethanol. I suppose she had the right to swallow whatever poison she wanted, just as she had the right to end her life when it became too unbearable. Some might view this choice, made by a mother of small children, as affecting others, and therefore, not hers to make. But between autonomy and maleficence, it seems, stretches a wide expanse of options. As a child who witnessed her attempts to die, I want to condemn her for this abandonment. But as a feminist, I ask myself: Why should a woman's decision to poison herself with vodka or to end her suffering with a handful of pills be condemned because of one anatomical difference between her and her male counterpart?

* * *

Tomek and I stand barefoot in the middle of our room. We are dressed in thin pajamas. The sky outside is pitch black, and the sheer curtains move slightly with each gust of wind even though the window is closed. We've been in the same spot for what feels like hours. If we move, Mother told us, we will get a beating.

Earlier that night, neither Tomek nor I could sleep, maybe because of the wind, maybe because of the fresh memories of Mother lashing out at Grandma with her fists when she realized her alcohol stash had been taken away again, maybe because we were both still fighting nightmares after Mother's latest unsuccessful suicide attempt (this time a rope, not pills or a balcony). We sang in our beds, played with our dolls in the dark, and finally one of us—who? probably me—came up with an idea: We would get up, get dressed for school, make our beds, and when Mother walked in the next morning, she'd see us ready to go, and she'd be happy. We were sitting at a particleboard desk, coloring and chatting, waiting for the morning, when Mother walked in, her flannel robe untied, and hollered "*Co tu się dzieje*???"

Mother's robe spreads behind her as she launches toward the desk. Like a Roman Fury she is all vengeance, all wrath. We disobeyed her command that we go to bed and stay in bed.

I step in front of Tomek's tiny figure and beg and explain and cry. Mother freezes but doesn't listen. Her eyes glitter, reflecting our small desk light.

"Very well then. You want to be up? You will be up. All night. It's 2 a.m. You will stand here, upright, right in this spot, no moving and no talking, until the morning." Mother's teeth are clenched, and she speaks quietly. "If I see you in beds or even sitting down on the carpet . . . *Manto.*"

Whenever Mother said "*Spuszczę wam manto*" or "*dam ci manto*" we knew violence was imminent. The colloquial expression means something like "hammer the opposing team" or "beat someone up." In her mouth, the phrase often accompanied a smile and a narrowing of her eyes, as if she were anticipating a treat. *Manto* sounds like a name of a soccer star from Real

Madrid or FC Barcelona. *Manto* sounds a little like Maradona or Messi or Mount. *Manto* should be running after a ball on a manicured turf to the ovations of the spectators. Instead, *Manto* meant sober and angry. *Manto* meant we had to flee or cower in the corner, covering as much of our heads as possible with our arms, coats, blankets.

So we stand at attention, spines upright, eyes darting toward the darkened door to the hallway, where Mother could emerge at any moment. We stand even though our legs hurt and our drooping eyelids are heavy. We squeeze each other's hands when one of us feels like we cannot stand upright anymore.

Years later, I will read on the bright rectangle of my phone screen this message from my brother: "You think things have changed, but we are still those kids standing at attention in pajamas in the middle of the night, scared and unmoving."

Mushrooms II

Four days after Reactor Number 4 in Chernobyl sends a radioactive cloud over Ukraine, Belarus, Poland, and the rest of Europe, my friend Dorota and I walk hand in hand on the uneven pavement snaking between cement buildings. Dorota spots an unwrapped, bright-red sugared jelly square on the sidewalk. Her eyes grow large. She picks it up, swinging her blond ponytails back and forth, blows on it, and stuffs it in her mouth. We climb down muddy stairs to our *szkoła*—one of the many colossal primary schools built in 1970s Poland—move along under the fading hallway slogan "*Ojczyzna to wielki zbiorowy obowią azek*" ("A nation is a grand collective duty"), and file behind the other uniformed second graders. There are 2,700 students in our *szkoła,* dressed in identical navy-colored polyester and told repeatedly not to run in the glistening 130-meter hallways. My uniform smells like cigarettes because I threw it down next to Mother the night before, hoping she'd wash it before her next bottle. She was smoking a filterless cigarette and nodded at me through a thick cloud, her eyes already narrow and unfocused.

In the line to our classroom, we are told to report to the nurse's office instead of seating ourselves behind desks. We are to drink iodine, our teacher says. *Jodyna.* Years later, I'll understand this to be potassium iodide, not that this distinction would have made a difference to us back then.

* * *

Four days before Dorota eats the foraged jelly square, on Saturday, April 26, 1986, at 1:23 a.m., a 1,000-megawatt reactor in the Chernobyl power plant explodes, sending a radioactive fireball into the night sky. I am in my bed at that time, unaware, as is everyone else in Poland, that a mushroom cloud of poison rises in the sky 400 miles east of my bedroom. But it isn't a mushroom cloud, is it? That's the image lingering in my imagination when I think about the nuclear accident. An image that lives in my brain ever since I saw photos of nuclear explosions, the mushroom clouds of Hiroshima and Nagasaki, thermal blasts we were taught to escape by ducking under our shiny new school desks. As it turns out, the radiation from the Chernobyl blast is 400 times higher than that of Hiroshima. And it isn't a mushroom cloud, or who knows, really, since the blast happened at night. The first photos of the still-burning Reactor Number 4 are grainy black-and-white images of mangled steel and crumbled concrete, smoke billowing from the debris.

* * *

It would take about twelve hours by car to get from Chernobyl to my city of Olsztyn, but the cloud moves more slowly. It travels north and west and passes over Prypiat, Minsk, Białystok, and then over unsuspecting bison and wolves in the primeval Biebrzanski National Forest, until it reaches the skies over my Soviet-style apartment building around Sunday evening and drifts northwest, over the Baltic Sea, and then to Sweden. It creeps. It sneaks. It lingers over my head and will linger until at least May 9.

* * *

On that first day, on April 26, unprotected firefighters at Chernobyl put down the flames by the time I wake up, but the blaze inside the radioactive core cannot be extinguished, and so it burns under the surface, sending out deadly plumes that will eventually envelop Europe.

What do I do all weekend? It's safe to assume my brother Tomek and I are mostly outside, avoiding the poisonous atmosphere in our apartment—weekend being the time Mother could drink without risking her employment. We roam the neighborhood, kick a soccer ball with other kids, play in a sandbox, explore the bowels of our eight-story apartment building that leans slightly toward the street even before all the tenants move in. We get into fights with snotty kids from another building, who knows why, the reasons are many—ownership of the only working swing in the neighborhood, a cussword thrown boldly in the direction of a freckled redhead, a water balloon dropped from the seventh floor, a territorial claim on a metal carpet-beating rack that doubled as our gymnastics bar. Someone bursts into tears. Someone returns home with a torn shirt collar. It's all a blur.

* * *

Later, as an adult, when I look at the map of radiation spread over Europe after the explosion, its conical orange shape over the map of Poland and the Baltic states will remind me of one of my favorite mushrooms—chanterelle. A rounded funnel shape, with forked folds tapering down the stipe.

* * *

By April 27, the cloud stretches across the Baltic, its cesium tail perched over my head. Initially, only our region is affected and the rest of Poland is spared, but by the end of April 29, the entire country is under the cloud, which now looks on satellite images like an enormous dragon spreading its wings—one over

Scandinavia and the other over the USSR, its heart beating over the Baltic Sea, its hungry stomach over Poland, its tail below the left wing, stretching toward Asia. The dragon expands and moves southward, over Czechoslovakia, Italy, then France, England, and other countries, and by May 7, it looks again like a gigantic chanterelle waiting to be plucked by a lucky hunter. By May 9, the cloud recedes from most of the western and central European countries, including mine.

* * *

On Sunday, April 27, in our grandparents' apartment, we watch the world cup in hockey, then our evening cartoon about a teddy bear, and then, at 7:30 p.m., Grandpa performs his daily ritual: He boils milk and adds egg-drop noodles, brings the soup to a folded table in front of the TV, and sits down to watch the Communist propaganda the Polish government calls *Dziennik Telewizyjny* (*TV Daily*). Window curtains are billowing in the spring breeze. The cloud is directly over our heads, but the news anchor, in his impeccable haircut and beige suit, is talking about pigs and quotas and preparations for May 1 marches across Poland. Or at least I think he is. The consensus among historians is that neither on Saturday nor Sunday nor even Monday do the Polish press and TV mention Chernobyl.

* * *

Thirty-five years after the core meltdown, when I try to check what exactly the content of the news was on that Sunday, I will learn that the current government in Poland is blocking access to TV archives. In my Indiana home, in the middle of a global pandemic, with a MacBook on my lap and a steaming cup of coffee on a side table, I will read tweets from opposition parties claiming that the reason the archives are closed to the public is the eerie similarity of the propaganda techniques of late Communism to those of the contemporary authoritarian regime. I am less annoyed by the plight of the Polish dissidents in the waning democracy than by the difficulty I face in attempting to deconstruct the events of Chernobyl, Poland's response to it, and the aftermath. I have a burning need to record specific dates, times, measurements, data, data, data. I want to order the history of Chernobyl's impact on Poland in a neat column of chronology, cause and effect, no speculation, no maybe, no perhaps, just order that will send its clear light toward the story of my childhood, a bright beam sent downward from a military helicopter.

* * *

After the news about pigs and quotas and preparations for May 1 marches, Grandpa walks us back to Mother's apartment, where he helps us get ready for bed. Mother is probably asleep in her room, or still drinking at the kitchen table, meditating over yellow cigarette marks on the smooth Formica surface. Perhaps Grandpa opens the window in our bedroom, depending on how warm the night is. After he leaves, Tomek and I play in our beds with my black doll Ania and his humanlike mouse stuffy, Zuzia. Then we tell each other stories about our imaginary family—the Modern Talking duo, Thomas Anders the mother and Dieter Bohlen the father. We sing "You're my heart, you're my soul"—only that's not what we sing because we don't understand the English lyrics, so what comes out of our mouths is something like "Yamaha, Yomaso."

The cloud stretches over our heads by 9 p.m.

* * *

On Monday, April 28, oblivious to the cesium-137 suspended above our city, to high-energy gamma radiation descending on our heads, rooftops, fields, and forests, I walk out on our tiny balcony overlooking the fields that will, a couple decades later, be covered with high-rises and a sprawling shopping mall. I squeeze myself between two clothes-drying ropes, prop my elbows on a planter, watch buses and little Fiats darting past my building, and then stare at the freshly flowering fields, at distant poplars, at the blue sky that does not portend any danger. I put on my navy polyester school uniform, lock the door with a key suspended on a yellow ribbon from my white-collared neck, and step into the elevator.

That day, Sweden detects large amounts of radiation in the air traced back to Ukraine. Scientists in Mikołajki, not far from my hometown, detect radioactivity levels half a million times higher than normal. One day later, a US spy satellite will confirm the Chernobyl explosion.

* * *

On Tuesday, April 29, we drink potassium iodide at school without knowing why. We're not too suspicious because sometimes we have to walk to the nurse's office to drink a shot of *tran,* fish oil, to supplement our horrible diets. *Tran* comes from whales, our teachers tell us, and once a month the nurse gives us a shot glass filled with oil and a piece of stale salted bread to bite into after. So on that Tuesday, things do not seem out of the ordinary when we have to line up in the hallway outside of the nurse's office. Someone behind me whistles Europe's "The Final Countdown," and I join in. Even the sight of classmates barfing all over the staircase doesn't faze me because that sometimes happens with fish oil, too. Most kids hate it. This time, though, the vomit is red, not yellow. And it has a strange smell. What is it that we're told to drink, again? *Jodyna?*

My closest classmates, Dorota and Gosia, who are directly in front of me, start fidgeting. What's iodine? Isn't it the stuff our mothers put on scrapes and wounds? The nasty, stinging purple liquid? You can drink that?

***

Płyn Lugola, or Lugol's iodine, is a solution of potassium iodide with iodine in water. It blocks the absorption of radioactive iodine. Polish scientists, faced with an information blackout from the USSR but hearing rumors of a nuclear disaster east of us, advised giving it to all the children under sixteen to prevent an excessive accumulation of radioactive isotopes in our organs. It was too late for it to make any difference anyway, but at least they tried. The Polish government, in rare defiance of directives from Moscow, decided to send the liquid to all the schools and clinics in the nation. So by the end of the day, people knew something was off, as soon as the kids who had to drink the thick, bitter iodine came home to tell the tale. But it was not until the next day that the official news channel reported on the nuclear catastrophe and the potential danger to the public. Five days after the explosion.

***

On April 30, an anchor appears on *Dziennik Telewizyjny* and reads an official statement from "the government commission" about Chernobyl. The day before, the USSR finally broke silence about the accident, though there was still little information about the scale of destruction. The anchor, stumbling over several words in the report, tells us that milk is safe to drink. That esteemed Soviet scientists are advising our government on safety.

Mother reaches for her beer and laughs.

"Well, if the Soviets are on it, why would we worry?"

I'm old enough to understand sarcasm. I'm old enough to detect panic in her voice. I'm not yet old enough to realize that the beer is there to soothe the panic. And to feed an enormous craving.

"Fucking Soviets." Mother closes the balcony door and all

the windows. She drops the empty beer bottle in the trash and pulls out a bottle of vodka. When I sit at the table next to her, the smell of alcohol is overpowering. I decide not to ask any questions.

* * *

I am in bed, my radio on the lowest volume, close to my ear. My brother is asleep across the room. After Modern Talking's "Brother Louie," which I already have on tape, I hear Cutting Crew's "Died in Your Arms" and press REC. I stop the recording when a man's voice starts droning again. Next is Berlin's "Take My Breath Away." REC.

Like the salted butter dropped from American planes, the evening program on Channel 3 is my gateway to the West. I memorize the sounds—because I don't really understand English yet—of songs by Samantha Fox, Peter Gabriel, Michael Jackson, Whitney Houston, George Michael, and later New Kids on the Block, Metallica, Alice in Chains, and the Sex Pistols.

I hear the front door open and close. Someone is in the hallway. I turn off the radio and hear our neighbor, a pediatrician and Mother's drinking companion, stage-whispering something with urgency. I crawl toward my bedroom door and press my ear against it. ". . . panic in Warsaw . . . iodine doses . . . May Day parade . . ." Then glass clinking in the kitchen. I slip under the cover and lie awake, listening to the hum of cars and buses outside my third-floor window, watching shadows dance on the asbestos ceiling.

* * *

"Mom, I want to go!" My voice is shrill, urgent.

"Not this year."

"You made me the costume! My whole dance group will be there!"

"Not this year. There will be another May Day."

* * *

On May 2, a *Washington Post* foreign correspondent visits a lakeside town not far from my city.

By scientific standards, a storm of lethal radioactive iodine blew in here Monday morning, wreaking unknown and perhaps incalculable damage on Mikolajki's 3,500 people. Yet as they anxiously think back on that day, all residents can remember is that the weather was beautiful, with brilliant sunshine and crisp spring breezes. Polish government experts have since told western reporters that the radiation here was 500 times greater than normal Monday and as much as six times above the accepted international daily safety standard. But Polish media available here censored the news, and shops, schools and even ice cream vendors have been working normally. Children were encouraged to turn out for yesterday's local May Day parade.

The only signs of trouble on May Day are the helicopters overhead and the nausea reported by many people. Children complain about headaches and stomachaches. But on Polish streets, people march in formations, waving white-and-red flags, waving red flags, waving pinwheels and ribbons. In the rolling hills of northeastern Poland, cows graze and swat flies with their tails. Babushkas line up in roadside ditches, selling mushrooms and herbs.

Today, one of the technicians could be seen hurriedly scooping up soil with special protective gloves as children who had been playing nearby crowded around to watch. "Those people, the scientists who have sent their own children out of here, are obviously the best informed," a resident said. "But we, the simple people of Mikolajki, we're stuck here, for better or for worse. There's no way to escape your shadow. There's no way we can escape what happened here."

* * *

In Poland, there are about 12,000 species of mushrooms, more than a thousand of them actually edible. Did we stop picking mushrooms after the Chernobyl disaster? Were we told not to eat vegetables from our gardens? When I search for archival warnings, there is little information, most of it sealed in hard-to-access archives. When I ask friends and family, everyone says that warnings traveled by word of mouth. Someone had an aunt in the Health Department, now regularly visited by secret police, and she said not to eat red currants and leeks. Someone's father, an engineer, kept his windows shut for weeks that summer and switched to powdered milk. Someone continued her mushroom-hunting escapades but avoided boletes. Why boletes and not chanterelles or buttermilk mushrooms? Who knows. We relied on whispered gossip, not facts. The official line was that food was not toxic.

* * *

The *Washington Post* again, reporting after the explosion:

Polish experts appointed to a special government commission told western reporters at a press conference yesterday that they expected an increase in cancer rates as a result of the radiation. The news was censored from the national media, however, and a communique today from the same commission said "no danger existed to the health of the population."

As it turns out, the long-term impact on the population of eastern and central Europe was not as dire as predicted. But tell it to the families of the children who have been fighting thyroid cancer and other illnesses related to radioactive iodine. In 2006 the World Health Organization released a report on Chernobyl's health impact. The *Washington Post* covered the findings in their follow-up on the thirtieth anniversary of the catastrophe:

"Researchers did find a higher-than-usual rate of thyroid cancer, particularly in children who were exposed to the radioactive iodine. The study also noted serious and widespread psychological trauma: Many people reported feelings of 'helplessness and lack of control over their future,' driving some to drink, smoke, and behave recklessly."

A totalitarian regime will do that. If you are not angry or helpless, or both, you are not paying attention. The secret police whose purpose is to create enemies of the state. The middle-of-the-night disappearances of activists. The murders of dissidents. The tell-tale clicks as you pick up the phone, indicating that your conversation is not private. The suppression of freedom of speech. The Orwellian use of language, where occupiers are liberators, bloody suppression of striking workers is peacekeeping, mindless propaganda is art, unpaid volunteer work is obligatory, spying on neighbors and family is honorable. The resulting self-censorship of students, professors, journalists, priests, artists. The constant self-censorship in lines for bread, in lines for toilet paper, in lines for sugar. Add a nuclear disaster, and it's no wonder Poland has had skyrocketing rates of alcoholism, disengagement from local communities, cynicism, distrust of others, widespread theft and vandalism of state property.

* * *

"Mama, do you ever feel like you are an actor in a movie and everyone else is acting, too, and you have the main role that you have to remember, and it's scary because your memory is not too good? Like nothing is real?"

Mother sucks on her cigarette, cheekbones in sharp relief as her jaw muscles cave in, and the outline of the veins on her neck looks like the Vistula River with its many tributaries. She looks at me in silence, then:

"It's very bad to think that way."

"Why?"

"Because everybody feels and thinks independently of you. They are not your props or puppets or shadows. They are humans, with free will, like you."

I lower my gaze, color rising to my face.

* * *

The pines in the so-called Red Forest, destroyed by acute radiation, were bulldozed and buried.

But fungi have had a billion years of evolution to refine one thing: consumption. Mycelium doesn't die. It simply waits until it can produce fruiting bodies—the mushrooms we hunt and eat. Those mushrooms are great barometers of the health of our environment because they "soak up" whatever there is to ingest, including radioisotopes in soil.

After the Chernobyl explosion, Sweden and Finland outlawed the sale and consumption of certain fish when scientists there detected high levels of radiation. Studies also proved that the main source of transfer of radiocesium into humans from the contaminated environment was cow's milk. Cesium-137 also bioaccumulated in mushrooms and wild animals that ate them—mainly boars and deer. But Poles' reliance on foraged mushrooms and wild blueberries for protein, vitamins, and antioxidants didn't change after the explosion. I imagine people in Sweden and Finland had other choices of food. For us, mushrooms and wild berries were a staple, as were vegetables and fruit we grew in our Communist-allotted gardens.

Cesium doesn't simply disappear with heavy rain. A 2010 magazine headline says "24 Years after Chernobyl, Radioactive Boars Still Roam Germany." A report commissioned by the European Parliament on the environmental effects twenty years after the disaster states: "In certain regions of Germany, Austria, Italy, Sweden, Finland, Lithuania and Poland wild game (including boar and deer), wild mushrooms, berries and carnivore fish from lakes reach levels of several thousand Bq per kg of caesium-137." Bq is becquerel, a unit of radiation. In Ukraine alone, about 80 to 95 percent of radiation has been from contaminated food—milk, meat, vegetables, forest foraging. In Great Britain, where sheep grazed on contaminated peat, lamb meat and mutton had to be tested for cesium until 2012.

In 2019 the Federal Office for Radiation Protection in Germany tested wild mushrooms in Bavaria and reported continued contamination of mushrooms with cesium-137, thirty-three years after the disaster. Among the most contaminated were wood hedgehogs, waxy caps, and bay boletus. The report explains: "In arable land, the radiocaesium is fixed onto clay minerals and plant uptake is significantly reduced. In forest soils, the radiocaesium is highly available for plant uptake, which leads to the observed contamination values in mushrooms."

Mushroom hunting continued in my family despite rumors that the fungi were contaminated. Hidden under the tree canopy, deep in the silent forest, there was a feeling of safety unavailable in crowded buses, shabby apartments divided by paper-thin walls, offices where everyone listened. Here, among pine trees and poplars and oaks, we could say whatever we pleased without risking arrest. There was mystery in the deep forest that the constant surveillance of the totalitarian state could not touch. And the mushrooms! They looked so innocent, robust, toothsome. How could we think of them as toxic when we bent over porcinis and boletes and inhaled their earthiness, when we squeezed their meaty flesh and cut the stalks close to the ground with a small knife, when we dropped them into a sizzling pan with salt, pepper, and onions?

* * *

Wild animals reclaimed the exclusion zone in and near Chernobyl. Nowadays you can spot Eurasian lynx, Przewalski's horse, gray wolves, brown bears, European badgers, bison, mice, voles, eagles, owls, and more species roaming the area that is very much like a nature preserve. Biodiversity in and around the evacuated area in Chernobyl has increased. Humans are gone. Nature thrives.

But I resist the temptation to turn this wildlife recovery into a simple story of nature's resilience. Barn swallows, for example, that returned to the area in much lower numbers, had a much higher frequency of physical abnormalities than before the explosion. Scientists note a higher occurrence of tumors in these birds as well as partially albinistic plumage and deformities in their toes, tail feathers, beaks, and air sacks.

A 2022 magazine article asks: "Is Chernobyl a radioactive wasteland reeling from chronic radiation, or a post-nuclear paradise with thriving populations of animals and other life forms?" The author, Katarina Zimmer, says that studies don't agree about levels of mutations and other ill effects in the aftermath of the explosion. She points to the debate in the scientific literature about "the health of the microbes, fungi, plants and animals that live around Chernobyl."

* * *

The first reactor in Chernobyl was launched in 1978, the year I was born. The core meltdown and fire happened when I was eight. After the fire was contained, ten days after the explosion, 400,000 cubic feet of cement and 7,000 tons of steel were poured over the surface of Reactor Number 4 to seal its radioactive corium, uranium, and plutonium and the toxic lava made of zirconium, graphite, and sand that had seeped into the basement. Ten years later, when I was writing my high school matriculation exams and planning escape from my increasingly unhinged mother, Ukraine started reinforcing the structure, whose shelf life was only a decade. In 2012, ten years after I moved from Poland to the US, specialists designed and began construction of a new sarcophagus on top of the old one, a cover called The Arc that is supposed to last a century.

But the sense of safety is illusory. Reactor Number 4 will remain highly radioactive for 20,000 years. Many scientists claim that the area will never be truly clean, that all we can do is contain the smoldering contents under the sarcophagus. Meanwhile, the 2020 wildfires that threatened the exclusion zone proved that danger can only be postponed until a new crisis arises. That crisis happened just a couple days before I wrote this paragraph, when Putin bombed the site and later took control over the exclusion zone.

Meanwhile, new fission reactions unknown to us form and transform under The Arc.

* * *

My family too built a sarcophagus. Mother's alcoholism and mental instability were taboo subjects even though alcoholism was as common in Communist Poland as a sneeze. The shame of her divorce, suicide attempts, drunkenness, violent behavior, and involuntary treatments in psychiatric hospitals was hidden under polite greetings and lukewarm smiles we exchanged with neighbors we didn't trust and classmates we wanted to impress. On the surface, my grandparents maintained the façade of Catholic respectability. Weekly pilgrimages to church in freshly ironed Sunday clothes, donations to the parish, First Communions and Confirmations, Easter blessings of baskets filled with eggs, bread, and salt, rules about whom Tomek and I could play with and who was not "our sort," theater tickets, dance tournaments, good grades in school, clean uniforms, new textbooks, spelling bees, math Olympiads, Grandma's accounting degree, Grandpa's master's degree in economics, Mother's master's degree in Polish literature and later certifications in English, rows and rows of books in Mother's home and in Grandma's home, classics, philosophy, history—our sarcophagus was well constructed and well maintained, most of the time. Except when cracks occurred and the fission could no longer be contained within the four walls of our apartment. But even then—when it was obvious that neighbors heard the demonic screaming and furniture crashing against walls, when Mother's gait was clearly unsteady as she returned from a two-minute trip to throw away trash, when she had to be dragged home from Uncle's birthday celebration kicking and spewing profanities that echoed against the drab high-rises, when window curtains moved, betraying the presence of witnesses to this spectacle—even then, the very next morning, we went on with our lives as usual. We said "*Dzień Dobry*" to neighbors we passed by on the stairs, and maybe they didn't quite look us in the eye, but they never asked any questions. Of course there must have been whispers and tongue clicking and shaking of heads. We chatted with friends during recess, avoiding the ones who lived in the same building and must have heard Mother yelling, "You whore! You fucking bitch!" either at Grandma or at me the night before, or maybe saw her throw a can of sardines at a checkout lady at the store. When Grandma's brothers and their families visited, we opened wine or vodka to celebrate our reunions as if there were not an alcoholic in our home, as if tempting Mother to have a shot and another and another was no big deal. Her suicide attempts were swept under the rug. Mushrooms, we said. Heart problems, we said. Not once did we acknowledge that underneath the pretense of respectable Catholic intelligentsia was violence, abuse, neglect, and vulgar name-calling that—Tomek and I were told at the dinner table—was the domain of the urine-soaked homeless drunks we sometimes passed by in our staircase, pinching our noses.

I dismantle the layers of concrete and steel, scratch at the radioactive bowels of the sarcophagus, resurrect the nightmares of the past, and begin the cleanup. Like the Ukrainian and Soviet "liquidators," I am told to take it easy, to work in short spurts lest the toxic dust settle in my lungs, my liver, my blood.

* * *

I reach for a clear round box of sugared jellies in a Polish shop on Chicago's Milwaukee Avenue. I can smell the smoked sausages lined up behind me, some with juniper, others with garlic, and I hear the checkout lady say to a customer, "*Wie Pani, bo w Polsce to by tego nie było.*" You know this wouldn't happen in Poland.

I listen in because I want to know what would not have happened in Poland. But then I'm distracted by the box again. The candies are shaped like an orange slice, arranged in a concentric pattern, colorful and bright. I know that my kids, who are waiting in the car with my husband, afraid to brave the late-spring snowfall, would love to eat the jellies on our way back to Indiana, but something stops me from putting the box in my cart. Instead, I grab milk fudge and *bezy,* the smoky smell from the meat counter still tickling my nostrils despite my N95 mask.

As we drive south on I-94 Express, I google my friend Dorota's name, curious what happened to her. Last time I saw her, we were both in college, a chance meeting at a bus stop after a decade of silence, an awkward "Hi, is this you?" followed by her rush to board a bus. To my untrained eye back then, the radioactive jelly had had no impact on her health as I watched her exhale cigarette smoke and balance her feet on an uneven curb.

I want to ask her now if she remembers that morning, the jelly, the iodine. But Google gives me no answers other than a public document assessing the value of her apartment, in the same building we grew up in, which she must have inherited from her parents. She could have changed her name, or maybe she's savvy about her online privacy.

My daughter screams in delight when she sees a sea of windmills along I-65, and my mind flies back to the Midwest, to my noisy children in the back seat, to our dinner plans. After eating out for almost a week in Chicago, I look forward to a home-cooked meal. There is a pint of puffball soup in the freezer, which I made last fall after loading the giant mushrooms into my trunk, to my tween son's embarrassment. The snow is no longer falling, but it's still cold for early April, and I think how perfect it will be to dip a spoon in the steaming garlicky mushroom soup once we arrive home.

Hunger

July 2015. My office phone rings in the morning silence. I take my fingers off the keyboard, annoyed to be interrupted so close to finishing my grant report.

"Agata? I think you need to come home." My husband's voice is quiet, hesitant.

"Wait . . . I just got in a couple hours ago. You know I have a deadline. Did you get sausages for the cookout?"

"I think we need to cancel the cookout."

"What happened? Are you okay?"

"Your brother called."

My breath catches. Why is he silent? I look at the tree branches outside the large arched window, at the empty parking lot, at the lush arboretum. Somewhere in the old building, a floor creaks.

"About your mom."

I know from his voice and from the silences between the words that this is the last dreadful phone call about Mother. I wait for more but want this pause to last and last and last because I know what comes at the end of the silence.

The sprawling magnolia is still, its leaves undisturbed by wind. After spring rains, its pink flowers blanket the path to the main entrance of the redbrick building with its high ceilings and large portraits of important men, benevolent and demure, looking down on the growing number of female professors in the all-male college where I teach. Now, in July, the magnolia is green, its branches spreading above the lawn where squirrels forage and chatter.

Just three weeks ago, Mother opened the heavy front door to her apartment, and I inhaled cigarette smoke and mint as she gave me a hug, squeezing me so hard her arms trembled. A kiss on the cheek and I walked in, my son following closely, attached to my dress hem. Mother had bought *szarlotka*—apple cake—and some eclairs that sat on a brown Pyrex plate I recognized from my childhood. The sheer lace curtains billowed, but the living room was still heavy with nicotine and something else, something like an old person's smell, though Mother seemed groomed and clean. Her hair was washed, though long black roots spread down almost to her ears, where the dark met yellow dye. Her face was ashen, sweaty. She wore a dark-purple blouse, light-purple vest, and plum skirt. Monochromatic, she used to explain to us whenever we questioned her insistence on wearing single-color outfits from head to toe.

"Ready?" I didn't want to sit down, worried how much smoke my son would inhale here if we lingered.

We walked to a neighborhood restaurant serving traditional Polish fare—pierogi, *bigos, schabowe, gołabki,* pork chops. She walked slowly, propping herself on my elbow, and I had to remind my boy not to run too far ahead. When summer sun hit the windows in the apartment buildings we passed, I almost forgot just how dreary my district was in the fall and winter. The slums of Olsztyn. The most densely inhabited area in the city, with four-to-ten-story buildings squeezed into a flattened top of a windy hill, uneven sidewalks, swastikas and anarchy signs graffitied on walls and trash containers, snotty kids swinging on *trzepaki*—the metal racks designed for carpet beatings that became social hubs for neighborhood drunks and free-range brats. As we crawled toward the restaurant, I noticed that some high-rise facades were freshly painted with pastel pink and cream colors more befitting a Miami neighborhood than the Communist-era concrete behemoths in northeastern Poland.

"Mama, you need to see a doctor. You can't live with daily stomachache and tremors. Do you eat enough?"

"*Oj tam.*" Whatever. "I eat."

"I'll buy some mint tea for you on our way back."

"I have mint. It doesn't help. I'll take more ibuprofen." She was sixty but walked as if she were a hundred years old, each step a challenge. Before we entered the restaurant, she pulled out a cigarette and told us she'd join us in a moment.

I ordered potato pancakes for my son and sauerkraut-mushroom pierogi for myself. Mother asked for pork chops. We sat in the beer garden and watched my son color Dora the Explorer sheets dappled with the afternoon sun. Mother ate a couple bites of her meat and lit another cigarette. She didn't ask why my son could suddenly eat potato pancakes, after several years of a special diet. Last time she'd seen us, he was thin, barely eating. Even then we didn't really talk about his illness, my desperate attempts to make his amino-acid-based formula palatable, the long nights I spent online, reading medical studies and statistics, exchanging tips on parenting forums.

* * *

This is what being unable to feed your child looks like:

Mickey button, you hear from the nurse. You sit in a pastel-colored room that could be mistaken for a family bathroom at Disney World, jungle animals smiling at you deliriously from the wallpaper, palm trees, split coconuts lying in the sand, waiting for you to dig into their fleshy white interior.

Fucking ridiculous name, you think. Fucking Mickey, insinuating himself even into a bleached hospital room. The GI specialist has already told you that your child's esophagus reacts to all protein with severe inflammation. A healthy esophagus is not supposed to have eosinophils—disease-fighting white blood cells. When a biopsy shows 15 to 20 of those little fuckers per high-power field, it means there's a problem. When it reveals over 120, something is really wrong.

It all started when your son refused to nurse. He refused to eat. He withered. His pediatrician called you hysterical when you asked for a referral to a specialist. A lactation nurse would not help. Your son's head bobbed above the carpet and fell down, his undernourished body exhausted, his muscle tone like a wilted parsnip. After each refused meal, you cry uncontrollably in your locked bedroom. What mother cannot find a way to feed her baby?

You scoured the internet for answers—moms' groups, message boards, university medical centers—while your son's pediatrician continued saying that he was okay, despite dropping below zero on his growth chart. You finally went to another doctor, who sent you immediately to a children's hospital. It would be a while before answers arrived. One day, you would be sitting in an office with a kind pediatric GI specialist who would tell you that your son's endoscopy and biopsy revealed an advanced case of eosinophilic esophagitis.

Food is pain. The first pediatrician tells you not to worry, that no child will starve himself to death. But one of the specialists you consult later will say: "Yes, kids with this condition will starve." Because starving is better than the excruciating pain in their throat, than constant choking and vomiting. Your child is put on steroids and an amino-acid formula, which he refuses. You can't blame him. The stuff is nasty, as if someone mixed vomit with metallic shavings and added sawdust to the mix, plus a dash of vanilla. It also costs a fortune—each can the price of your weekly grocery bill.

And throughout this battle to save your son from starving, you think back to Communist Poland with nostalgia—to its humane maternity leave, generous sick leave, its free health care.

On the door to the hospital room where the nurse tells you about the Mickey button, there is a laminated sign, red and angry: "ABSOLUTELY NO FOOD AND DRINK IN THIS ROOM." Not that you'd want to dig into a sandwich or milkshake in a place smelling of chlorine. But this is a room visited by children and adults who cannot dig into anything—french fries, chicken nuggets, pizza, juicy steak, a bowl of cereal, white coconut flesh. This is all out of reach, forbidden. This is a room where inexperienced mothers of nine-month-olds who simply refuse to nurse or eat their mashed peas and carrots and applesauce and rice pudding learn how to operate all the components of the feeding tube attached to the box on one end and to their children's stomachs on the other. This is a room where parents experience defeat. This is a room where denial ends. This is a room where grief begins.

Your infant son has refused everything that came near his mouth—breast milk, special formula, homemade organic GMO-free mashed winter squash, sweet potato mush straight from a glass jar with a delightfully chubby Gerber baby smiling right at you, intentional and malicious. That chubby little fucker looks at you, jeering: *My mama knew how to feed me. But you? You failed at the most basic function of motherhood. You cannot feed your baby.*

In that pastel-colored room in the hospital for children, where everyone is trying to help you, you resent the nurses for being so kind and sympathetic. You want them to slap you in the face and yell, *Wake up, you've been doing it wrong, it's such a simple thing, feeding a baby, here's how you do it without Mickey buttons drilled into your son's flesh, without rubber tubing, with-*

out hypoallergenic amino acid–based formulas that cost as much as a luxury car.

"He hates food," you tell one feeding therapist, then another. You learn how to do vestibular exercises. You learn the word *vestibular.* You watch the therapist swing your son in circles before a meal, singing: "Vestibular, vestibular, vestibular!" She dips a bright-yellow banana-shaped fork in a bowl of mashed bananas, only to see it land on the floor after a swipe. You watch her scooping mashed potatoes with a tractor-shaped spoon only to see it fly toward the wall. You hear her say, "Poke, poke, poke" in a sing-song voice to encourage your son to at least touch his food only to hear him cry when the plate is too close to his fingers. You see her kiss a silicone spoon and then encourage your son to kiss his silicone spoon dipped in chocolate ice cream only to trace the arc of the spoon as it bounces against the pantry door. You pump breast milk into hundreds of plastic and glass bottles, large baggies, small baggies, and then put the milk in the fridge. When the fat separates on top, you scoop up the rich layer and consolidate. Then you try feeding this enhanced, nutrition-packed breast milk to your son with a bottle, which he slaps in anger. You pump more. The rhythmic sucking and releasing of air on your hospital-grade Medela breast pump sounds like a simple Polish verse: *i chuj, i chuj, i chuj.* Fuck this, fuck this, fuck this. Repeat.

So in that hospital room, you agree to learn how to use a feeding tube. That fucking Mickey button.

"Can you show me?" you ask, leaning closer to the nurse, all tense, all tired, all sad.

And your child senses the fear in you, and he also sees the coiled tubing and the complicated instruction manual, and so he grabs the bottle from your hand, downs eight ounces of the nasty metal shavings on his own, no help, no coercion, no crying and begging, no vestibular. And you look at your husband and then at the nurse, and you say you will be back, but right now you want to go home and celebrate. And once home, you will call your son's feeding therapist and scream into the receiver, "He drank eight ounces! He drank eight ounces!" And she will know that this moment is as important to you as a child's first step, and she will cry with you, wiping her snot on a sleeve.

* * *

If I had known in the summer of 2015, when I slowly walked with Mother to eat pierogi at a neighborhood restaurant, that it was my last meal with her, would I have made it special? Would we have gone somewhere else, perhaps to a Greek place by a little waterfall, or a fancy white-cloth restaurant in the old town? Would I ask whether she had any regrets, or what she was proud of, when she was happiest, what she would have changed?

Instead, I chewed my greasy pierogi in silence, interrupting only to cut another pancake bite for my son. I watched Fiats and Opels and Hyundais drive by. I waved flies away.

"Do you want to take the rest of the pork chop home? You didn't eat much."

"I'm not that hungry. I think I just need to lie down and rest." Mother tapped on the cigarette, and the ashes fell down on the pavement.

"Should I call a taxi?"

"No need to pay for a taxi. We can walk back."

Back in her place, she popped two ibuprofen in her mouth and covered herself with a duvet despite the heat. I stood in the hallway, one hand on the door handle, another on my son's head.

"Say *do widzenia to babcia*. We are flying back in two days."

My son hugged Mother through her thick duvet. I think I kissed her temple. I want to believe I kissed her temple. I hope I kissed her temple. As we walked to a bus stop, my son and I passed by a dry cleaner's and laundry service, and I inhaled the familiar smell of freshly pressed cotton. Next door, in the same building, there used to be Klub Muza, a dance studio where I spent years practicing sambas, rumbas, and paso dobles in front of large mirrors, sweat steaming off my skin. My son and I moved past a youth club where I had taken my first guitar lessons, where I lip-synched to a song from *Dirty Dancing* during a karaoke contest, where I fell in and out of love with neighborhood boys. We waited for a bus to take us to my brother's place at the same stop where I began my commute to high school every dark morning.

"It's a good thing we didn't get lost, Mama!" My son's large eyes reveal a sense of accomplishment. My little country boy who runs barefoot through grass and thistles, fearlessly jumps into Indiana lakes infested with water snakes, and hops on his trampoline in driving snow has now reached another level: He didn't get lost in the dense maze of concrete where everyone spoke Polish and looked at him suspiciously when he shouted "Hi!" to strangers loaded with plastic bags or tugging their dogs away from other dogs' poop coiling on narrow strips of grass.

* * *

I knew the concrete maze through and through. No pastel pinks and creams would fool me into taking a wrong turn. I had spent most of my free time in these streets, on *trzepaki,* running after or away from someone along the cracked sidewalks, munching on sunflower seeds on muddy curbs and spitting the shells out into gutters, drinking vodka straight from the bottle at abandoned bus stops, playing stalking games with rival gangs, breaking up fights, starting fights, teasing neighborhood drunks. Blindfolded, I would know where I was: The smell of fresh bread would lead me to the bakery; the smell of fish to the local market; the smell of old urine to the underground crosswalk where skinheads drank cheap wine. If I followed the screeching of bus breaks, I'd find the bus stop. Even the sound of bus doors opening and closing could tell me which number it was because Number 2 buses were shorter and older, and their doors rattled, whereas the longer articulated buses, usually Number 11, had doors that closed with a sigh. Back in Mother's apartment, I could tell which floor the elevator stopped at based on the intensity of its click, what hour of the morning it was as long as I could hear the cars outside, which family had a birthday celebration when I heard the *Sto Lat* echo through our staircase. I knew what my neighbors ate for dinner because I could smell their boiled cabbage or fried mushrooms.

Even the streets leading out of our district and toward more exciting parts of the city—to theaters and cinemas, to dance clubs and dive bars, to universities and parks and beaches—were no match for my friends and me. We knew the route of all the buses, and we knew at which stops the conductors were likely to check tickets, and we knew which door to kick out and in which direction to run. Sometimes we biked to the old town. Sometimes we walked.

On days when I skipped school, I stayed on the bus two additional stops and got off in the old town by the fourteenth-century Upper Gate, a massive gothic structure that used to serve as an armory, a customs point for people entering the city, a jail, and finally a hotel. I often stopped for tea and *pączki* at a café overlooking a narrow cobblestone street, next door to a brothel. I walked through streets flanked by gingerbread houses, shops, and restaurants, still empty and quiet, toward the fourteenth-century castle that once housed Copernicus. If I didn't see anyone I knew in the *fosa*—the punk moat—I'd keep walking through a park toward a viaduct, climb the grassy hill toward the train tracks, and look at the city.

I was rarely alone, though. Friends skipped school with me.

We smoked menthol cigarettes and talked about poets and rock bands. The artists that impressed us the most were drug addicts and rebels. We read their biographies and liked to think of ourselves as nonconformists and rejects. We were punks. We were children fleeing booze-soaked homes, fleeing strict teachers and tedious homework assignments, fleeing dress codes and church doctrines.

In all this flight, we had each other. Like geese flying in formation over long distances, we traveled through the city along familiar migratory paths, resting for a time at *trzepak*, the *fosa* or the viaduct or an old cemetery, some of us knowing we couldn't return home just yet. Sometimes my brother joined me in this wandering, but he had his own tight-knit group of friends as he got older and didn't require much handholding on my part. Some of our homes were uninhabitable because of addiction, some because of poverty, some because of overcrowding, some because of violence. When kids from a "good home" joined us at a punk concert or drank cheap wine with us at a riverbank, I would look at them with wonder. Unicorns among cement slabs and filth, the kids got high on our lawlessness and returned to their Equestria filled with stories.

We? We were slime mold making our way through labyrinthine streets, extending our tentacles toward sources of nourishment—a *bułka* pilfered from a bakery, a bottle of wine, a handful of pills.

* * *

Sheldrake says in *Entangled Life* that Japanese scholars once made models of Tokyo in petri dishes, with oats representing urban hubs, and bright lights (the enemy of slime molds) standing for obstacles. The mold, without the aid of a central nervous system, found the most efficient route to oat flakes within one day, replicating Tokyo's existing public transportation network.

Someone apparently did a similar experiment with models of IKEA stores, slime mold moving steadily toward the exit and avoiding obstacles. Then researchers used slime molds to design efficient fire evacuation routes from buildings.

Fungi always find ways to nutrition. They find ways out of labyrinths. They devour. They escape.

The process of fungal hyphae seeking other hyphae to merge with is called "homing." It's a pleasant-sounding word, *homing,* like a wave that gently lifts you up and carries you toward safety. An exhale followed by *ooooeeee* like an *ommmmmmm,* the mantra chanted at the beginning of yoga sessions, the nasal consonants vibrating with possibility.

Without homing, there could be no fungi.

If I had left Mother's apartment to wander city streets alone, if I had not had my grandparents' safe space to return to when I was tired of smoking and drinking, when I was hungry and cold, I would have ended up in one of the abandoned houses with heroin addicts strewn on the floor. Homing happens because the fungus searches for nourishment. I found mine in Grandma Iza's kitchen, in my friend Paula's apartment, on a bench with Gosia and Dorota and Darek when we split bread and *kiełbasa* and chased them down with *kefir.* I found nourishment in conversations with my brother even when we grew apart as teens, each seeking our own network. And I sought meaning and acceptance in my first relationships with boys and men, relationships Mother turned a blind eye to and Grandma was too innocent to suspect me of.

* * *

There were men, but oh, what's the point of naming the awkward grammar teachers, fiery-haired drummers on motorcycles, pot-bellied jazz guitarists smelling of horseradish, draft-dodging doughnut bakers, Italian veterinary students, and the unsuspecting classmates who confused my braided blond hair with innocence? I clung to them with the zeal of a hungry inmate. I yearned for attention and love, and that's what they gave me. One called me a guitarist's mascot, not a guitarist, even though I practiced for him each morning, repeating arpeggios with increasing speed until my fingers bled, but he wasn't interested in my fingers unless they clutched his flabby penis in the back seat of his Volvo.

* * *

In my adopted home of small-town Indiana, I sit in my cavernous reading chair and reread Sheldrake's *Entangled Life.* The book opens to page 40, where I previously marked a simple pencil-drawn illustration of a nematode being devoured by fungal mycelia coiling around the worm, starving it of nutrients, taking up its space, trapping it in a series of rapidly produced nooses. It's a black-and-white drawing, shaded in parts to distinguish the prey from the hunter. Why am I drawn to it?

* * *

During the COVID-19 pandemic, paralyzed by my inability to act, I eventually decide to Marie Kondo my house. As I look through books I haven't seen in years, I find two small, square hardbacks in Polish: *Matki i córki: miłość która łączy* (*Mothers and Daughters: The Love That Binds*) and *Moja córka, moja radość* (*My Daughter, My Joy*). I vaguely remember receiving these as birthday gifts from Mother.

On the covers are reproductions of paintings: Amedeo Bocchi's *In the Meadow* and Dora Hitz's *Girl in a Poppy Field.* Inside them, decontextualized quotations about mothers and daughters from Mae West, bell hooks, Maya Angelou, Margaret Drabble, Louisa May Alcott. Also a Navajo song. On the back cover of one book, a neon-orange price sticker: 17 zł 90 gr.

Both gift books were first printed in China for the US audience. These are Polish translations, and now I attempt to find the original sources for the quotes. This circuitous exercise leads me to less saccharine truths about motherhood. In 1976 Rich wrote: "That earliest enwrapment of one female body with another can sooner or later be denied or rejected, felt as choking possessiveness, as rejection, trap, or taboo; but it is, at the beginning, the whole world." In "It Is Hard to Write about My Own Mother," she admits that "the institution of motherhood finds all mothers more or less guilty of having failed their children" and recalls her own anger at her mother, "the ancient, unpurged anger of the child."

Rich continues:

But if a mother had deserted us, by dying, or putting us up for adoption, or because life had driven her into alcohol or drugs, chronic depression or madness, . . . or if she had simply left us because she needed to live without a child—whatever our rational forgiveness, whatever the individual mother's love and strength, the child in us, the small female who grew up in a male-controlled world, still feels, at moments, wildly unmothered.

* * *

In one of the gift books, there is a reproduction of Frank Dicksee's *The Mother*. It's hard to distinguish between a mother and a daughter in this painting, but the one who looks a little older is cradling a rosy-cheeked young woman in her arms, her hand smoothing the daughter's hair, as if to say, *Hush, don't cry, I'm here.*

* * *

I'm tempted to think of Mother in black-and-white terms. Some evenings, when I'm exhausted by chasing my kids around the house and reach for a can of beer, I feel compassion spreading through my veins for a woman who simply responded to biochemical triggers telling her to drink. Our bodies are chemically irritable and fragile. It takes effort, a reliable support network, a sense of purpose, to disentangle from addiction. And then on other days, when I snuggle with my children while we watch *Encanto* for the forty-seventh time, when I breathe in their smell and worry about their vulnerability, I feel angry, cheated out of this experience of closeness and safety when I myself was a child.

Mother was not simply an alcoholic whose only longing was to satisfy her chemical craving. Neither was she a lost soul whose erratic and aggressive behavior could only be explained by epigenetic trauma and illness. I want to know her, now that she is dead. I want to study the underground currents behind her decisions and rejections, the gentle streams and treacherous vortexes of her soul, the emotions strong enough to keep her alive, to botch her suicide attempts, yet not strong enough to make her present for her children and parents. The easiest way to explain her behavior is to blame it all on the biochemistry of alcohol addiction and mental illness. But Mother was more than an addict. She was a petulant child. She was a shy but inquisitive teenager. She was a student of Polish literature, an avid reader of biographies and crime novels. She was a good friend to other lost souls, other broken people—neighbors with addictions and mental disorders, her students who struggled in broken homes, her lovers who appreciated her subtle beauty and voracious appetites, lost and sick animals that came to our apartment to heal. Who was she, really? And how much of her do I have in me? How much of that inheritance should I be grateful for, and how much should I fear?

* * *

Back to Sheldrake: "Imagine that you could pass through two

doors at once. It's inconceivable, yet fungi do it all the time. When faced with a forked path, fungal hyphae don't have to choose one or the other. They can branch and take both routes." I, too, passed through two doors at once. I was a devout Catholic girl—Communion, Confirmation, mass, church songs, and all—and a rebel getting drunk and experimenting with drugs and sex. I was a good student, straight As until about eighth grade, always reading, praised for good behavior at school, but also a pathological truant, a loudmouth saying *kurwa* a lot, as long as teachers didn't hear me. At Grandma's I did my homework and practiced scales on my guitar, but at Mother's I turned into a feral teen disappearing from home for days.

As an adult I wanted to leave Mother behind, cut off contact, heal. I fled across the Atlantic to facilitate this healing. Yet I was unable to turn away. I called, even though I knew she'd pick up and slur "*Słucham*?" in a drunken stupor that made my blood boil. I sent her money for bills and food only to see it spent on vodka for herself and her crowd. On my annual visits home, even if I stayed with my brother, I still went to see Mother only to turn away at the door at the sight of her stumbling and bleary-eyed, at the overpowering smell of cigarettes and booze.

Pathway branching benefits fungi. But it stunted my healing. Whatever trite metaphor I choose to describe what I should have done—burn the bridge, turn off the light and shut the door, buy a one-way ticket—it wasn't trite enough, I guess, to impress itself on my brain back then, first in South Carolina, then in Indiana. I reached out to her again and again like an addict seeking poison.

* * *

I reach deep in my memory to excavate ways in which I can love and support my children. I reach back to the nights when I wetted my bed and was soothed by Grandma's gentle voice, the nights when I lay feverish and clammy, with Grandma by my side, singing about brave soldiers dying for Poland, the afternoons I spent in the kitchen while she made red currant juice. I reach back to her patience and forgiveness and love, and I still draw from that source, as an imperfect mother who is learning. This constant becoming is what Sheldrake points to when he talks about mushrooms: "A mycelial network is a map of a fungus's recent history and is a helpful reminder that all life forms are in fact *processes* not *things.*"

* * *

"Your brother called."

Magnolia branches, a large arched window, an empty parking lot, a lush arboretum, a creaking floor.

"About your mom."

"Oh my god." I exhale.

Josh's voice is now so quiet I guess at the sounds.

"Please don't drive now. We will come get you in ten minutes. Stay where you are."

* * *

A red-eye Lufthansa flight, bread rolls with butter, Arcade Fire and Massive Attack on my iPod, no sleep, no tears. I replay my brother's voice in my head: She was taken to the hospital with burst ulcers. Ripped out the IV lines she was hooked up to and walked out of the hospital in her nightgown. Took a taxi home. Probably couldn't stay away from alcohol long enough to allow the doctors to treat her. This kind of hunger you don't play with. This kind of hunger can kill you.

Three days after she walked out of the hospital, her boyfriend climbed into her apartment through an open window and found her dead in her bed. Police, coroner. My brother thought it was a sick joke when the police asked him to the precinct to testify.

* * *

A photo: A black-and-white snapshot of Mother, dressed in a stylish turtleneck sweater and a jacket, leaning over my cot, awkwardly reaching for my plump arm, her mouth open, but not in a smile. Is she saying something to me? It doesn't look like she's cooing, but then I wouldn't be able to tell for sure because her eyes are covered by her hair. I look straight up at her, my fists balled up, as infants' fists often are, and I look like I'm readying myself to fend off a blow in a boxing match. We're both frozen in time, alert, eternally waiting for what's going to happen next. This is how I remember my entire childhood—always waiting. I anticipated a drunken yell, or a thud against the floor in Mother's bedroom, or the sound of breaking glass. I learned to read silences. There was the silence of Mother's sleeping, when I knew I should just go ahead and try to clothe and feed myself and my brother. There was the silence of Mother's lonely drinking at the Formica kitchen table as the ashtray filled with cigarette butts. There was the silence of Mother gone to look for alcohol or perhaps to stand in line for bread or sugar or a scrap of meat.

* * *

"Mama, did your mother ever hug your brain?" asks my preschooler as we munch on our noon quesadillas.

* * *

So now I'm writing about that which I can no longer delay: Mother's death, the real death, not the attempted and botched ones we experienced so often as children and teens. I wanted to start with her death but couldn't will my fingers to type up any reflection about Mother's passing. Instead, I wrote about mushrooms and blood and fat, and I delayed. It took five years of therapy and growth to write these sentences: Mother did not directly kill herself, but she willed her death. She chose to go home and drink rather than heal. She did not love herself enough to save her own life. Her hunger for alcohol was stronger than her hunger for life.

What did she feel in those final moments? I imagine searing pain. I imagine fear. I imagine immense loneliness one can drown in, lungs filled with aloneness. I don't imagine regret. She would have thought, *Hurry up now, hurry up.* She would have clenched her teeth with impatience at the slowness of dying, the discomfort and indignity of going in and out of consciousness as the pain spread across her abdomen, as blood seeped into her organs, as the alcohol entered her veins and coursed inside her withering body, as her hair, wet with sweat, clung to her forehead and ears. She did not call the hospital. I don't think she wanted to be saved.

Six years after her death, I will open a news article about Rep. Debbie Dingell (D-Mich.), who woke up at night with intense abdominal pain and after an emergency surgery learned that it was a perforated ulcer caused by her long-term use of ibuprofen. As it turns out, ibuprofen reduces our ability to make a layer of mucus protecting our stomach from gastric acid. Dingell, who was sixty-seven at that time, said that the pain from the perforated ulcer was intense: "I was just on fire. I could barely walk, it hurt so much."

Doctors say that apart from ibuprofen use, there are other risk factors for ulcers: smoking and using alcohol heavily, both of which Mother had done for decades. The police found a lot of empty vodka and beer bottles in her apartment, lots of pills. Right before her death, she drank and took a handful of ibuprofen. Not enough to kill a healthy person but enough to kill her.

* * *

While reading up on fungi, I come across a song from the Central African Republic, performed by Aka people: "Women Gathering Mushrooms." I listen to the recording. Among the chirping of birds and high-pitched calls of cicadas, the women's voices rise and fall, following different but compatible melodies that twist and turn and twine around each other. A multitrack song emerges even though there is no lead tune, like mycelium.

Mother's life was a polyphony, too, often set against the sounds of nature, sometimes against Polish libation songs, or Leonard Cohen, or the Beatles. It was certainly a song composed of many melodies, without a seeming plan or design, without much forethought, without an awareness or fear of consequences, but out of these disparate melodies a song emerges, a terrifying, sublime song of a broken yet beautiful human being, a song whose meaning I will never be able to parse no matter how many pages I cover with feeble attempts.

Mother's impact on me was not just toxic, though that's the side of her I remember most vividly. I catch glimpses of her youthful enthusiasm, her love for animals, her sensitivity and creativity that were mostly hidden from me. To do that, I have to dig, hunt, and disturb the quiet surface of my family's life several years after her death.

* * *

Her imprint on the bed. Her scarves. The peeling wallpaper. *Melina.*

I stand on the peeling linoleum floor with my back to Mother's closet. Tomek asked me to pick items from her apartment that I wanted to keep. I grabbed a couple of books, a black scarf with a red rose pattern, and a pair of burgundy sunglasses. Her bed hasn't been touched since the coroner's office took her body. I see a gentle indentation in the sheet, an almost imperceptible dip. Someone must have flung the duvet to the side to pick her up, and now, several days later, all that is left of my mother is this imprint of her body on the bed.

I imagine her lying there, still alive.

And I'm assaulted with a memory. *Mama, wake up. We're hungry.*

What was she thinking back then, when we were children, as she poured the pills into her cupped palm like a handful of dry lentils, as she felt their fullness in her mouth, as she moved them to the back of her throat with her tongue, as she swallowed and swallowed and felt her esophagus expand with the sheer weight of death? She must have put her head down on the pillow while she waited for oblivion, our voices drifting from the bedroom as Tomek and I molded zebras and hippos out of clay and argued who was going to be the zookeeper and smeared our fingers with glue, making a fence for alligators out of matchsticks. In that interval between swallowing and drifting off into nothingness, was she relieved? Did she panic for a moment? Did she regret? I imagine her anguish so unbearable that she welcomed the wave of inertia and the world slowly receding behind a veil of silence and darkness. I have to imagine it because I have no comparable experience to latch onto, no pain so deep that I would willingly abandon my children to make it end.

Only later will I learn, from the medical records my brother sends me, how she explained that first—was it the first? who knows?—suicide attempt. The records are poorly copied case history documents and intake forms from one of the hospitals in which Mother was treated.

May 5, 1986
Diagnosis: depression

The patient overdosed pills and was treated at the City Hospital. The consulting psychiatrist suggested the transfer to the psychiatric hospital for observation. There is no history of mental illness or anxiety in the patient's family. The patient is a high school teacher. Married, for a few years separated from her husband. Mother of two children.

The reason for the suicide attempt was "probably a series of minor problems . . . I assessed my situation as meaningless . . . I watered my little plants and . . ."

Psychomotor drive and mood balanced. Maintaining verbal contact. Allopsychic orientation maintained. Train of thoughts logical. Answers spontaneous, sometimes laconic and dismissive. The patient was not at all interested in therapy suggested by the hospital.

Demonstrative behavior. Egocentric. Careless.

Podlałam kwiatki i . . . I watered my little plants and . . . If she told the truth to the attending psychiatrist, Mother did care about something enough to nurture it before swallowing the pills. Houseplants.

***

Where does a mother's self end and her children's selves begin? New research indicates that fetal cells remain in mothers' bodies even after pregnancy, sometimes for decades. *The Smithsonian*, for example, reports that "during pregnancy, cells from the fetus cross the placenta and enter the mother's body, where they can become part of her tissues." Mother is part of me, and I was part of her. By trying to kill herself, she tried to kill me, too, that little part of me that hoped I would one day be enough for her to love me, but also possibly, and quite literally, the cells I passed on to her own body.

Did she try to liberate me from her own toxicity?

Why do we expect all mothers to nurture and sacrifice? Why do they have to relinquish the vestiges of autonomy they have in the already restrictive world of patriarchy? Where does a mother's autonomy begin and end? Merlin Sheldrake's *Entangled Life* brings up lichens—symbiotic organisms composed of fungi and algae—and asks, impossibly: Where does one organism stop and another begin?

Is a blood-related family an integrated whole? Should it be? Does the presence of Mother's DNA in my cells tie her to me in unbreakable ways? Does it determine my future as much as it influenced my past? Recent research proves that embryos and fetuses shed DNA inside their mother's bodies. When we exchange coils of self-replicating material, do we also exchange vows of loyalty?

I revisit *Mad Mothers, Bad Mothers*: "A mother may have a longing for independence that is at odds with caretaking, revolt against the relentless empathy with one's child, and mourn the loss of her maiden self." Some mothers report "an impulse to either fight or flight. They have a sudden urge to kill their child, to run away, to kill themselves, or otherwise reverse the fact of their child's existence." So Mother was not alone in feeling this way. Combine this postnatal abnegation of the self, postnatal depression, with material worries and preexisting mental health issues, and the result could be homicidal and suicidal behavior, neglect, escape. After all, in *Becoming a Mother,* Ann Oakley says that "one in three women have definite psychiatric symptoms of depression" and that the "likelihood of becoming depressed is crucially related to motherhood."

Rozsika Parker writes in *Torn in Two: The Experience of*

Maternal Ambivalence: "There is, however, a spectrum of maternal feeling, from thoughtful containment to retaliatory abuse, a spectrum from pulling a zipper roughly to outright acts of violence. It is perhaps reassuring to think in neatly bifurcated terms of those mothers who contain and those who retaliate, but small moments of aggression will well up and pepper even the most caring of mothers."

Could Mother have sent signals we all missed? Plants attacked by aphids, for instance, emit infochemicals that signal their distress to the world. In the case of broad beans, the signal attracts parasitic wasps that feed on the invading aphids. Trees, too, send distress signals to other plants via roots. What were Mother's signs of distress, before she started drinking? Since I don't remember her before her alcoholism, and I can't ask my grandparents, I have to imagine: Tantrums as a child? Withdrawal from others into books? Avoiding company? Exploding at home at minor inconveniences?

* * *

May 15, 1986
The patient feels tired and irritated. Difficulties sleeping. Stays in bed and is not taking care of her children. To improve her mood she drinks beer. She missed work yesterday. Patient smells oil paint, violets, and soil. Contact and orientation correct. Sometimes laconic, strange, eccentric, prone to irritation. Smell hallucinations. In hospital ward, grandiose, careless, sometimes bizarre. Complaints of anxiety, fears, and sleeplessness.

* * *

Sheldrake ponders the fungal "ability to cling on—and often flourish—through periods of catastrophic change." They are resilient and restorative. In Colorado, for example, native fungi are used to restore forests ravaged by fire. *Science Daily* explains that fire-spawned fungi are the first to rise from the ashes after a wildfire obliterates a forest. In fact, some species cannot complete their life cycle without fire. "Scientists have long argued about where and how such pyrophilous (fire-loving) fungi survive, sometimes for decades, between fires. A new study finds that some of these fungi hide out in the tissues of mosses and lichens."

* * *

July 15, 2015
SAW:
The lady at the front desk of the funeral parlor has neon-green and neon-orange nails
HEARD:
Joyful pop music—I'm a Barbie girl in a Barbie world, life in plastic, it's fantastic—in an office where Tomek and I picked up Mother's death certificate
DID:
Picked cremation urn

* * *

In one of the mother-and-daughter gift books I see a cropped version of Gustav Klimt's allegorical *Death and Life* painting. Mother and child entwined, content, peaceful, mother's hand on the baby's bare back, gentle and protective, against a backdrop of Art Nouveau grass and flowers. The cropped part? Death. The left side of the oil painting represents a skull, grinning with anticipation, draped in a dark cape with a cross pattern, a grim reaper looking at Life—the mother and child, a muscular man, an older woman.

* * *

I walk to my laptop and check Messenger. I had asked Tomek whether his memories could fill the gaps in mine. I sent him some questions. Instead of his reply, I see a message from his wife: “Please don’t ask Tomek about your childhood. Whenever he has to think back, he falls apart. Please let him forget.”

In a selfish attempt to weave a coherent story of my childhood, I tore a nasty gash in the protective fabric he had worked hard to keep between his adult self and the little vulnerable child holding my hand. Guilt swells in me and something else, the old desire to protect him, to shield his tiny limbs and large, inquisitive eyes from the blows coming our way, from the unloving silences and brutal words, from Mother’s clenched teeth, from the sight of her feet dangling in the air as he opened a bathroom door.

* * *

After an afternoon of Mother slamming cabinet doors, we finally heard: “Go to Grandmother! Nothing to eat here.” Midsentence, we stood up. Mother shoved an umbrella in my hand and reminded me to hold Tomek’s hand when we crossed the streets. Fifteen minutes later, Tomek and I sat by Grandma Iza’s open balcony door, smelling the rain to come, shelling peas, lifting our eyes from the bowl each time we sensed a distant flash of lightning on the horizon. Finally, the smell of rain gave way to the smell of potato pancakes from Grandma’s sizzling cast-iron pan.

“I don’t want pancakes.” Tomek wrinkles his nose, his ribs clearly outlined under his tight T-shirt. “I want lard, with onions.”

Grandma emerges from the kitchen, wiping her hands on the apron.

“Children in Africa are starving, and you turn up your nose at *placki*???”

* * *

When Father came back from his European tours with the Baltic Opera loaded with sweets, Mother would give us one tiny chocolate square a week, on Sundays. I never saw her eat any.

But oh, the things we ate while playing outside with neighborhood kids! These were as adventurous as the bananas and real chocolate from German boxes: tasteless, stiff chewing gum with crushed graphite filling from coloring pencils to help us blow colorful bubbles; chewing gum, gooey and slightly sweet, made from wheat and other grasses we found on a nearby escarpment and fields; milky substance sucked from the inside of dandelion stems when we played house on our rusty playground; all kinds of hard berries from shrubs and bushes around the city, some of them possibly poisonous; coarse gray sand, dry or wet, depending on what was served in the sandbox—crunchy cereal or perhaps mud cake; meds stolen from our parents' cabinets: Chlorchinaldin, Relanium, diazepam, APAP, aspirin; cheap acidic wine from Grandpa's basement, consumed somewhere behind a bus stop or in an abandoned construction site amid rolls of asbestos insulation, after which we once started spraying the wall of the local power station with burgundy paint. I spray-painted a gigantic leg of a woman, and on that sexy thigh was a strap, and behind the strap was a dollar bill. Next to my gigantic leg, my friend wrote "GUNS'N'ROSES KINGS."

* * *

Intake date: October 27th 1996
Several days after checking out of the hospital patient "reached for alcohol." Her mother got very sick—heart attack. The patient's father and brother maintain that "at home there were hair-raising and shocking scenes, she demolished the apartment while under the influence of

> *alcohol." The patient denies these allegations. She maintains that she drank one beer a day and performed all the household duties.*
>
> *Staff educated the patient again about the problem of alcoholism.*

***

In my Indiana kitchen, as I sink my hands into bread dough and squeeze the lumps between my fingers, I feel tiny hands on my apron. A tug. Then another. My daughter wants me to draw Rainbow Dash for her so she can color it in with her new crayons. I bought the crayons so I could have a little peace at home. It's a bribe, in a way, or a ploy, to carve out time for baking and writing. Both, I realize as I kneel on the kitchen floor and grab a pencil with sticky fingers, are always just out of reach. Both, I also realize, will never take precedence over my children's well-being.

My own childhood was a series of evasions and flights from an abusive single parent, and I had never been able to shape these early experiences into creative nonfiction, not with empathy and nuance anyway, until I had to respond to my own children's constant demands, until I felt the tug and release of their little hands.

All I can offer is this fragmented meditation on parenting, love, and addiction. Unanswered questions about the reliability of a fragmented, traumatized memory and the value of gaps and silences in our personal narratives. Even after combing through hundreds of hours of recordings to extract a narrative about childhood, totalitarian regimes, hunger, and substance abuse, my recollections have large blank spaces and erasures. Research cannot fill the black holes in my memory. Can one heal from adverse childhood experiences without a coherent narrative? Can one heal from love hunger?

* * *

When you're a mother of a special-needs child, on top of the expected sleeplessness and anxiety of first-time parenthood, you feel anger whenever your son's pediatrician dismisses your reports of his constant vomiting ("All kids spit up!"), his reluctance to nurse for more than one minute ("You're doing it wrong, go to a lactation specialist to learn"), his delayed physical development and delayed milestones ("All kids develop differently"), his bloody poop ("All infants have fragile digestive systems"), and finally his being so weak that he can't lift his head back up from the carpet ("All kids get tired"). Your friends who deliver their babies around the same time will come for playdates, and your eyes water whenever you look at the three infants lying next to one another on organic cotton blankets in your backyard—two of them plump and healthy and one so thin that you could count his bones through his pale skin, just lying there, smiling but not moving much. Something is terribly wrong with your baby, and everyone thinks you're nuts.

* * *

When I think of Mother, I think of her eyes, always hungry for something I couldn't give her, looking past me. As a child I was a walking seismograph, detecting every tremor and predicting earthquakes.

Mother's hunger was all-consuming. There is no greater hunger in the world than that of an addict.

So I'm on guard. There is no second beer. When I share a bottle of wine with a close friend going through a difficult divorce, I wake up the next morning in a panic: Am I an alcoholic now that I had more than one glass? When we visit friends who offer us a juicy joint, I say no—my kid is asleep in another room. C'mon, they say. You can have a little. I know I can. I also know that my genes make me more likely to want another. And another.

***

Intake date: October 22nd, 1998; 11:30 PM
The patient was admitted to hospital after a conflict with her mother. The family says she is irritable, explosive. The patient tried to commit suicide with Pernazyna, 8 pills 25 milligram each.

***

As I browse the internet to relax after work, dinner, and my son's bedtime, I come across an article in the Polish press. A two-year-old boy who shares my son's name was found dead in his crib in a *melina.* He weighed less than twelve pounds when the police discovered his emaciated body. The coroner didn't find any food in his digestive tract—only hair and splinters from his wooden crib. For two weeks, the boy did not eat anything. The boy's mother was arrested. Expert witness: "I confirm psychopathic tendency in the mother, manipulative and neurotic behavior." And: "At the time of the child's death, she was sound of mind."

I dissolve into sound. It's not exactly crying or sobbing, more like a wild wail, long and loud, exiting my body without any warning. Ripples of acoustic waves scream away from my throat. My skin is sound waves. My lungs are sound waves. My lips are sound waves.

My husband, startled and wide-eyed, runs into our bedroom. It takes a long time to calm me down so I can tell him about the boy.

* * *

When I was a child, I loathed crouching over our patch of strawberries, pulling nettles, surrounded by mosquitoes. Now weeding is one of the few calming things I can do without flooding my body with toxins. Weeding my strawberry patch in Indiana, I reach with gloved fingers deep into the earth to loosen the soil and find the lowest point where I can grab the roots of creeping Charlie, crabgrass, or thistle, and I pull them out whole, to purify the earth and let good things grow. The strawberry patch is covered with viny weeds, and when I pull some of them, a single white root comes out from deep in the patch, all twisted and hard and long, and it keeps coming out, and I can pull it easily without breaking the root. Other times the vine underneath the surface of the soil spreads in different directions, and I pull it gently at an angle to see the soil move across the raised bed, making fault lines in the dirt.

* * *

Intake date: July 5, 2013
Release date: July 17, 2013
Diagnosis: Alcohol withdrawal syndrome
The patient has been hospitalized in the Psychiatric Hospital 12 times since 1986. Last hospitalization July 20, 2009. Currently patient requests detox. Initially apathetic and withdrawn. Hands shake visibly. Patient says she feels helpless, complains about memory and focus problems. Sleeplessness. Self-criticism low.

* * *

Creeping Charlie is everywhere. I pull and pull to save my spinach and young tomato plants from suffocating, and for a while, things look tidy and safe, but then a storm passes through and I go outside and creeping Charlie is back, already winding its way across my garden beds, sneakily rooting underground, snaking around delicate stems, stealing water and nutrients from the soil.

Weeding and working through trauma are like that. After a good therapy session or when my meds kick in, life unfolds in front of my eyes clearly, predictably—oh, how I crave predictability! And then an email arrives with Mother's medical records from one of the hospitals and—behold—I'm back to pulling at the weeds.

About the Author

Agata Izabela Brewer was born and raised in Poland. A teacher, a mother, an activist for immigrant rights, and a Court Appointed Special Advocate, she is Professor of English at Wabash College. Her creative writing has appeared in *Guernica* and *Entropy*. *The Hunger Book* is her first book of creative nonfiction.

21ST CENTURY ESSAYS

David Lazar and Patrick Madden, Series Editors

This series from Mad Creek Books is a vehicle to discover, publish, and promote some of the most daring, ingenious, and artistic nonfiction. This is the first and only major series that announces its focus on the essay—a genre whose plasticity, timelessness, popularity, and centrality to nonfiction writing make it especially important in the field of nonfiction literature. In addition to publishing the most interesting and innovative books of essays by American writers, the series publishes extraordinary international essayists and reprint works by neglected or forgotten essayists, voices that deserve to be heard, revived, and reprised. The series is a major addition to the possibilities of contemporary literary nonfiction, focusing on that central, frequently chimerical, and invariably supple form: The Essay.

*The Hunger Book: A Memoir from Communist Poland**
AGATA IZABELA BREWER

Night Mother: A Personal and Cultural History of The Exorcist
MARLENA WILLIAMS

Twenty Square Feet of Skin
MEGAN BAXTER

*Mistaken for an Empire: A Memoir in Tongues**
CHRISTINE IMPERIAL

Everything I Never Wanted to Know
CHRISTINE HUME

Engine Running: Essays
CADE MASON

Ripe: Essays
NEGESTI KAUDO

*Dark Tourist: Essays**
HASANTHIKA SIRISENA

Supremely Tiny Acts: A Memoir of a Day
SONYA HUBER

Art for the Ladylike: An Autobiography through Other Lives
WHITNEY OTTO

The Terrible Unlikelihood of Our Being Here
SUSANNE PAOLA ANTONETTA

---

* Annual Gournay Prize Winner

*Warhol's Mother's Pantry: Art, America, and the Mom in Pop**
M. I. Devine

How to Make a Slave and Other Essays
Jerald Walker

Don't Look Now: Things We Wish We Hadn't Seen
Edited by Kristen Iversen and David Lazar

Just an Ordinary Woman Breathing
Julie Marie Wade

My Private Lennon: Explorations from a Fan Who Never Screamed
Sibbie O'Sullivan

*On Our Way Home from the Revolution: Reflections on Ukraine**
Sonya Bilocerkowycz

Echo's Fugue
Desirae Matherly

This One Will Hurt You
Paul Crenshaw

The Trouble with Men: Reflections on Sex, Love, Marriage, Porn, and Power
David Shields

*Fear Icons: Essays**
Kisha Lewellyn Schlegel

Sustainability: A Love Story
Nicole Walker

Hummingbirds Between the Pages
Chris Arthur

Love's Long Line
Sophfronia Scott

The Real Life of the Parthenon
Patricia Vigderman

You, Me, and the Violence
Catherine Taylor

Curiouser and Curiouser: Essays
Nicholas Delbanco

Don't Come Back
Lina María Ferreira Cabeza-Vanegas

A Mother's Tale
Phillip Lopate